The Bicycle Touring Manual

The Bicycle Touring Manual

Using the Bicycle for Touring and Camping

Second, fully updated and expanded edition

Rob van der Plas

Illustrated by the author

Bicycle Books – San Francisco

Copyright © Rob van der Plas, 1987, 1993

Second, fully updated and expanded edition

Printed in the United States of America

Cover Design Kent Lytle, Lytle Design
Photograph: Dan Gindling
Frontispiece photograph: Kimberlee Caledonia, at Hole in the Rock, Utah

Index Paul Kish, Kish Indexing Service, Mendocino, CA

Published by: Bicycle Books, Inc.
PO Box 2038
Mill Valley, CA 94942 (USA)

Distributed to the book trade by: USA: National Book Network, Lanham, MD
Canada: Raincoast Book Distrib, Vancouver, BC
UK: Chris Lloyd Sales and Marketing Services, Poole, Dorset

Cataloging in Publication Data: Van der Plas, Robert, 1938 —
The Bicycle Touring Manual
Using the bicycle for touring and camping,
2nd. updated and expanded edition
Bibliography: p. Includes Index
1. Bicycles and Bicycling, Manuals and Handbooks, etc.
2. Bicycle Touring, Manuals and Handbooks, etc.
3. Camping and Backpacking, Manuals and Handbooks, etc.
I. Title.
II. Authorship

Library of Congress Catalog Card Number 92-83821

ISBN 0-933201-52-4

About the Author

Rob van der Plas is a professional engineer and a lifelong cyclist. He has toured by bicycle extensively in Europe and America. As a child, he was taken on bicycle camping trips by his parents when he was old enough to sit upright in a child's seat on the bike, and continued to do so ever since he could ride a bike of his own. In this book he shares with his readers the experience gained over many years of active bicycle touring and camping.

In addition to the present book, Rob van der Plas has written extensively on all matters related to bicycles and cycling. His *Bicycle Repair Book, Bicycle Technology*, *Mountain Bike Book*, *Mountain Bike Magic* and *Roadside Bicycle Repairs* also appeared in this series, published by Bicycle Books. His technical contributions regularly appear in the form of books and articles with major publishers and in specialized periodicals on both sides of the Atlantic.

Today, he works as a full-time writer and editor, and lives in Mill Valley, California.

Author's Preface

The first edition of this book appeared back in 1987. Although the first printing was sold out within a year, it soon seemed the subject had lost much of its appeal. Simultaneously with the surge in popularity of purely recreational mountain biking, bicycle touring seemed to have died.

That's the way it seemed until 1992. Then suddenly you started seeing cyclists with luggage, touring over longer distances again, and the remaining copies of the book were grabbed up in short order. The time had come to reissue *The Bicycle Touring Manual*.

In this new edition of the book, all the equipment-related information is brought up to date for what is available today. I have made every effort to include all the information that seems relevant. If you, the the reader, know of better ways to tackle certain jobs, I would appreciate hearing from you.

Send any comments you may have to the author, care of the publisher (see copyright page for the postal address). Your suggestions for improvements, expansions or corrections may be incorporated in subsequent editions of the book.

Table of Contents

Part I. Selecting Your Equipment _____ **13**

Chapter 1
Bicycle Touring
is Back *15*

Advantages of Bicycle Touring 15
Goals of This Book 16
Organized and Individual Cycling 17
Commercial Tours 18
American and British Cycling Clubs 18
Sources of Supply 19
Buying or Renting 20
A Personal Note 20
Sharing Knowledge and Experience 21
About This Book 22
Organization of the Text 22
Choice of Words 23

Chapter 2
The Bicycle's Frame,
Steering System
and Saddle *25*

Parts of the Bike 26
Touring Bike Philosophy 27
Bicycle Manufacturers 28
The Bike and Its Parts 29
The Frame 29
Materials, Strength and Rigidity 30
Tubing Materials 33
Frame Dimensions 33
The Steering System 34
The Headset 35
Handlebars and Stem 36
Saddle and Seatpost 37
The Mountain Bike for Touring 37
Other Mountain Bike Details 39
Suspension 40

Chapter 3
The Bicycle's Other
Components *41*

The Drivetrain 41
The Gearing System 45
The Wheels 46
The Brakes 52

Chapter 4
Touring Bike
Accessories *55*

Braze-ons, Lugs and Eyelets 55
Clamps and Clips 56
Luggage Racks 57
Fenders 57
Lights 59
Pump and Tire Gauge 62
Water Bottle and Cage 63

	Locks	64
	Warning Devices	64
	Tools and Spares	65
	Covers and Pouches	66

Chapter 5
Luggage Carrying
Equipment *67*

	Dividing the Load	67
	Luggage Racks	69
	Types of Bags	71
	Bag Details	74
	Bicycle Trailers	76

Chapter 6
Clothing On and Off the
Bike *77*

	Shoes and Socks	77
	Shorts and Slacks	78
	Shirts and Other Tops	79
	Gloves	80
	Head Protection	80
	Rain Gear	81
	Cold Weather Wear	82
	Street Clothes	83
	Campsite Wear	84

Chapter 7
Selecting Camping
Gear *85*

	Sources of Information	85
	Sleeping Bags	86
	Sleeping Bag Designs	87
	Sleeping Bag Care	88
	Tents and Shelters	89
	Tent Materials	91
	Sleeping Pad and Air Mattress	92
	Cooking Equipment	93
	Other Camping Equipment	94

Part II. The Art of Bicycle Touring   **95**

Chapter 8
Bike Fit and
Riding Style *97*

	Riding Posture	97
	Bike Fit	98
	Saddle Height	99
	Saddle Position and Angle	101
	Saddle Adjustments	102
	Handlebar Height and Position	102
	Handlebar Adjustments	103
	Adjusting Special Bikes	104
	Basic Bike Handling	104
	Safe Stopping and Slowing Down	105

Chapter 9
Selecting and Using
the Gears **107**

The Derailleur System 108
The Need for Gears 109
Gearing Practice 110
Gear Designation 111
Gear Selection 113
Derailleur Care and Adjustment 114
Selecting Chainrings and Sprockets 115

Chapter 10
Bike Handling Skills . . . **117**

The Steering Principle 118
Bicycle Balance 118
The Natural Turn 119
The Forced Turn 120
Braking Techniques 121
Basic Riding Techniques 123
Getting up to Speed 124
Maintaining a Constant Speed 124
Accelerating 124
Riding Against the Wind 125
Hill Climbing 125
Climbing out of the Saddle 126
Avoiding Obstacles 126
Jumping the Bike 127

Chapter 11
Safety and Health **129**

The Risks of Cycling 130
Traffic Hazards 131
Regular Accidents 131
Bicycles as Vehicles 132
Falls and Collisions 133
How to Treat Injuries 136
Other Health Problems 138

Chapter 12
Cycling in Any
Weather **143**

Clothing for Touring 144
Other Equipment 146
Riding Style 147
Touring Techniques 148

Chapter 13
What to Take and
How to Pack It **151**

Packing Smartly 152
What to Take 152
Saving Weight 153
Different Loads for Different Trips 154
The Art of Packing 155
Tying Things Down 156
The Inside Package 157
Containers 157
Carrying Your Bike 159

Chapter 14
Planning Your Tour 161

Basic Rules 161
Learning to Cope 162
Where and When to Go 163
Time and Area 163
Detailed Route Planning 164
Reaching Your Starting Point 165
Direction of Route 165
Reading the Map 165
Map Features 167
Other Sources of Information 168

Part III. The Practice of Bicycle Touring _____ **169**

Chapter 15
Expanding Your
Horizons 171

Getting Ready to Tour 171
From Casual Rides to Day Trips 173
Overnight Trips 174
Longer Tours 175
Bike Touring as a Way of Life 176

Chapter 16
Finding Your Way 179

Preliminary Orientation 179
Orientation Aids 180
Reading the Map 181
Recognizing Map Features 181
Map Use in the Field 182
Other Orientation Aids 183
Getting Help 184

Chapter 17
Food for the Road 185

Diet for Endurance 185
The Tasks of Food 186
Types of Food 186
Food for Energy 190
Your Energy Needs 191
RQ: Fat or Carbohydrate 192
Caffeine 192
Carbohydrate Loading 193
Weight Loss 193
A Meal Planner 193
Snacks 194

Chapter 18
Bicycle Camping 195

Choosing and Packing Your Gear 195
Campsites 196
Free Camping 197
Pitching Your Tent 197
Inside and Around the Tent 198
Meal Preparation 199

Sleeping in the Tent 200
Breaking Up Camp 201
Ride and Meal Timing 201

Chapter 19
Bicycle Touring
Abroad **203**

Preparation 204
Sources of Information 205
Tourist Boards 205
Foreign Maps 206
Getting There with Your Bike 207
Choosing Maps 208
Understanding One Another 209
Timing Your Tour 210
Where to Travel 211
Where to Stay 212
Hostels and Private Rooms 213
Staying Healthy Abroad 213

Chapter 20
Touring with
Children **215**

Age and Ability 216
Ways to Carry the Child 217
Gerry-Pack 218
Children's Seats 218
Trailers 219
Children's Bikes 219
Riding with Children 220
Tandems 220
Overnight Stays with Children 221

Chapter 21
Tandem Touring **223**

Tandem Skills 223
Transporting a Tandem 224
Renting a Tandem 225
Mechanical Problems 225
Tandem Frames 226
The Tandem Drivetrain 227
Tandem Wheels 229
Tandem Brakes 230

Chapter 22
Mountain Bike
Touring **231**

Rough Trail Cycling 232
Off-Road Cycling Skills 233
Cross-Country Touring 233
Mountain Biking on the Road 234
Mixed Touring 234
Staying Off-Road 235

Chapter 23
Keeping a Record
of Your Tour *237*

The Photo Log 237
The Touring Log 238
The Mapping Log 239
Getting Published 240

Back Matter _____ *241*

Appendix *243*

Table 1. Frame sizing 243
Table 2. Gear in inches 244
Table 3. Conversion from inch gear to development 244
Suggested Packing List 245
List of Addresses 247

Bibliography *248*

Index *250*

Part I.

Selecting Your Equipment

CHAPTER 1

Bicycle Touring is Back

Suddenly, bicycle touring is popular again. During the late 80s, it seemed the only respectable way to ride a bicycle was with a fancy racing or mountain bike, showing off the latest fashion in lycra bicycle togs. Whereas the introduction of the mountain bike had brought increasing popularity to cycling as a whole, it did little for bicycle touring specifically. Yes, all the touring companies replaced their touring bikes with mountain bikes, because that seemed the way to go. But individuals cycling long distances with luggage had become a rare sight. Now suddenly they're back: bicycle touring is *in* again.

Advantages of Bicycle Touring

There is probably no greater way to appreciate the delights of riding a bicycle than by using it for touring. Nor is there a better way to appreciate nature on its grander scale. No offense to hikers and mountaineers, skiers and canoeists—all folks who are similarly self-propelled and closely in touch with nature. Yet all seem to get only a thin slice of God's greatest works, as compared to what is meted out to the touring cyclist.

The cyclist travels at some speed through the vastness, finding himself now following a river, now ascending a mountain slope, now skirting a town, getting the full experience of nature's variety. The other muscle-powered tourists are mostly limited to a small region, characterized by either one type of terrain or the other. Whereas the cyclist can travel quite significant distances,

Touring along the Dempster Highway, Yukon. (Photo Dan Gindling)

crossing entire continents in a matter of weeks or at most months, the others usually make very slow progress indeed, not venturing far from their starting point.

Yet bicycle use for touring purposes is not restricted to continental crossings and other major expeditions. In fact, a lot of bicycle touring may be done much closer to home. You can start cycling right outside your own front door. Be it for a long trek or a short trip. By bicycle, you may choose to go for months, a week, a weekend, a day, or just a few hours. The bike gives you the freedom to use even the tiniest bit of time and the most unlikely starting points for your trips. The bicycle makes you free.

Goals of This Book

This book is written to help not only those who have little cycling experience, but also experienced cyclists who want to get the most out of their hobby. I shall try to help you make optimal use of the bicycle, by sharing with you the experience I and others have gained over many years of active bicycle touring. I shall try to cover all the many facets of cycling over longer and shorter distances. I'll show you how to choose your equipment, ranging from the bike itself to accessories, such as racks, packs, tents and sleeping bags.

Not only will you learn to choose your equipment, but also to get the best use from it and to expand your cycling skills. You will be shown how to ride your bike safely and efficiently, how to plan your tour and how to choose your route. I'll show you how to maintain the bicycle itself and the rest of your equipment, how to pack the bike and how to find your way at home and abroad. You will learn to be self-sufficient and you'll find out where to get help when you need it.

I also hope to share something else with you—namely the feeling of inspiration and the sense of true freedom that for me and many other touring cyclists will always turn the activity of cycling into something more than merely using a bike to get around, instead of a car. If all is well, with the aid of this book you will discover the oneness with nature and the peace with civilization that I have found make bicycle touring one of the best things man has ever learned to do.

It matters little whether you go on long tours or on short trips. Although different kinds of rides and distances do involve varying levels of preparation and involvement, the quality of these is the same each time. On the long tour, you generally have to carry more luggage than on a shorter trip, you will need more aids to orientation and you may encounter more diverse experiences. Yet anything that helps you on one kind of ride will also help you, more or less, on any other kind of bicycle tour.

Sure, all these things can be learned without a manual. I never read any of this in a book. Instead, I assimilated it from my parents, and I have continued learning from my own experiences and from other cyclists with whom I have kept company ever since. Others have learned mainly from their own mistakes—perhaps the most thorough, though also the most time-consuming, frustrating and sometimes dangerous way of gaining proficiency in any skill.

Organized and Individual Cycling

For many years, cycling has been largely a club activity, especially in Great Britain, but to some extent also in the United States and a number of other countries. Cycling clubs preceded motoring organizations by many years. More recently, cycling was regarded as such an anachronism, in a society geared to motorized transportation, that those who participated in it seemed most at ease in the company of others who shared their interests. Active membership in a bicycle club was, certainly in those days, the most effective form of schooling for beginning cyclists.

Even today, joining others in a club remains a great way to enjoy the sport. However, with the remarkable revival of interest in biking, and the similarly spectacular influx of new cyclists since the early 70s, two factors have reduced the overall benefit of the potential propagation of skills via the cycling clubs. In the first place, more people for whom club membership is either impractical or unappealing have joined the sport. Secondly, the average level of skill and experience in many clubs has suffered in direct proportion to the increase in membership.

In the mid 70s a brand new organization, established by longtime bicycle PR genius Dan Burden, mushroomed in America. Called Bikecentennial, this group set out to celebrate the second centennial of the United States and the first centennial of organized cycling with bicycle tours across the North American continent. An enormous amount of work, both physical and mental, was rewarded with an unbelievable increase in the popularity of bicycle touring in the U.S., which would never have achieved its present popularity without Bikecentennial. Today this organization is still active and helps its members with their bicycle touring needs.

At about the same time quite a number of local and regional bicycle organizations of a different type were formed. These coalitions, associations, cooperatives and whatever else they may be called, all have as their major purpose either the propagation of cycling or the defense of the real or presumed interests of cyclists—objectives that are by no means always identical. Most of these groups are very loosely organized, and members almost invariably do more talking than cycling together. Necessary and useful work is done by several of these groups. Yet only a handful of them really serve to help or educate their newer members

A different way of cycle touring: mountain biking in the Rockies. (photo David Epperson/Bicycle Sports)

in practical matters associated with cycling, whether touring or otherwise.

A much older and more general nationwide organization, one that has represented cycling in the United States for well over a hundred years, is the League of American Wheelmen. In the mid 80s this national association, with chapters in most states, experimented with a new name and a new image. Calling itself Bicycle USA, the old League ventured away from helping existing cyclists to promoting the image of cycling and trying to attract newcomers to the sport. The outcome was disastrous, with sympathies lost and goals missed, but since then the League has honorably recovered from its losses. By whatever name, I hope the League will continue to play a prominent part in the American cycling scene, and that similar organizations establish themselves in other countries.

Commercial Tours

Another form of bicycle touring that should not be ignored is initiated by commercial tour operators. In many states, one or more such establishments organize bicycle tours, some only at home, others also abroad. They supply all the necessary route planning and take care of the accommodations, food and luggage transportation problems for their patrons. Certainly for inexperienced riders, who would like to try out bicycle touring without wanting to jump in at the deep end, this form of touring can be highly recommended. All this assuming we're talking about a serious agency that is well established in the field and can keep its promises. The advice in this book will apply as much to those who travel alone as to those who prefer to tour under any such form of expert guidance.

American and British Cycling Clubs

Although much of this book is written primarily for an American audience, I hope it will prove equally useful to other readers. Great Britain remains a wonderful place to go touring — for natives and foreign cyclists alike. It is an area that can also be highly recommended as a goal for U.S. touring cyclists. And no account of bicycle organizations active on behalf of bicycle touring can be complete without mentioning the British CTC (Cyclists' Touring Club), which is probably internationally the one with the highest proportion of really competent touring cyclists.

Cycling clubs continue to exist and have indeed experienced an increase in membership throughout the last one or two decades. Many clubs cater to racers, others mainly to casual or recreational cyclists. They organize local rides over various distances—ranging all the way from afternoon trips to day tours of 100, 200 and even 300 miles, referred to as single, double and triple centuries, respectively. Most of these rides are open to

Organized bicycle tours range from day trips, such as the one photographed here, to all-inclusive month-long tours. (Photo Dan Gindling)

members and outsiders alike. They are well organized, replete with food stops, repair service and a so-called *sagwagon* to transport stragglers and their equipment. Patches or other mementos are usually offered to those who complete such an event.

But even among the many active clubs, only a few have enough really experienced people available to help and advise all those who want to take up bicycle touring. Neither can they organize educational programs, nor can they offer adequate help to those who would like to become more effective at pulling off their own tours. In fact, there isn't even very much going on by way of regular club riding in the U.S., as I know it from England, where new members were quickly and effortlessly coached in a truly social manner.

Although I still heartily recommend joining a bicycle club today, the proportion of adequately competent cyclists in many clubs is at an all-time low. So, not as much can be learned there these days as used to be the case. Furthermore, the modern trend of wanting to be self-sufficient, of learning alone, with or without the aid of written instructions, applies as much in cycling as it does elsewhere. Perhaps it is a loss, because the social aspect of community in its many diverse forms is more and more receding from our lifestyle.

Today's cyclist should be entitled to get the best help that can be offered in the form of written instruction. That's what this book is intended to achieve. Even so, I hope it can be a little more than a kind of cookbook on bike touring. I would also like it to whet your appetite for bicycle use, and increase your spontaneous awareness of the many wonderful aspects of this unique form of transportation, whether for touring or for more mundane purposes.

Sources of Supply

Throughout this book, I shall describe and discuss various kinds of equipment, ranging from clothing to bike parts and camping gear. In general, the best places to buy either the finished products or the materials used in their construction will be in specialized shops. I recommend you shy away from non-specialized sources, such as department stores and general mail order establishments, as much as possible. Go to a bike shop to get bikes and bike parts, to an outdoor equipment shop for camping gear, to a book shop for books or maps.

Just the same, there is a place for the mail order business. I myself keep several catalogs of specialized mail order suppliers handy, even if only as a source of reference. They inform me every six months of what is available, and there is hardly a better place to get general information about many useful items of equipment. You will find such mail order establishments advertised in cycling, backpacking and camping magazines, which are also an excellent additional source of information.

Especially among bike shops, you will find great differences. There are some that stock only the basics, others that offer an adequate choice only for a particular type of bike and matching accessories. Some stores specialize more than others in touring equipment. Chances are that somewhere near your home there is such a store with an excellent collection of the kind of materials you need. Otherwise, you may have to venture farther out. As you patronize various shops, you will find that many are run by people who will gladly go out of their way to oblige you by offering useful advice and assistance, while others are interested only in a quick sale.

It will be worth your while to choose your suppliers as carefully as you select your equipment. Look around to find the best sources, both for bike parts and other items. I suggest you try several stores and ask other people who are active in bike touring. On your search for good suppliers, it will be best to start closest to your home. Only in very rare cases, perhaps when you live many miles away from a major town, or for items that are just not available locally, should you fall back on the several major specialized mail order companies. Once you have found a good source, continue to patronize it and give the operator some feedback with your experience.

Buying or Renting

If you are not sure the whole thing is for you, you may consider renting all or at least some of the equipment. Certainly if you entertain the thought of bicycle camping, but have never tried camping before, you would be well advised to obtain some of the rather expensive pieces of the necessary equipment through a rental outlet. Once you have established whether it really turns you on, you can always decide to buy your own gear. In some instances, such as when traveling abroad or when mountain bike touring in certain areas, bikes and some accessories may also be rented locally. For addresses of reputable rental outfits, check the advertising pages of the major national cycling and camping periodicals.

A Personal Note

Perhaps you wonder what gives me the crazy notion of wanting to write a book about bicycle touring, and what gives me the qualifications to speak with authority on the subject. Sometimes I wonder myself. Though a keen and experienced cyclist, I lack some of the talents that make bike touring a natural to some. I am not the world's greatest adventurer. While I have toured extensively in Europe, New Zealand and North America, I have never had the ambition to venture into the unknown. In fact, I have the awful habit of getting lost in my own town, and I have

European touring cyclists. Unlike their American counterparts, they rarely wear a helmet. (Photo courtesy Agu-Sport)

at times been caught improperly prepared for what I was doing myself.

Even so, the combination of many years of personal experience, spiced with humiliation, together with the advice from other, more organized cyclists and the forced inventiveness that I had to develop to get by despite my own shortcomings, has probably prepared me well for the task at hand. Yet when I first came to America in 1967, I never imagined I would finish up eking out a living by writing bicycle books. At that time hardly a soul seemed to ride a bike, and the few who did seemed to know a lot about the subject.

I myself had been touring by bike in Holland and later in England since I was a kid, accompanying my cycling parents on summer tours all over Europe. As a youth, I started touring with friends or alone, learning more from my own and my companions' mistakes than any other way. Over the years I became a truly competent touring cyclist, one who can solve all of the many problems he ever encounters. But above all, experience had made me inventive enough to solve problems that I had not faced before.

During my first few years in the U.S., in the late sixties, I seemed to have forgotten all about cycling, living the life that was typical for the urban young in San Francisco, as it was probably elsewhere too. I mostly drove a car, and cycling seemed just a happy memory of a quickly receding earlier age — until bicycles started cropping up everywhere around me. Within a short time, bike shops seemed to open up everywhere. Soon enough I decided to replace the bike I had left in Europe upon the recommendation of Americans, who had convinced me that one just could not ride a bike in the New World, something I had blindly believed, though never really accepted.

Sharing Knowledge and Experience

By the middle of the seventies, lots of people were riding bikes, and I found what I had learned over the years could benefit many others who were newer to the sport. The bits of knowledge, skills and experiences that I had taken for granted, even though their accumulation had taken many years of conscious and unconscious learning, appeared to be treasured morsels of wisdom to the less initiated. Soon I found myself giving advice, and it was a short step to writing articles for the then-emerging bicycle periodicals.

Eventually, it became obvious that the most important facts about cycling could be wrapped up systematically in the form of a book. That is how my first English book, *The Penguin Bicycle Handbook*, evolved. But oddly enough, this book, covering perhaps 90% of the things most cyclists wanted or needed to know, left as many questions unanswered as it addressed. What about obscure details of bike maintenance, what about mountain bikes, what of training practices, commuting, racing, touring? My efforts to answer those additional and more detailed questions resulted in a number of books, each addressing quite specific fields of interest.

Whereas the initial reaction to my proposal to write a bicycle book had been that one couldn't possibly fill a whole book about such a trivial subject, the attitude soon changed. As cyclists became more knowledgeable, they also became aware of their need to know even more. So this book is just one in an extended series of books, each of which tries to adequately address one aspect of cycling. Other books published by Bicycle Books in this series include Kameel Nasr's *Bicycle Touring International* and my *The Mountain Bike Book, The Bicycle Repair Book, Bicycle Technology, Mountain Bike Maintenance,* and *Roadside Bicycle Repairs.* The latter book may be of particular interest to the reader, being a companion volume to the present book: compact enough to be carried on the bike.

About This Book

Like the other books in this series, the present volume makes no claim to being the complete manual on everything worth knowing about cycling. Instead, it tries to give the absolute maximum of really relevant information on the subject at hand. If you really want to know about training or history, about diet or wheel building, there are excellent guides on those subjects available, and this would be the wrong place to look for that kind of information.

Some of the points raised here could perhaps also be found in other manuals on bicycles or cycling. But I have tried to concentrate the information to maximize its usefulness with regard to the subject. Consequently, I have selected the topics very carefully, excluding only what is trivial or irrelevant to the touring cyclist. I have included all the related material that will be useful both to people with a minimum of previous exposure to cycling, and to those who have used bikes for other purposes but not for touring. Though I have done my utmost to strike a good balance, I welcome any comments from readers, both regarding the choice of subjects and their treatment.

Organization of the Text

The book is divided up into three distinct parts and an appendix. Each of the main parts covers as fully as I consider practicable one of the three major stages of involvement in bicycle touring. In the first part, you will find all the help I can offer you on the subject of equipment selection. Here you will be shown how to choose items ranging from the bike itself to major components and auxiliaries, including racks, packs, clothing and camping gear.

Modern bicycle bags are well designed and don't interfere with your movements. (photo courtesy Eclispse)

The second part of the book is devoted to the basics of bicycle riding and touring. Although many people will think immediately of heavily loaded touring with camping gear and survival methods, I shall first make you familiar with all the techniques you have to master in order to enjoy any kind of bike touring, be that for a continental crossing or for short evening or day trips, whether heavily loaded or carrying nothing but a credit card. You will be shown how to ride safely and effectively, how to adapt to the weather and how to go about planning your trip.

In the third part, I shall concentrate on some of the less everyday aspects of cycling and touring. Here I cover those problems that are peculiar to bike touring in general and to quite specific forms of this pursuit. This applies to information that is perhaps useful or important on one trip but not necessarily on the other, let alone on every tour. Included will be advice on orientation, feeding yourself, and bicycle camping. Also covered will be special forms of bicycle touring, such as off-road and tandem touring, cycling with children and touring abroad.

The appendix, finally, contains some information that would make dull reading, though it is essential to have easy access to such facts. Here you will find tables and summaries, ranging from frame sizing and gearing tables to packing lists. Also included are a list of addresses, a bibliography and an extensive index.

Choice of Words

Let me conclude this introductory chapter with some remarks about the language that will be used in this book. Since the book is purposely written for both American and other English-speaking readership, it would be nice to offer a different version to each market. However, the hard facts of publishing dictate that the same version has to be offered on both sides of the Atlantic. Consequently, I must ask my British readers to put up with the peculiar version of the English language as it has become modified in the New World, since I will be using American spelling conventions throughout.

Thus, you will find words like *center, fiber, tire* and *aluminum,* where the British reader expects to read *centre, fibre, tyre* and *aluminium.* On the other hand, my proofreaders and I have done everything possible to avoid the use of words and expressions that make sense only one side of the Atlantic. Some things are known by different names in the two countries. Wherever several distinct names are in common use for the same concept, I will endeavor to explain both the first time they are used, and thereafter only the American term will be used.

Finally, there is the subject of gender. Bicycle touring, like most other activities, is equally accessible to people of either sex. Though I am probably as open to equality of the sexes as any male can be expected to be (which is perhaps still not quite enough), I also feel expressions such as *he/she, him/her* and composites with *-person* are monstrous constructions that stifle any language. That's not the way any sane person speaks, so why should anyone want to write that way? In short, I ask you to accept that the masculine form is typically used to include both sexes, while I use the feminine form only when a statement applies specifically to women only.

CHAPTER 2

The Bicycle's Frame, Steering System and Saddle

In the late 80s, it seemed the conventional touring bike was dead and had been replaced by the mountain bike for good. Yes, mountain bikes are suitable for some forms of touring. But no, for most tours, they are not the best equipment to use. And then it happened: suddenly the touring bike came back, and today it is once more readily available — in fact, some of the equipment available today is better than ever before, thanks to many of the developments pioneered in conjunction with the mountain bike.

In the present chapter and the two that follow, you will be shown what to look for when choosing and buying a touring bike. This chapter will deal only with the bicycle's backbone: its frame with the steering system and the saddle. The next two chapters will describe the many components installed on the bike, such as wheels, drive system, gears and brakes. The fourth chapter, finally, will deal with the accessories that make a touring bike particularly suited to its specific purpose.

Of necessity, all this will involve some rather basic explanations and definitions of terminology, in addition to specific advice about touring bicycles and their components. The former is especially required reading for those who are not fully familiar with the details of the bicycle. Readers who are quite familiar

California frame builder Bruce Gordon not only makes the finest luggage racks available, he also builds some fine touring bikes. This model can be used either with regular touring tires or with fat ones for off-road riding. Additionally, the drop handlebars can easily be exchanged for flat bars, because the derailleur cables can be separated with a latch mechanism.

with the bicycle for other uses may be tempted to skip these chapters, assuming they contain nothing new.

Yet even if you fall into the latter category, you would do well to take this material to heart, since it contains quite a bit of information that will help you to select bike and components specifically for touring. Furthermore, it will be helpful to at least check the illustrations and their labels, so you become familiar with the terms I shall be using to identify parts of the bike throughout the book. Often some of these things are called by different names in different parts of the world and indeed by different people in the same area. Thus, confusion can only be avoided if we agree on the terminology that will be used elsewhere in this book.

Parts of the Bike

Fig. 2.1 gives the names of just about all the major parts of the bicycle. The model illustrated is a fully equipped derailleur bike as might be used for touring. This illustration is chosen because it shows so many different parts, even though not all the components shown will be installed on every bike. In a subsequent part of this chapter and the next, I will more specifically examine the criteria which each of these parts should satisfy to qualify the bicycle for touring.

Before I get into such details, however, here is a summary of the way the bicycle is built up, and what the various parts are called. The easiest way to do this, at the same time explaining roughly how the bike works, is by organizing the many different parts together in functional groups. Thus, one can distinguish the following major component groups:

☐ The frame, to which all the other components are attached.

☐ The steering system, required for balance and control.

☐ The drivetrain, comprising all the parts that transmit power to the rear wheel.

☐ The gearing system, allowing the rider to adapt the transmission ratio to the terrain and weather conditions.

☐ The wheels.

☐ The brakes, together with their controls.

☐ The saddle with the seat post that attaches it to the frame.

☐ The various accessories, which distinguish a touring machine from any run-of-the-mill bike.

Frame, steering system and saddle will be treated here. The other functional groups of components will be examined in Chapter 3, while the accessories will be dealt with in Chapter 4.

Touring Bike Philosophy

There are two basic ways of looking at what makes a bike or any of its components suitable for touring: specialized or general. If you never venture into the unknown, the most specialized equipment will be just fine—if it breaks down or if you have any other trouble, you can hitch a ride home and get your ultimate touring machine put back into operation by your bike shop. But for real touring, that's not the way to go, because you want the independence that comes with equipment that can be fixed or replaced anywhere.

This approach may seem at odds with the current craze for highly specialized high-tech materials. My 40 years of experience in cycle touring suggest it's the only way to go, though. When you break a spoke far away from home, you may have a couple of spares with you, but when it's a more serious problem, you don't want to be stuck with a wheel that can't be straightened, a front derailleur that can't be attached, or a headset that won't fit on your high-tech bike. The moral is, make sure standard components can be installed on the bike; often the simplest ones will do just fine.

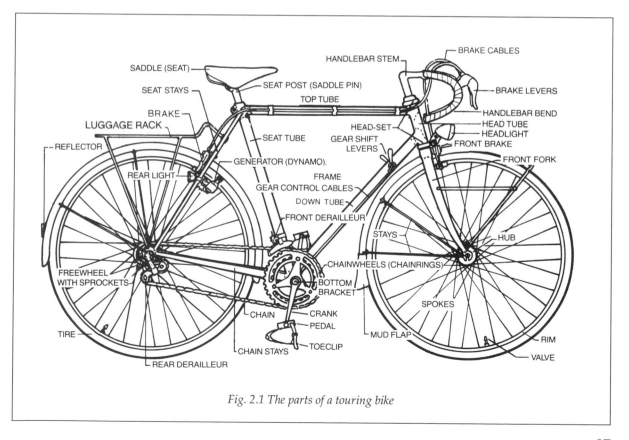

Fig. 2.1 The parts of a touring bike

Bicycle Manufacturers

Most bicycles sold these days are made by major bike manufacturers. Although there still is a domestic bicycle industry in the U.S., the majority of quality bikes sold through the specialized bicycle trade are imported these days. For many years most domestically made bikes were the low-end mass products sold through non-specialized outlets, but that has changed during the last ten years, with manufacturers like Trek and Cannondale building most of their bikes in the U.S., even though some older, established manufacturers, such as Schwinn, have fallen on hard times. Even so, most bikes are now imported from places like Taiwan.

In addition to these American and East Asian manufacturers, the Europeans are not quite dead, although even bikes with European names may well be made elsewhere. Thus, you will find presumably Italian Bianchis with a sticker proclaiming, *Made in Taiwan*. Many of these bikes, wherever they may be manufactured, are perfectly good quality machines. What matters more than the country of origin is the care that went into making them. I will try to show you what to look for to recognize products of satisfactory quality.

Besides factory bikes, there are custom-built machines, based on frames made either to the rider's specifications or at least built by a specialist frame builder. Though this is a very personal way to go, and assures you will get a distinct looking machine that generally costs a lot of money, there is no absolute certainty it will necessarily give you a better bike than you could have bought off the rack for less money. In recent years so many manufacturers have introduced and perfected special touring machines that it should be no problem to find one to suit your needs at an affordable price.

It is not realistic to think of most custom-built bikes as being made to measure. Most frame builders also use standard sizing tables with fixed proportions, even though theirs may be a little

Left: a typical French touring bike.
Right: British touring bikes.
Unlike their American counterparts, most European women prefer to use a bike with a special frame, such as the mixte design with twin lateral tubes, which unfortunately make it less rigid than the conventional "men's" frame is. For loaded touring, you want the stability that only a rigid frame can offer.

different from those used by others. However, when you order a custom-built frame, you can usually specify just which components should be used and what kind of attachments for the installation of accessories you want to have installed. That may be interesting for a very experienced rider, who has tried all the standard solutions and knows exactly what he wants. For most of us, though, it will be smarter to choose one of the standard touring bikes now offered by many manufacturers.

The Bike and Its Parts

Now for an overview of the bike. It consists of a frame to which the other parts are installed. Virtually all frames for the same type of bike are made with similar materials, and all the other components come from the series production lines of a limited number of specialized component manufacturers (one of which, Shimano, has a market share for components as high as 90%, with all other manufacturers scrambling for the rest). On bikes from many different manufacturers, even custom-built machines, you will find the same frame tubes, brakes, gears, tires, handlebars and a hundred other parts that all come from one of a limited number of manufacturers who specialize in those particular items.

Even so, not all parts made by the same firm are of the same quality. A maker of brakes, for instance, may have half a dozen or more different models, ranging in price, type, size and quality from one end of the spectrum to the other. It will be impossible to give you very detailed information indicating which make and model of any part will be better than other ones, if only because manufacturers change their product specifications and designations from time to time. Instead, I shall explain which general types are suitable and what to look for to make sure you are getting a satisfactory product.

The thing to check is the part's ultimate functionality on the finished bike. To give but one example, the Campagnolo C-Record brake is a superb mechanism—on a racing bike. Mount the same model on a touring machine, and you'll find it won't even clear the tires, let alone provide good braking. When buying a complete bike, you should try out all the various components as they work on that bike. When replacing any component, make sure to take the bicycle on which it must be mounted, or at a minimum the matching parts, to the bike store. This way the sales person or mechanic can help you select an item that is really satisfactory for your specific application.

The Frame

The bicycle's frame, shown in Fig. 2.2, is its biggest single component. It consists of the main frame, built up of relatively large diameter tubes, and the rear triangle, consisting of double sets of tubes with smaller diameters. The main frame comprises top tube, bottom tube, seat tube, and head tube. The pairs of tubes that form the rear triangle are called seat stays and chain stays, respectively.

On most bikes, the large diameter tubes of the main frame are joined by lugs, though these tubes may be joined directly on some bikes. The seat lug, which connects seat tube and top tube, is slotted in the back, allowing it to clamp around the saddle there. The lug that connects the down tube and the seat tube is called the bottom bracket or chain hanger and accommodates the bearings for the crankset. The two forward lugs are called head lugs and connect the head tube to the down tube and the top tube, respectively, accept the headset bearings. These and hold the bike's steering system. Fig. 2.3 shows the difference between different types of frame joints.

The rear triangle's pairs of seat and chain stays each come together in flat plates, referred to as drop-outs or (rear) fork-ends, in which the rear wheel is installed. At the top, the seat stays are usually attached directly to the seat lug, while the chain stays run to the bottom bracket. The pairs of stays are each connected (and stiffened) by means of short transverse tubular bridge pieces.

Materials, Strength and Rigidity

Although some manufacturers now offer very attractive bikes with frames made of aluminum tubing, welded or bonded together with or without lugs, the majority of touring bikes continue to be made with more traditional materials: various qualities of steel. On cheap bikes, the frame is made of simple carbon steel tubes that must have significant wall thicknesses

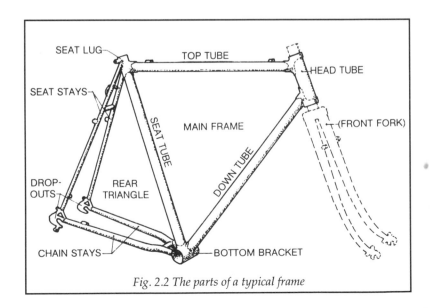

Fig. 2.2 The parts of a typical frame

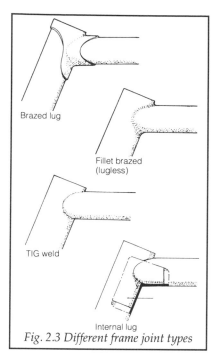

Fig. 2.3 Different frame joint types

(about 1.4 mm) to give adequate strength for a touring bike. This results in a rather heavy and "dead" bike.

For more expensive machines, stronger steel alloys are used. These alloys contain small percentages of other materials, such as chrome, molybdenum and manganese. Generally, their strength is further increased through the tube forming operation. Due to these materials' greater inherent strength, the resulting frame is strong enough for touring even when the tube wall thickness is much smaller. On the highest quality frames, these materials are used in tubes that have a greater wall thickness towards the ends (for adequate strength and resistance to the heat when joining the tubes) than elsewhere along the length of the tube, as shown in Fig. 2.4. The use of such tubes, referred to as butted tubes, results in a lighter, more responsive and comfortable bike.

Given adequate strength and rigidity, the lighter bike is distinctly more enjoyable to ride, even if the difference seems minor relative to the total weight of bike, luggage and rider. This is due to the fact that, unlike the rider's own body weight, most of the weight of bicycle and luggage should be considered "dead" weight or mass. Essentially, it is unsprung mass, which is not cushioned, as is the equivalent weight of a car or motorcycle. Nor can it be transferred or shifted, as is the case for the rider's weight, which can be raised off the saddle in response to anticipated road shocks. This not only applies to the weight of the frame, but to virtually all parts of the bike and the luggage carried on it when touring.

Another desirable feature of the bike, besides high strength and low weight, is adequate lateral and torsional rigidity. Rigidity means absence of flexibility, and on a rigid bike, there is little deformation in response to a force applied to it at one point. Inadequate rigidity leads to vibrations, oscillations and swaying, particularly while riding fast on poor road surfaces or when changing direction abruptly. For a real touring bike, used to carry luggage in difficult terrain, rigidity is of particular importance.

Unfortunately, rigidity is largely affected by some of the same factors as weight: for a given material and tube diameter, the rigidity decreases with decreasing wall thickness. Thus it is harder to get an adequately rigid bike with strong, light and expensive tubes, due to their smaller wall thickness. In consequence, good touring bike frames should be made of tubing materials that are as strong as those used on racing bikes, yet built with thicker walls to be adequately rigid. The down tube is particularly sensitive to undesirable flexing, and should therefore have a considerable wall thickness, even if that makes the frame a little heavier.

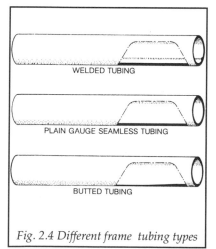

Fig. 2.4 Different frame tubing types

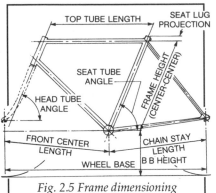

Fig. 2.5 Frame dimensioning

There is an even more effective way to achieve greater rigidity: increase the diameter of the tubes. Whereas a 20% increase in wall thickness only leads to a proportional 20% increase in rigidity, the effect of a 20% greater outside diameter, even with an unchanged wall thickness, is on the order of 70% (or conversely, it can be made equally rigid with thinner, and thus lighter tubes). Both methods lead to the same 20% weight increase. This is the reason why the frame's down tube, which is most heavily subjected to torsional forces, is always made with a greater diameter than the other main tubes.

A third factor to keep in mind with regard to rigidity is the material used for the tubes. On the one hand, all types of steel, from the cheapest and weakest to the strongest and most exotic, have the same inherent rigidity. Given the same diameter and wall thickness, the tubes are equally rigid, whatever kind of steel is used. On the other hand, aluminum with all its alloys is considerably less rigid. Consequently, an aluminum frame should have tubes that have a greater wall thickness (required to compensate for this material's lower strength anyway) as well as a greater outside diameter, if it is to be satisfactory for touring use.

In addition to the tube diameter, the wall thickness and the tubing material, the bicycle's frame geometry also affects its rigidity. The longer the individual tubes, the more flexible they become. And the frame for a touring bike must be made to more generous dimensions than that for a racing machine, to accommodate fatter tires and allow the installation of certain accessories. A real rigidity nightmare is of course the tandem frame, which is at least 65 cm (26 in.) longer than that of a regular bike. The problems of tandem frames will be addressed separately in Chapter 21, *Tandem Touring*.

Within certain limitations, the bicycle manufacturer is at liberty to select greater wall thicknesses and diameters for certain tubes, to achieve the desired combination of strength, weight and rigidity. Especially for heavily loaded touring on a bike that should itself be kept as light as possible, it should be obvious that only the diamond-shaped "men's" frame gives the required rigidity. That applies to bikes for men and for women alike, and all special women's models without a horizontal top tube are potentially dangerous at higher speeds when loaded. Oddly enough, that applies particularly if they are made with high strength tubing, since it will have thinner walls.

Many women have particular difficulties getting a bike to fit them properly. That is due to the manufacturers' desire to standardize. They provide off-the-rack frames to fit the averagely proportioned male. However, the typical woman has different proportions that don't fit this standard scheme. Women's legs tend to be longer than men's in relation to their trunks. Their

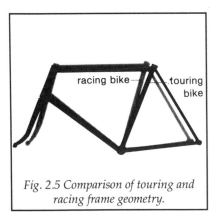

Fig. 2.5 Comparison of touring and racing frame geometry.

arms are generally shorter and weaker and their hip area is heavier. In addition, women tend to be shorter, though short men have at least as much trouble finding a properly proportioned bike. At least one American manufacturer (Georgina Terry) offers a special series of bikes that are right for the averagely proportioned woman. They are very fine machines that are available in many of the more sophisticated bike shops around the country.

Tubing Materials

For quality bikes, virtually all major bicycle manufacturers and individual frame builders use butted alloy steel tubing. These materials are made by specialized manufacturers, such as Reynolds, Columbus, True Temper, Mannesmann, Vitus, Tange and Ishiwata. Since each of them offers a wide range of different tubing sets of various strength levels and different wall thicknesses, it is important to find out whether the variety intended for touring bikes has been used for the frame in question. The lighter thin-walled tubes intended for racing frames would not be rigid enough, even if their strength may be adequate.

If you should get a custom frame built, ask the frame builder to give you details on the various tube sets available, so you can select one that is beefy enough. This is especially critical for the down tube and the chain stays, which must be pretty hefty on a touring frame. Whether the frame is custom built or not, I would say for a normal touring bike with conventional tubing diameters (i.e. 1⅛ in. seat tube and down tube, 1 in. top tube and ¼ in. head tube), the down tube should nowhere have a wall thickness less than 1 mm, while the seat stays should have a diameter of at least 15 mm.

Special frame designs and materials should be considered carefully. Mountain bikes, quite suitable for many touring uses, tend to have tubes of greater diameters, usually welded together without lugs. This makes them quite satisfactory, despite their generous dimensions. Aluminum frames must also have tubes of greater diameters, as well as a greater wall thickness. Since aluminum is so much lighter than steel, the overall weight will still be quite low.

Frame Dimensions

A bicycle's nominal size is determined by the frame size, which is defined as the length of the seat tube. Unfortunately, different manufacturers measure this dimension differently, as shown in Fig. 2.5. In the English-speaking world, the distance between the center of the bottom bracket and the top of the seat lug used to be quoted. Today, it is becoming more common to follow the French custom of measuring between the center of the bottom bracket and the center of the top tube. The same frame will be

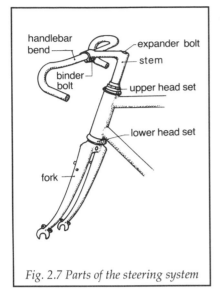

Fig. 2.7 Parts of the steering system

quoted as being 15 mm (about ½ in.) smaller in the latter case than in the former.

To select a frame of the right size, you can either use the advice contained in Table 1 in the Appendix, or you can try out some frames for fit. With wheels of the correct size installed, the top tube should be at such a height that you can straddle it with both feet flat on the ground, wearing thin-soled shoes with minimal heels. Most people seem to buy a bike that is too big. Though less critical for a touring bike than for a racing machine, I would suggest you deviate on the smaller, rather than on the larger side. See Chapters 20, 21 and 22 for the size selection of special children's bikes, tandems and mountain bikes, respectively.

A good touring bike's frame distinguishes itself from that designed for a racing machine in the following details:

☐ The touring bike frame comprises relatively thick-walled tubing of the same high quality butted alloy steels and a greater seat stay diameter.

☐ The touring bike frame should have slightly more generous dimensions and clearances, including shallower angles between the horizontal plane and the seat tube and head tube.

☐ Corresponding to many touring cyclists' choice to sit more upright, the touring frame may perhaps be selected about an inch bigger than the optimal racing bike size, which should be kept rather small to allow a really low handlebar position. Table 1 in the Appendix suggests a range of frame sizes as a function of the rider's leg length, measured as shown there. Whatever else applies, you should be able to straddle the frame with both feet flat on the ground.

☐ The touring bike frame should be equipped with a number of threaded bosses and lugs for the installation of accessories such as racks and fenders (in Britain called carriers and mudguards, respectively) and for water bottles, lighting equipment, racks and special brakes.

The Steering System

This is the assembly of parts that keeps the bike on track and balanced, by allowing the rotational plane of the front wheel to pivot relative to the rest of the bike. As shown in Fig. 2.7, it comprises the fork, headset bearings, handlebar stem, and the handlebars.

The Fork The front fork consists of two blades, terminating in fork-ends or front drop-outs, a fork crown and a steerer tube or fork shaft, which is threaded at one end to accept the adjustable parts of the headset. The fork should be of similar materials to those used for a good frame: strong alloy tubing, brazed onto the fork crown

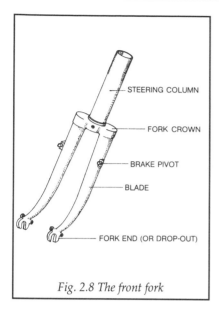

Fig. 2.8 The front fork

and with relatively thick fork-ends. The latter should have threaded eyelets for the installation of a rack and a mudguard. There should be additional threaded bosses on the fork blades to accept a rack, and pivot bosses may be provided for the special brakes used on most touring bikes. Even on bikes with aluminum frames, the forks should be of steel tubing to stand up to touring abuse.

Due to the shallower angle of the steering system axis relative to the horizontal, the touring bike's fork should have a greater off-set or rake than what is customary on a racing bike. This is necessary to achieve the same steering characteristics. Typical values for a touring bike are a steerer tube angle of 70–72 degrees and a rake of 45–55 mm.

This combination of greater rake and shallower angle results in more clearance between the pedals and the wheel. This allows for the installation of fenders without interference with the rider's toes when steering around a steep curve at low speed. It also gives better shock absorption, which is essentially a function of front fork design and construction (at least on a bike without suspension). On the other hand, the touring bike's fork should be made of thicker wall tubing for adequate strength, which tends to detract from its shock absorption qualities.

In a collision, the fork will generally be the first thing to get damaged, being bent back. Although such a bent fork can sometimes be straightened again, it will be smart to check with a qualified bike mechanic, rather than experimenting around yourself. When in doubt, have a new fork installed.

The length of the fork's steerer tube is a function of the frame size. It is determined by adding the head tube length to the headset bearing's stacking height, deducting 2 mm (about 1/16 in.). There are two distinct threading standards in use: French and English. The latter standard is used on most bikes. Nowadays, even frames made for export by French manufacturers are supplied with English threading. Just the same, it will be a good idea to take the old fork and a matching threaded part of the headset along when replacing a bent fork. If the bike has cantilever brakes (as explained under *The Brakes* in Chapter 3), pivot bosses for their installation must be present, in addition to the threaded eyelets and bosses required for the installation of rack and fender.

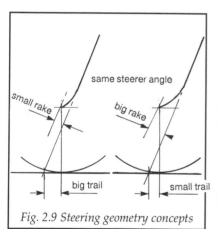

Fig. 2.9 Steering geometry concepts

The Headset

The headset consists of a double set of ball bearings. These are installed at the upper and lower ends of the head tube, with the matching parts fixed on the fork crown and screwed onto the threaded part of the steerer tube, respectively. The headset should be adjusted if the steering is either too loose or too tight. Refer to Fig. 2.10 and proceed as follows:

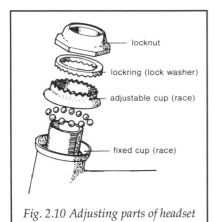

Fig. 2.10 Adjusting parts of headset

Handlebars and Stem

1. Loosen the big locknut on the upper headset bearing by about 3–4 turns.

2. Lift the lock washer far enough to allow turning the bearing race immediately below.

3. Tighten or loosen the adjustable race as required, by turning it clockwise or counterclockwise, respectively.

4. Put the lock washer in place and tighten the locknut, while holding the adjustable race.

5. If problems persist, see a bike shop for lubrication or part replacement, or learn to do it yourself with the aid of a technical manual, such as my *Bicycle Repair Book*.

The handlebars are attached to the fork's steerer tube by means of an L-shaped piece called the stem. The lower end of this device fits inside the steerer tube. A wedge- or cone-shaped part can be pulled into the stem to clamp the two parts together by tightening the expander bolt. The latter is reached from the top and is generally operated by means of an Allen key. If you are using a relatively high handlebar position, as many touring cyclists do, the extension should be quite long, since at least 65 mm (2½ in.) must remain contained inside the steerer tube for safety reasons.

The handlebars proper are held in a split or otherwise clamped portion at the forward end of the stem. Here they are clamped by tightening a second bolt, referred to as binder bolt. The stem is either made of aluminum alloy or welded up from steel tubing. Stems a available in various extension lengths, measured horizontally. A different size may be necessary to adapt the distance between saddle and handlebars to the rider for maximum comfort, as will be described in Chapter 8, *Bike Fit and Riding Style*.

The handlebars are generally made of aluminum tubing. They are available in several distinct shapes, ranging from the wide flat ones installed on mountain bikes to the narrow and deep models used on pure racing machines. For touring, most riders prefer bars similar to those used on racing bikes, referred to as drop bars, though with less depth and greater width. One popular touring model is the Randonneur type, on which the curved sections are raised relative to the straight center.

The center section of the handlebars should be reinforced by an interior or (preferably) exterior reinforcing sleeve, resulting in a section of greater diameter over a length of at least 5 cm (2 in.) to eliminate the chance of breaking the bar at the point where it projects from the stem. Handlebar bend and stem must be

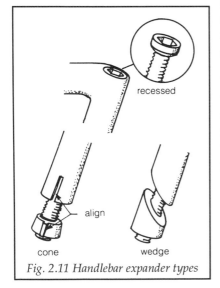

Fig. 2.11 Handlebar expander types

matched, since diameters vary from one make and model to the other.

Drop handlebars are finished off by wrapping cloth or plastic handlebar tape around them. Alternately, you may choose installing flexible foam plastic sleeves. The latter solution appears to be most comfortable for bike touring on less than perfect road surfaces. The open ends are closed off by inserting plastic plugs.

Saddle and Seatpost

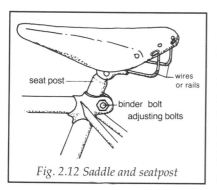

Fig. 2.12 Saddle and seatpost

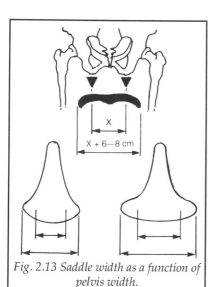

Fig. 2.13 Saddle width as a function of pelvis width.

The Mountain Bike for Touring

On a touring bike, the saddle, or seat, had better be comfortable. Most touring cyclists prefer to sit more upright than is customary for bicycle racing. This riding style results in more weight resting on the saddle and more difficulty lifting the weight to relieve pain. Consequently, a different saddle design may be required.

In general, a good touring saddle should be somewhat wider in the back, though still as long and narrow in the front as the racing saddle. In particular women, who usually have a considerably wider pelvis then most men, may need an extra-wide and more generously padded model. Although I and many other experienced touring cyclists prefer leather saddles, the trend is towards nylon-based seats with some padding in the main pressure areas, covered by thin leather.

Fig. 2.12 also shows the way the saddle is attached to the frame at the seat lug by means of a seatpost, referred to as seat pin or seat pillar in Britain. The attachment bolts that hold the saddle to the seatpost may be either on top, underneath or by the side of the clip that holds the saddle wires to the seatpost.

The seatpost should be of a model that allows fine adjustment of the position and the angle relative to the horizontal plane. Nowadays, most models are of aluminum and have a micro-adjustable head, with which the saddle angle can be fine-tuned. The seatpost diameter should match the inside diameter of the seat tube, which can vary from 26.6 mm to 27.2 mm on frames built with butted tubing. The seatpost is held at the right height by clamping the split seat lug around it when the binder bolt is tightened. The seatpost should be so long that at least 65 mm (2½ in.) is held inside the seat lug for safety reasons. Consequently, a tall rider on a relatively short frame may need a particularly long model, though a better fitting frame is preferable. See Chapter 8, *Bike Fit and Riding Style*, for a step-by-step description of the saddle adjustment procedure.

During the late 80s, the touring bike as we know it temporarily disappeared off the market and the presumed virtues of the mountain bike were extolled for touring. Meanwhile, it has become clear that on regular roads, you'll be better off with a dedicated touring bike. What the mountain bike has done, though, is open up unpaved trails and poorly paved roads to bicycle touring. Off-road cycling makes some demands of its own, most of which will be covered in Chapter 22. In this section, we'll take a closer look at what distinguishes the mountain bike before going into all the technical details.

Essentially, the mountain bike is nothing but a derailleur bicycle with fat tires and flat handlebars. In practice, these machines are generally characterized by a few additional features, though most of these may be lacking on one machine or the other, without disqualifying it as a true mountain bike.

In addition to the things you can recognize immediately, there are some more subtle features, which will be covered here. In the first place the frame on a good mountain bike is not identical to that of a regular bike. To increase stability, to accommodate the fat tires, and to allow using it on very uneven terrain, it should be dimensioned differently: longer, with shallower angles and bigger clearances. In addition, it should be constructed with tubes and other components of slightly larger diameters and wall thicknesses than what is typical for regular bikes of comparable quality.

Typically, the mountain bike's frame is chosen 2½–5 cm (1–2 in.) smaller than a regular bicycle for the same size rider. This is also in part predicated on the frame's different geometry. Since the bottom bracket is higher, to clear obstacles, and since the rider may want to sit low enough to put a foot on the ground, the seat tube may be up to two inches shorter than that on a touring bike for the same rider, as listed in Table 1 in the Appendix.

The mountain bike's frame is also equipped with the pivot bosses that allow it to take cantilever or other frame-mounted brakes, but these are dimensioned differently from the ones used on regular touring bikes: mountain bikes are equipped with larger versions of the same types of brakes to clear the fatter tires. The pivot bosses must be positioned to accommodate these larger brake arms and to accept the different rim sizes used for the mountain bike's differently dimensioned wheels.

The rims are of a dimension to fit the special fat, knobby tires designed for them. The industry standard is rims with a rim shoulder diameter of 559 mm and a width of 22–25 mm. These rims are designed for tires of 26 inch nominal size in the American designating system. The international size will be, e.g.: 54-559. That means the tire has a cross section of 54 mm (2.125 in.) and fits a rim with a shoulder diameter of 559 mm. That will be one of the fattest models; narrower tires are also available, and perhaps more suitable for on-road touring.

Just the same, for people who really do cycle more off-road than they do on the road, especially if they travel on loose dirt or sharp rocks a lot, the thickest tires are the ultimate. The secret to low rolling resistance, as well as rim and tire endurance, is tire

Mountain bike in action. Although suitable for some uses, the real touring bike has proven itself more suitable for most uses. (photo David Epperson/Bicycle Sport)

pressure. Skinnier tires are more easily constructed to endure the higher pressure. In addition, they will weigh a little less, although I have also seen some really fat tires that were beautifully light and flexible, while accepting a pressure of 5 bar (72 psi) without problems.

Other Mountain Bike Details

The gearing set-up for a mountain bike should be similar to that of a good touring machine: widely-spread derailleur gears with 21 or 24 speeds. However, in general, these gears will be selected by the manufacturer so that the entire range is significantly lower than it would be for a regular touring bike. This is necessary to account for the greater incidence of really hard cycling, either uphill or on ground that provides a higher rolling resistance.

The handlebars are flat and wide, although narrower ones are getting increasingly popular. Some riders actually have started using drop handlebars that are only slightly modified by flaring them out a little to make them wider overall. The very wide, flat handlebars can be cut down to a more civil dimension with the aid of a hacksaw. Unless your name is King Kong, 55 cm (22 in.) is probably as wide as can be comfortably handled. The narrower bars make it much easier to ride sharp curves, since you don't have to twist your upper body as far. Mountain bike handlebars are not wrapped with handlebar tape; instead, they are equipped with closed cell foam grips. These grips dampen road shocks quite a bit, while still allowing excellent control over the steering and handling operations.

Typically, the mountain bike has an easily adjustable saddle. A quick-release binder bolt allows height adjustment in combination with a very long and (hopefully) strong seat post. If a spring support, such as the Hite-Rite, is installed between seat post and binder bolt, the height adjustment can actually be carried out while riding. I question the need for all this, even on a mountain bike, since most riders never adjust their saddle position while riding, but it can help prevent the theft of the too easily removable combination of saddle and seatpost.

Since more of your weight rests on the saddle than would be the case on a regular derailleur bike, on account of the high handlebars, the saddle should be particularly comfortable and a little wider than usual. To my mind, the ideal mountain bike saddles are the Brooks 66 Champion and Conquest models. Unfortunately, these sprung saddles do not fit a regular adjustable alloy seat post, due to their double-wire construction. However, it can be used on one of these with a filler piece, such as the one marketed by Joe Breeze. This accessory is available at some of the bike stores that deal in quality mountain bikes.

Modern mountain bike with suspension. Yes, the front suspension does make a bike more comfortable, so you may consider it for use on really rough roads. To date, I have not seen a model that allows you to install a front luggage rack.

The same kind of accessories used on regular touring machines are available in special versions for mountain bike use as well. These should indeed be specially designed for mountain bikes. Special luggage racks for the front and the rear, matching bags and packs, map holders, fenders, warning devices and lighting equipment will be just as useful on a mountain bike used for touring as they are on a regular touring bike.

Suspension

Flexstem: the one suspension method that is maintenance-free enough for a touring bike.

Many of the latest mountain bikes come complete with a suspension system—typically a telescoping front fork. For riding at speed on rough terrain this is wonderful, but I don't consider it useful for bicycle touring. This kind of equipment is often quite sensitive, and getting it replaced or repaired when away from home may be next to impossible. I would suggest sticking with more conventional and generally available equipment. If you do want to keep vibrations at bay, your best choice will be a sprung handlebar stem, such as the Girvin Flexstem or the Softride Frankenstem. These are remarkably effective and are virtually maintenance-free.

Most other suspension methods contradict my touring philosophy. Not because I am masochistic, but simply because these devices are more trouble-prone than conventional equipment. Whereas your regular fork requires no maintenance, and can easily be replaced at any bike shop if you should damage it far from home, you're not likely to get a quick solution to any problem that affects a suspension fork. This applies even more in the case of full-suspension bikes, which also have a specially adapted frame with one or more springs in the rear.

CHAPTER 3

The Bicycle's Other Components

Having considered the overall configuration of the bicycle and its main structural parts in the preceding chapter, we shall now look at the remaining regular components. These will be grouped into several major categories: drivetrain, wheels, gearing system and brakes. The accessories—those items that adapt a touring bike to its particular purpose—will be treated separately in Chapter 4. In addition, the gearing system, which is handled here briefly, will be covered more fully in Chapter 9, *Selecting and Using the Gears.*

Some elementary repair and maintenance instructions are included here for the components discussed. This is only done in those cases where it seems relevant in the context of a touring book. When you get into trouble en route because you have a flat (referred to as a puncture in Britain) or the chain comes off, you'll want to know what to do about it. On the other hand, there are numerous other possible maintenance or repair jobs that are not relevant in the context of this book. Those who want to do these jobs themselves can get full information from a complete repair book, while the less ambitious may choose to take their machine to a bike shop to alleviate the problems.

The Drivetrain

Two types of component groups. Left a conventional derailleur system group with cantilever brakes. Right an uncommon system with drum brakes from Sachs.

The bicycle's drivetrain comprises all the parts that transmit the power from the rider's legs to the rear wheel. The gearing system, which allows adjusting the transmission ratio, can be considered part of the drivetrain as well. I have chosen to treat it separately, not only in the present chapter, but also in conjunction with a discussion of its theoretical and practical implications in Chapter 9, *Selecting and Using the Gears.*

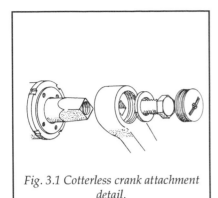

Fig. 3.1 Cotterless crank attachment detail.

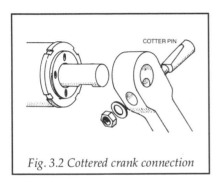

Fig. 3.2 Cottered crank connection

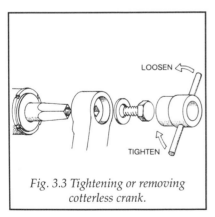

Fig. 3.3 Tightening or removing cotterless crank.

The heart of the drivetrain is the crankset, referred to as chainset in Britain, which is installed in the frame's bottom bracket. It turns around a spindle, or axle, that is supported in ball bearings. The two types of bottom bracket bearing systems used on quality bicycles are the adjustable cup-and-cone type and the non-adjustable cartridge type, usually referred to as a sealed bearing units. Although the cartridge bearings tend to be very good, I would shy away from them for a long-distance touring bike: on a long trip in faraway places, you don't want anything but the most common and simply adjustable parts on your bike.

On virtually all quality bikes built nowadays, the bottom bracket spindle has tapered square ends, matching correspondingly shaped recesses in the cranks. The cranks are held on the spindle by means of a bolt, covered by a dust cap in the crank. This method of attachment is referred to as cotterless and is shown in Fig. 3.1. Spindle lengths, bottom bracket widths, screw threading and taper shape all may differ, even if (different) models of the same make are installed. Consequently, all parts of the bottom bracket can only be replaced when the original and the matching parts are taken along to the shop, to make sure they fit as a system. For touring in less developed parts of the world, you may well be better off with an old-fashioned steel cottered crankset, which works just fine if you can find a high-quality model. It has the advantage that the cranks can be straightened without risk of breaking when bent and replacement parts can be found, or if necessary custom-made anywhere in the world.

On a new bike, the cranks tend to come loose after some use, as they may at more infrequent intervals later on. For this reason, and for other maintenance or replacement work, I suggest you obtain a matching crank tool for the particular make and model of the crankset installed on your bike. Check and tighten the crank every 50 km (30 miles) during the first 200 km (120 miles), and perhaps once a month afterwards. On models with a one-key release, which were popular for a while, only a matching Allen key is required, which is simply used to tighten the crank insert bolt like any other bolt. For all other models, proceed as described below:

Tighten Cotterless Crank

1. Remove the dustcap with any fitting tool (on most models a coin may be used).

2. Using the wrench part of the special crank tool, tighten the recessed bolt firmly, countering at the crank (see Fig. 3.3).

3. Reinstall the dustcap.

The cranks are generally made of aluminum and are available in several different lengths. Unless you have particularly long or

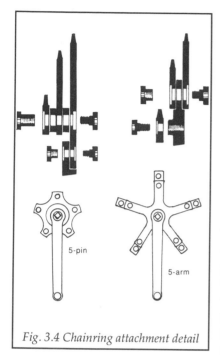

Fig. 3.4 Chainring attachment detail

short legs, the standard size of 17 or 17.5 cm (about 7 in.) will be quite satisfactory. The RH crank has an attachment spider for installation of the chainrings, also called chainwheels. On touring bikes you will generally find three chainrings installed, just like on the mountain bike. In many types of terrain, a 12-, 14- or 16-speed gearing system, with only two chainrings, will be adequate. This set-up tends to cause fewer problems and uses more readily available replacement parts. Check the attachment screws of the chainrings from time to time, and tighten them evenly if necessary.

Whatever the number of chainrings, make sure the spider is of such a type that quite small chainrings, down to perhaps 26 teeth or so, may be installed—more under *The Gearing System* below and in Chapter 9. The other point to watch out for is that the RH crank and the attachment spider must be formed in one integral part, rather than two parts swaged together, as often used on cheaper bikes. Swaged attachments usually do not stand up to heavy use in hilly terrain. Although there is some standardization, some manufacturers use differently dimensioned attachment spiders, making it mandatory to be cautious. Make sure you get perfectly matching parts when replacing anything.

The Pedals The pedals are installed at the ends of the cranks. They come in several different models. The platform model is probably most suitable for touring bikes, although many riders are quite satisfied with quill pedals.

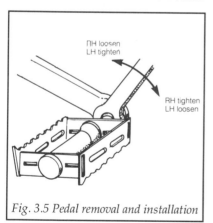

Fig. 3.5 Pedal removal and installation

The pedals may have to be removed from the bike when it is transported, particularly if it has to be placed in a box, as is demanded by many airlines. First check whether your pedals have only flat wrench faces or also a (more convenient) hexagonal recess reached from the back of the crank. In the latter case, use a matching Allen key to unscrew and install them. Otherwise, you will need a thin open ended wrench of the appropriate size (usually 15 mm). The LH pedal has LH thread, so it is loosened by turning to the right, fastened by turning to the left. Put some lubricant on the thread to protect the screw thread and to make it easier to loosen the pedals next time. I like to place a thin steel washer between the pedal spindle stub and the crank to ease removal and prevent damage.

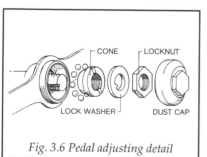

Fig. 3.6 Pedal adjusting detail

Whether or not you use special bicycle shoes with shoe plates, or cleats, which hold the shoes accurately in place on the pedals, the installation of toeclips seems a must for comfortable cycling over longer distances. I prefer the regular type which has a strap to wrap around the shoe. If you don't like the idea of being semi-permanently wired up to your bike by the feet, install the short open type of toeclips, which at least stop the feet from slipping forward off the pedals.

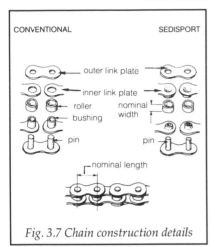

Fig. 3.7 Chain construction details

The Chain

In recent years, so-called clipless pedals, which clamp the (special) shoes in with a device similar to a ski binding, have become popular with racing and fitness cyclists. They require the use of special matching shoes. To the touring cyclist, these are even more cumbersome than cleated shoes and are not recommended.

The chain connects the crankset with the rear wheel, where a freewheel block with several different size sprockets is installed. The chain must be routed as explained below under *The Gearing System*. It must have the right size, which means it should neither hang loose nor tighten up excessively when using either of the extreme gearing combinations (big chainring with a big sprocket or small chainring with small sprocket, respectively).

Fig. 3.7 shows how the two methods of chain construction. On derailleur bikes an endless chain is used, which may be parted by removing one of the pins connecting two links. The same method is used to add or remove links to adjust the chain's length. It may be necessary to remove the chain for cleaning and lubrication, which will be frequently required under dusty or wet conditions. You will need a chain rivet extractor tool.

Chain Maintenance

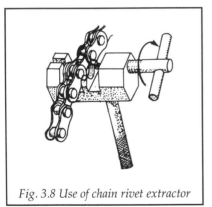

Fig. 3.8 Use of chain rivet extractor

1. Put the chain on a combination of a small chainring with a small sprocket, to release its tension.

2. Place the tool on one of the pins connecting two links, and turn it in by 6 turns.

3. Turn the handle of the tool back out and remove the tool from the chain.

4. Wriggle the chain apart.

5. Reinstall the chain, routing it around the derailleur's little wheels, or pulleys.

Note: This description applies to the removal of the chain for cleaning or replacement. To remove or add links (must be done in pairs), one pin must be pushed out completely, turning the tool in as far as needed.

The Freewheel

Depending on the make and type of rear wheel hub, the freewheel is either a separate unit screwed on, or it is integrated in the (special) hub, referred to as a cassette hub. Among the former variety, the solution with a special easily detachable screw thread, such as the Maillard Helico-matic, is particularly suitable for touring, since it can be easily removed en route. Yet despite the universal acceptance of this equipment in Europe, I hear nothing but disparaging remarks about it in the U.S., so you may have difficulty finding it. Removal of the freewheel block may become necessary to replace a broken spoke, and is hard to do with other screw-on types.

The Gearing System

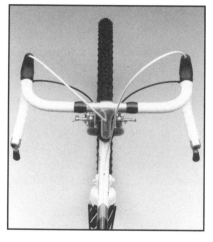

Touring bike gearing:
Above: Most modern touring bikes with drop handlebars are equipped with bar-end shifters.
Below: Typical rear derailleur.

In this section we'll discuss only the hardware, while the niceties of the system, including selection and handling, are described in some detail in Chapter 9, *Selecting and Using the Gears*. Whereas hub gearing systems may be suitable for many touring purposes, they have been essentially eliminated from the American market. Consequently, I shall confine my remarks to derailleur gearing.

A typical derailleur system is shown in Fig. 3.9. It consists of a front derailleur, or changer, and a rear derailleur, which are operated by means of shift levers. The shifters may be installed either on the down tube or, in the case of a bike with flat handlebars, on the bars. Other shift lever locations, such as the stem, though seen on some bikes, are inherently unsuitable for touring use, since they are not easily accessible under touring conditions. The shift levers are connected to the derailleurs by means of flexible cables that run over guides and, in the case of handlebar-mounted shifters, partly inside flexible outer cables.

The front derailleur, or changer, is installed on the seat tube, either by means of a clip around the tube or a brazed-on lug. The latter solution restricts you to the use of derailleurs of the same make as that lug if you ever have to replace it. The rear derailleur is installed on the RH drop-out, which should have a threaded eye for this purpose, though adaptor plates are provided with most derailleurs, to allow installing them on a bike without a derailleur eye. The chain is routed around the rear derailleur's little wheels, while it is guided through the changer's cage in the front.

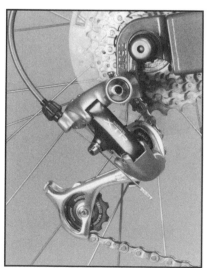

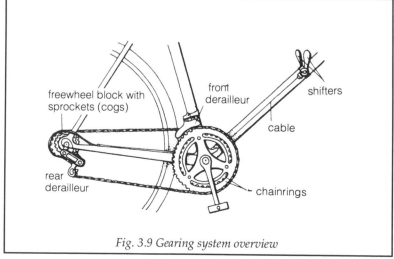

Fig. 3.9 Gearing system overview

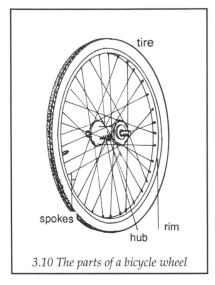

3.10 The parts of a bicycle wheel

The derailleurs are used to shift the chain over sideways to engage a smaller or bigger chainring or sprocket, while you continue to pedal forward with reduced pedal force. A combination with a large chainring and a small sprocket provides a high gear, suitable for easy terrain conditions. Engaging a small chainring and a large sprocket provides a low gear, required to go up an incline, starting off or riding against a head wind. A thorough explanation will be found in Chapter 9.

For serious touring, especially in hilly terrain, carrying luggage, both front and rear derailleurs should be models suitable for use with wide-range gearing. This may be defined as gears ranging from very low to very high, characterized by big differences between the numbers of teeth (and hence the sizes) of individual sprockets and chainrings. You can recognize these wide range models by the greater size of the cage through which the chain is guided.

Virtually all modern derailleurs are indexed, meaning that they shift in distinct steps from one gear to the next. Although I agree that this has greatly eased shifting, I suggest you look for a system that can be shifted from the indexed to the so-called friction mode. In the friction mode, the shifters don't stop at the distinct settings but can be moved gradually, which makes it possible to shift correctly, albeit a little slower, even when the derailleur is out of adjustment or is damaged—something that invariably happens on a longer tour.

The Wheels

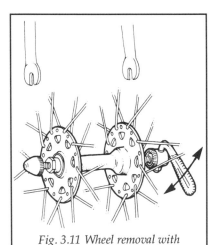

Fig. 3.11 Wheel removal with quick-release.

A typical bicycle wheel is shown in Fig. 3.10. It is a spoked wheel with regular wired-on tires, which consist of a separate inner tube and a casing that is held tight in a deep-bedded metal rim by means of metal wires in the side of the tire casing. The other components of the wheel are hub and spokes. Wheel problems are perhaps the most common category of incidents while touring, and their repair will be covered in some detail below.

The hub may be either a high flange or a low flange model (referred to as big and small flange, respectively, in Britain). Like the rim, it must be designed for a minimum of 36 spokes per wheel. Smaller sizes, as used on children's bikes, are an exception. On most touring bikes the hubs have quick-release levers, allowing easy wheel removal. For mountain bikes and tandems, but even for heavily loaded normal touring machines, quick-releases are not such a good idea, since these have hollow axles. The hole weakens the axle somewhat, which is an important drawback, especially for the rear wheel.

The spokes should be of stainless steel. Each spoke is held to the rim by means of a screwed-on nipple, which should be kept tightened to maintain the spoke under tension, which actually prevents a lot of spoke breakages. The spokes run from the hub

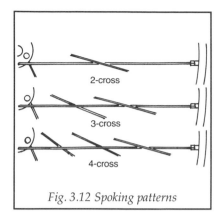

Fig. 3.12 Spoking patterns

to the rim in one of several distinct patterns. Fig. 3.12 shows three-cross and four-cross spoking patterns. The latter appears to be most suitable for the rear wheel, as it has been demonstrated to result in fewer spoke breakages.

A problem on the rear wheel is the fact that the rim with the tire must be centered over the ends of the bearing locknuts. This normally creates a significant off-set relative to the hub flanges, on account of the presence of the freewheel on the RH side. Fig. 3.13 shows several ways the wheel may be centered. The usual off-set in the rear wheel results in much higher forces (and somewhat shorter spoke length) in the spokes leading to the RH flange than in those on the other side of the wheel.

The length of the spoke is measured as shown in Fig 3.14. It depends on the wheel size, the type of hub and the spoking pattern. Make sure you know which sizes are needed for your wheels (they may be different for front and rear, and in the rear even for both sides). The strength is a function of the thickness—at least 2.0 mm or 14 gauge is required for a touring bike. Butted spokes have a thinner section in the middle. They are as strong as regular spokes that are as thick as their thickest section (the lower gauge number in their size designation). If a spoke should break, carry out a repair according to the following description:

Replace Broken Spoke

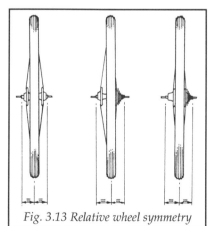

Fig. 3.13 Relative wheel symmetry

1. Remove the freewheel, if the hole in the hub that corresponds to the broken spoke lies inaccessibly under the freewheel.

2. Remove the old spoke. If possible, unscrew the remaining section from the nipple, holding the latter with a wrench. If not possible, the tire must be deflated and lifted in the area of the broken spoke first, after which the nipple may be replaced by a new one.

3. Locate a spoke that runs the same way as the broken one: every fourth spoke along the circumference of the rim runs similarly. Check how it crosses the various other spokes that run the other way, using it as an example.

4. Thread the spoke into the nipple until it has the same tension as the other spokes of the wheel.

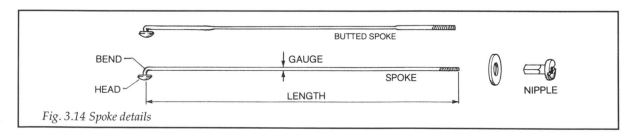

Fig. 3.14 Spoke details

5. If the spokes do not seem to be under tension, tighten all of them half a turn at a time, until they all seem equally taut and the wheel is reasonably true—if necessary, follow the instructions for *Wheel Truing* below to correct the situation.

The Rims For a touring bike of any quality, the rims must be of aluminum, which is reasonably light and strong. In addition, aluminum provides much better braking characteristics than heavier chrome-plated steel rims. The rim should match the tire, which will be discussed below. For touring, a relatively strong model should be selected. Stronger models tend to be those that are a little heavier.

If weight is to be saved—and lighter wheels definitely run better than heavier ones—keep it down by selecting a relatively narrow model, within the limitation that it must accept the tire selected. The spoke holes should be reinforced by means of ferrules, which on a "box section" rim design should connect the inner and outer bottom, as shown in Fig. 3.15. To protect the tube, a piece of tape should cover the part of the rim bed where the spoke nipples would otherwise touch the inner tube.

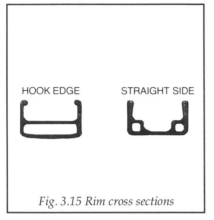

HOOK EDGE   STRAIGHT SIDE

Fig. 3.15 Rim cross sections

Wheel Truing If the wheel is bent, which may or may not be the result of a broken spoke, proceed as follows to straighten it by retensioning certain spokes, as shown in Fig. 3.16:

1. Check just where it is offset to the left, and where to the right, by turning it slowly while watching at a fixed reference point, such as the brake shoes. Mark the relevant sections.

2. Tighten LH spokes in the area where the rim is offset to the RH side, and loosen the ones on the LH side—and vice versa.

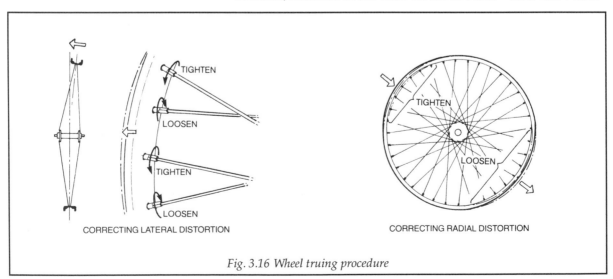

CORRECTING LATERAL DISTORTION   CORRECTING RADIAL DISTORTION

Fig. 3.16 Wheel truing procedure

3. Repeat steps 1 and 2 several times, until the wheel is true enough not to rub on the brakes. This will get you by but, unless you are quite good at it, I suggest you get the job done properly by a bike mechanic as soon as possible.

Tires and Tubes

The size of the tire defines the nominal size of the wheel. Adult touring bikes usually have 700 mm tires of various tire widths, although 650 mm (26 in.) wheels are actually more suitable for heavy touring use, since their shorter spokes tend to hold up better, and the old 27-inch wheels are still available. These nominal sizes are a far cry from their actual dimensions. To give an example: the supposed 700 mm tires normally measure anywhere from 666 mm to 686 mm, depending on the tire width. Although they are also known as 28 in. tires (based on the outside diameter with the use of a rather fat tire), the types in use today are actually smaller in outside diameter than those of nominal size 27 in. The inner tube should be of a size to match the tire. For any given size, it seems the lighter and thinner tube and tire give a better ride. Only in terrain with thorns and other frequent puncture causes, should the very thick thorn-proof tubes be used.

Tire and rim must match. The critical dimension determining tire interchangeability, especially important if you ever run into trouble on a trip abroad, is the rim bed or rim shoulder dimension. For 27 in. and 700 mm tires this diameter should be 630 mm and 622 mm, respectively. Mountain bikes that roll on 26 in. tires have rims of 559 mm rim bed diameter. At least the European tire and rim manufacturers now quote these critical dimensions in mm on tires and rims in the form of the ETRTO designation, illustrated in Fig. 3.17. On tires this is, e.g. : 25- 622 for a 25 mm wide tire for use on a 622 mm rim. On a rim the ETRTO code may read 622 x 19 for a 622 mm diameter tire that's 19 mm wide.

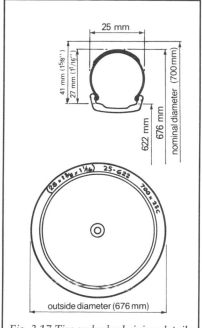

Fig. 3.17 Tire and wheel sizing details

As for the recommended tire width, it depends on the terrain encountered. The minimum width suitable for any kind of touring is probably 25 mm, while 28 or even 32 mm are good choices for heavily loaded bikes on good road surfaces, 35 to 40 mm for mixed road surfaces. If you want to tour off-road or in regions where roads are maintained less scrupulously than they are in the U.S. or Western Europe, mountain bike wheels with tire widths anywhere from 42 mm to 54 mm are an excellent choice, as they are for tandem use. Whenever long life and resistance to abuse are required, select a tire with plenty of rubber in the tread area. Even in that case, look for a model with flexible sidewalls, which I have found to roll significantly lighter, especially on rough surfaces.

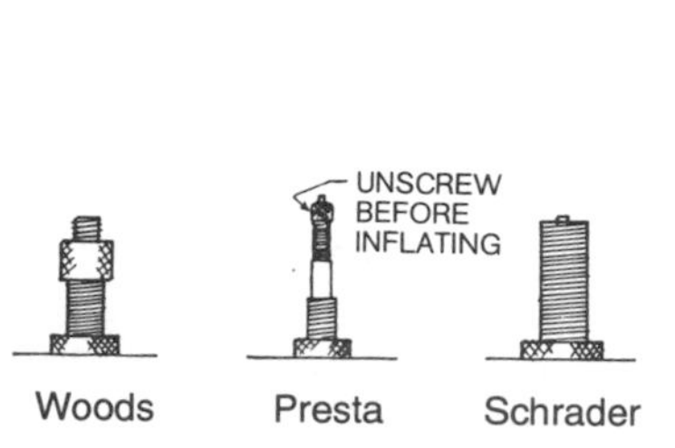

The tube is inflated by means of a valve, several types of which are illustrated in Fig. 3.18. By far the most suitable is the Presta valve, which requires much less force to inflate properly,

Fig. 3.18 Valve types

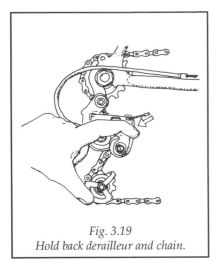

Fig. 3.19
Hold back derailleur and chain.

though it can't be done by means of a gas station air hose, unless you buy an adaptor nipple. Unscrew the round nut at the tip before inflating, and tighten it again afterwards. Inflation pressure is the key to low rolling resistance and immunity to puncturing. Maintain at least the pressure quoted on the tire sidewall, and don't hesitate to inflate at least the rear wheel by about 20 percent more than that minimum value. On the road, use a hand pump and regularly check the pressure with the aid of a tire pressure gauge, both described in Chapter 4.

Sooner or later, every cyclist gets a puncture—a flat tire. When you are touring, you must be able to handle this repair yourself. Carry a patch kit, three tire levers, a pump and perhaps a spare tube. The adhesive quality of the patches in your kit deteriorates over time, so I suggest replacing them once a year. Proceed as follows to fix a flat:

Fixing a Flat

1. Remove the wheel from the bike. On a rear wheel, first select the gear with the smallest chainring and sprocket, then hold the chain with the derailleur back.

2. Check whether the cause is visible from the outside. In that case, remove it and mark its location, so you know where to work.

3. Remove the valve cap and locknut, unscrew the round nut (if you have a Presta valve).

4. Push the valve body in and work one side of the tire into the deeper center of the rim.

5. Put a tire lever under the bead on that side, at some distance from the valve, then use it to lift the bead over the rim edge and hook it on a spoke.

6. Do the same with the second tire lever two spokes to the left and with the third one two spokes over to the right. Now the first one will come loose, so you may use it in a fourth location, if necessary.

7. When enough of the tire sidewall is lifted over the rim, you can lift the rest over by hand.

8. Remove the tube, saving the valve until last; then push the valve back through the valve hole in the rim.

9. Try inflating the tire and check where air escapes. If the hole is very small, so it can't be easily detected, pass the tube slowly past your eye, which is quite sensitive. If still no luck, dip the tube under water, a section at a time: the hole is wherever bubbles escape. Mark its location and dry the tire if appropriate. There may be more than just one hole.

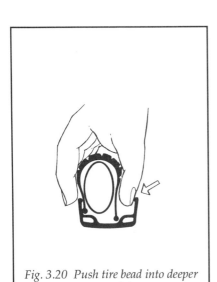

Fig. 3.20 Push tire bead into deeper center of rim.

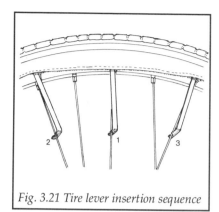

Fig. 3.21 Tire lever insertion sequence

10. Make sure the area around the hole is dry and clean, then roughen it with the sandpaper or the scraper from the puncture kit and remove the resulting dust. Treat an area slightly larger than the patch you want to use.

11. Quickly and evenly, spread a thin film of rubber solution on the treated area. Let dry about 3 minutes — half as long in dry, hot weather.

12. Remove the foil backing from the patch, without touching the adhesive side. Place it with the adhesive side down on the treated area, centered on the hole. Apply pressure over the entire patch to improve adhesion.

13. Sprinkle talcum powder from the patch kit over the treated area.

14. Inflate the tube and wait long enough to make sure the repair is carried out properly.

15. Meanwhile, check the inside of the tire and remove any sharp objects that may have caused the puncture. Also make sure no spoke ends are projecting from the rim bed—file flush if necessary and cover with rim tape.

16. Let enough air out of the tube to make it limp but not completely empty. Then reinsert it under the tire, starting at the valve.

17. With your bare hands, pull the tire back over the edge of the rim, starting opposite the valve, which must be done last. If it seems too tight, work the part already installed deeper into the center of the rim bed, working around towards the valve from both sides.

18. Make sure the tube is not pinched between rim and tire bead anywhere, working and kneading the tire until it is free.

19. Push the valve through the hole in the rim; install the valve locknut and inflate the tire to about a third its final pressure.

20. Center the tire relative to the rim, making sure it lies evenly all around on both sides.

21. Inflate to its final pressure, then install the wheel. If the tire is wider than the rim, you may have to release the brake (and make sure you tighten it again afterwards). On the rear wheel, refer to step 1 above.

Note:
If the valve leaks, or if the tube is seriously damaged, the entire tube must be replaced, which is done following the relevant steps of these same instructions. Replacement of the tire cover is

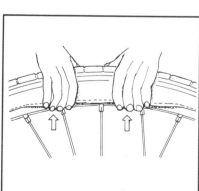

Fig. 3.22 Reinstalling tire over rim

The Brakes

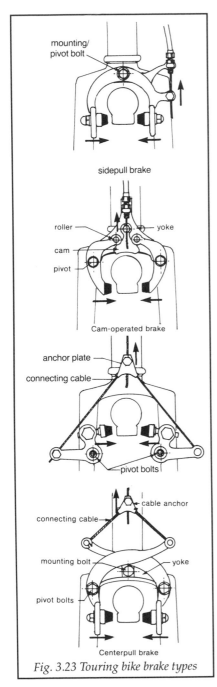

Fig. 3.23 Touring bike brake types

done similarly. Always make sure the rim tape that covers the spoke ends is intact.

There are three different types of rim brakes suitable for touring bicycles. In some countries hub brakes are also used, but only rim brakes are commonly applied for serious cycling of any kind in the English-speaking world. Fig. 3.23 shows the various types, referred to as centerpull, cantilever, and cam-operated brakes, respectively.

On the centerpull brake the brake arms pivot on bosses mounted on a yoke that is part of the brake unit. On the cantilever brake and the cam-operated model, the pivots are installed on bosses that are attached directly to the fork or seat stays, which must be welded on in those locations. The cantilever brake is generally considered the most suitable for touring bikes, because it is the most rigid and reliable even under extremely heavy conditions. Not shown here is the conventional sidepull brake used on most regular road bikes — it is not designed for the wide tires and large clearances required on a touring bike

With any rim brake, the force applied by pulling the lever is transmitted to the brake unit by means of flexible cables. These cables are partly contained in flexible outer cables, or casings, and restrained at anchor points on the frame. The force is transmitted to the parts of the brake unit to which the cable is attached. A pivoting action then pulls the ends of the brake arms with the brake blocks against the sides of the rim to create the drag that slows down the bike.

Touring cyclists are fortunate compared to racing cyclists, because the best brakes for their application are relatively reasonably priced. The paramount criterion for a good touring brake is that it must be rigid, while still opening up far enough to clear the rather fat tire and leaving enough space for fenders. Of the models shown, the cantilever brake is generally considered to be the best, since it can easily be designed that way. My second choice would be the centerpull brake.

The brake lever should be quite rigid. It must match the handlebar type used and it should be easy to reach, while allowing full application of the brake. The type of levers designed for mountain bikes are suitable for any bike with flat handlebars, providing the attachment clamp matches the bar diameter. If you like to hold drop handlebars in the top straight portion, you will be best served with *guidonnet* models shown in the lower detail of Fig. 3.24. Models with extension levers are not satisfactory, since they are insufficiently rigid and often shorten the regular handle's range of travel.

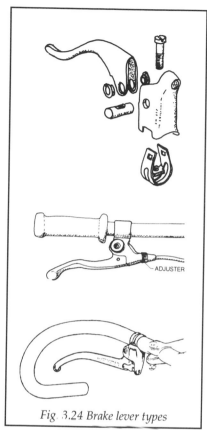

Fig. 3.24 Brake lever types

All brakes have an adjustment mechanism to shorten the cable, which allows you to apply more force. It may be installed at the handle, at the brake unit or at one of the cable anchor points. The adjustment is described below. Most brakes have a quick-release mechanism to allow easy wheel removal and installation, without affecting adjustment of the brake. Brake cables should not be elastic or 'spongy', to allow applying adequate force. Relatively thick inner cables with non-compressing outer cables, such as those by Campagnolo, are best for use with any make or model of brake. Brake cables should be routed as short as possible, providing they are not forced into excessively tight bends in any position of handlebars or brake.

The brake blocks should be of a composition material that provides adequate braking even in the rain, which is just not the case with any kind of plain rubber brake blocks. Contrary to popular belief, longer brake blocks are not better but poorer than shorter ones, given the same material.

To make sure the brakes work properly, it is enough to test them at low speed. Try them out separately at walking speed, which is perfectly safe and still gives a representative test of the deceleration reached with each brake. Used alone while riding the bike, the rear brake must be strong enough to skid the wheel when applied firmly. The front brake should decelerate the bike so much that the rider notices the rear wheel lifting off the ground when the brake is fully applied. If the braking performance is inadequate, carry out the adjustment described below.

Adjust Brake We will assume the brake must be adjusted because its performance is insufficient. In this case, the cable tension must be increased by decreasing its length. Should the brake touch the rim even when not engaged, the opposite must be done to lengthen the cable slightly.

Before starting, check to make sure the brake blocks lie on the rim properly over their entire width and length when the brake is applied. Ideally, the front of the brake block should touch the rim just a little earlier than the back. If necessary, adjust by loosening the brake block bolt, moving the block as appropriate. Retighten it while holding the brake block in the right position. If necessary, the brake block may be replaced, after which the adjustment steps that follow must be carried out as well.

1. Release brake quick-release.

2. Loosen locknut on the adjusting mechanism for the brake cable, which may be installed on the brake, on the lever or at a cable anchor point.

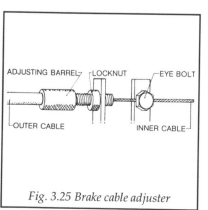

Fig. 3.25 Brake cable adjuster

3. While holding the locknut, screw the barrel adjuster out by several turns; then tighten the quick-release again.

4. Check the brake tension: the brake must grab the rim firmly when a minimum of 2 cm (¾ in.) clearance remains between the brake handle and the handlebars.

5. If necessary, repeat steps 1–4 until the brake works properly.

6. Tighten the locknut again, while holding the adjusting barrel to stop it from turning.

Replace Brake Cable   To avoid the unsettling experience of breaking your brake cable just when it is most needed, I suggest you replace it as soon as individual strands show signs of damage at the end nipple. Since a cable may have to be replaced while you are touring, it will be smart to carry a spare. Make sure the spare cable has a nipple that matches the particular brake lever used on your bike. Proceed as follows:

1. Loosen the brake quick-release.

2. Loosen the eye bolt or clamping bolt that holds the cable at the brake, until you can pull the old cable out.

3. Push the old cable out, working towards the lever, where you can dislodge the nipple. Then pull the entire inner cable out, catching the outer cable sections, as well as any other parts, memorizing their installation locations.

4. Lubricate the new cable. Loosen the locknut, then screw the adjusting barrel in all the way.

5. Starting at the lever, push the new cable through, securing the nipple by pulling it taut. Thread the cable through the various anchor points, outer cable sections and other parts, and through the adjuster. Finally push it through the eye bolt at the brake, and clamp it in. Secure the nipple into the lever by pulling the cable taut from the brake end.

6. Tighten the eye bolt while continuing to keep the cable taut.

7. Adjust the cable tension, following the preceding instructions under *Adjust Brake*.

8. Test the brake in operation, followed by a final adjustment if necessary.

9. Finally, cut off the free end of the cable until about 2.5 cm (1 in.) projects, using sharp cutters.

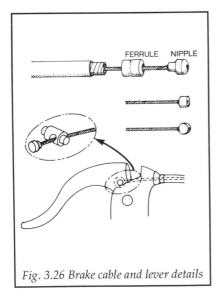

Fig. 3.26 Brake cable and lever details

CHAPTER 4

Touring Bike Accessories

Having examined the bicycle itself with its essential components in the two preceding chapters, we shall now look at its accessories: the additional equipment that can be installed to advantage on the touring bike. In recent years quite a few manufacturers have re-introduced purpose-built touring bikes, more or less completely equipped with such accessories. In some cases, any more or less regular derailleur bicycle, whether a model with drop handlebars or a mountain bike, can be turned into an acceptable touring machine by merely installing additional equipment, such as luggage racks, fenders, lights etc. Either way, the following descriptions deal with all those accessories that turn a regular bicycle into a real touring bike.

Braze-ons, Lugs and Eyelets

Ideally, the touring bicycle should be equipped with a number of attachment points for the installation of accessories. In most cases that is not only the most convenient solution, it is also the safest way: reliable and secure. Even if sold without the actual touring accessories, the bike should preferably have the following attachment provisions:

☐ Double threaded eyelets on front and rear drop-outs, to attach the stays for front and rear luggage racks and fenders simultaneously.

Cannondale touring bike with accessories. Still missing: lights, lock and pump.

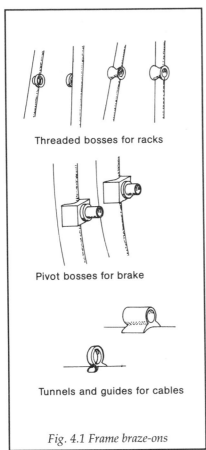

Threaded bosses for racks

Pivot bosses for brake

Tunnels and guides for cables

Fig. 4.1 Frame braze-ons

Clamps and Clips

☐ Threaded bosses on the fork blades and on the seat stays, to attach the upper supports for front and rear luggage racks.

☐ Tunnels and guides for the brake and gear cables on the frame.

☐ Anchors or stops for the outer brake cables. One should be in the form of a bridge between the seat stays to act as a stop for the cable to the rear centerpull or cantilever brake, and a similar device either on the handlebar stem or integrated in the upper headset bearing for the front brake.

☐ If the bike will be equipped with cantilever brakes or cam-operated brakes, pivot bosses for these on the fork blades and the seat stays. If a cam-operated brake with fixed pivots will be used, those for the rear wheel may be installed at the bottom of the chain stays, instead.

☐ Threaded bosses on the frame's down tube and seat tube for the installation of two or more water bottles.

☐ Threaded bosses or lugs for the installation of front and rear lights and a dynamo, or generator.

☐ A boss or chain hanger on the inside of the RH seat stay, to accept the chain when the wheel is not installed.

If the pertinent accessories are not installed initially, bolts should preferably be installed in the threaded parts to protect the internal screw threads. These bolts should be greased slightly and kept tightened. Some frame builders use nylon screws here, which is quite acceptable, but they will have to be replaced by (steel) bolts of a different length when the accessory is installed.

To install accessories on a bicycle without such special provisions, you will have to rely on provisional clamps and the like. It will be advisable to install a rubber patch from the bicycle tire patch kit around the bike's tubing before mounting such a clamp. This not only protects paintwork or metal finish, it also prevents the clamp from slipping or twisting. Do not use self-adhesive tape for this purpose, since it will slip over time, whereas a tire patch, applied just like you would do to repair a puncture, will stay in place firmly.

By way of maintenance of most accessories, you merely have to make sure they are not broken or loose. Tighten the various attachment bolts from time to time, preferably on a regular basis—even daily on a longer tour. To make sure bolts do not come loose, I suggest you use washers and locknuts wherever possible.

Luggage Racks

Small but adequately rigid luggage rack made of welded aluminum rod, with adjustable mounting hardware.

It may be possible to go on shorter trips (up to weekend rides, if you stay in hotels) with no more luggage than can be carried in bags directly attached to the bike or carried on the back. However, you will need luggage racks, or carriers, for any serious touring over longer distances. The dilemma of carrying luggage, and the details of bags and racks, will be covered in much more detail in Chapters 5 and 13. Here we'll merely introduce the basic types of racks available.

Luggage racks are available for the front and the rear. Generally, the rear rack allows carrying relatively large bags by the side and on top, while the one in the front is smaller, being attached to the fork. Their details of construction and the preferred way to combine the various types of racks and bags will all be covered in the next chapter.

Whatever their type, make sure the racks can be attached very firmly to the bike. Preferably, brazed-on attachment lugs or bosses should be installed on the bike, exactly matching the dimensions of the particular rack used. That may become a bit of a problem when replacing the rack on a used bike or when installing a rack on a bike for the first time. However, a certain degree of standardization has taken place. Most manufacturers of touring bikes and racks nowadays design their equipment in line with the attachment details of the racks produced by Jim Blackburn—including his many cut-price competitors.

Do not skimp on the quality of your luggage racks, since they are essential load-bearing parts. As in so many things related to the bike, the price difference comes either out of the weight or the quality. Consequently, you should expect to pay a lot for a good light rack made of steel tubing or aluminum rod, or save quite a bit on a well-built, though heavier, steel rack. Just don't look for a rack that is both light and cheap: it probably won't be much good. See the next chapter for more details on recognizing quality and suitability.

Fenders

Although many cyclists in America abhor the idea of installing fenders, or mudguards, on their bicycle, I suggest no touring bike is complete without them, unless you do all your cycling in one of those areas where it simply doesn't rain for a period of several months. Even then, you would be well advised to get fenders, though you may hold off on installing them until the rainy season starts. Cycling in the rain or on wet roads after it has rained is not as bad as some people think, and it will certainly be less miserable when you are equipped for it.

Yes, you can ride in the rain, or on a wet road after the rain, on a bike without fenders. But you'll be miserable. A spray of muddy water will stain your back and your luggage; another jet of water will be shooting at your feet. Although you may still

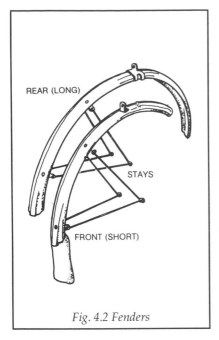

Fig. 4.2 Fenders

need rain gear to keep the rain off the top, you'll find fenders at least keep you reasonably dry and clean from below.

At the top, the fenders are attached to the brake bolt behind the front fork and in front of the bridge connecting the seat stays, for front and rear fenders, respectively. In the rear, a second point of attachment is by means of a clip over the bridge just behind the bottom bracket. Finally, they are held on by means of rather thin stays, to the front fork-ends and rear drop-outs, respectively.

Install plain washers between bolts or nuts and the various clips or stays. The fenders should be mounted in such a way that about 2 cm (¾ in.) radial and at least 1 cm (⅜ in.) lateral clearance remains between the tire on the one hand and the fender or its mounting hardware on the other. If the fender is either crooked, too close to, or too far from the wheel, do not adjust it by bending the stays. Instead, undo the clamping point and move the stays in or out to suit, after which the bolt is tightened again. Any excessive protrusions should be cut off. On the fenders approved by the CPSC (Consumer Product Safety Commission) sold in the U.S., the stays are attached on the inside, which means the stays must be cut to size before they are installed.

If you choose to install fenders only occasionally, removable attachments are easy enough to make, as shown in Fig. 4.3. To attach the stays at the fork ends-and drop-outs, make your own wing bolts by soldering a sizable washer into the slot of a normal slotted-head screw. If the bike has caliper brakes, attached by means of single bolts in fork crown and rear brake bridge, replace their attachment nuts by two thinner nuts (locknuts), between which the fender clip is clamped. Install and tighten both nuts, even when the fender is not installed, since a single thin nut is not adequate to restrain the brake.

On a bike with pivot boss- mounted brakes there is no central brake mounting bolt bolt, and in that cas you can attach the fenders to the fork and the rear stay bridge by means of a similar home-made wing bolt with a nut at the other end.

Fenders may be either of plastic or of metal. The lightest satisfactory fenders available are the plastic models that used to be made by Bluemels of England. Since this company's production facilities were taken over by SKS, a major German competitor, the future of these fenders is not assured, but they'll probably be around for a while. The problem is that SKS is used to doing business in a market where a rear light is commonly installed on the rear fender, and even the strongest plastic fenders invariably break after extended use when they are loaded by anything like that in the back. This kind of failure mode is known as fatigue, which will be explained in the next chapter, as it also applies to structural members of luggage racks.

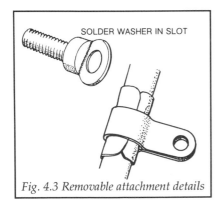

Fig. 4.3 Removable attachment details

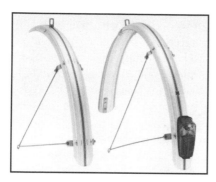

Fiber-reinforced plastic fenders by ESGE, with pre-wired rear light for a system with generator or central battery.

Much more expensive fiber-reinforced fenders, such as those made by ESGE, oddly enough do not last any longer than the lightest and cheapest plastic ones. Much stronger are most metal models, and it is generally agreed that the relatively wide aluminum versions, particularly those made by the French Lefol company, are the ideal touring fenders. On the latter models, the wire stays and other mounting hardware are solidly attached to the metal of the fenders, while such items are only clamped or loosely riveted on most plastic fenders. If you choose aluminum or other metal fenders, make sure the edges are rolled to eliminate potentially dangerous protrusions.

Fenders with unguarded edges are not legal as original equipment in the U.S. To protect children, the American CPSC has the authority to regulate the sale of toys. Curiously defining all bicycles as toys, this agency has instituted some far-out criteria for bicycle equipment, of which this is one of the very few sensible examples. You will, for instance, find out that the mounting hardware for fenders as sold in the U.S. is often highly impractical—simply to satisfy one of the many less sensible CPSC regulations.

To really keep the water that is splashed up from the road at the front wheel from your feet, you will need a mud flap installed at the bottom of the front fender. Very few models available have one of these things attached, but you can make your own, using a 15–20 cm (6–8 in.) square piece of flexible, but relatively thick vinyl attached to the bottom of the front guard.

Lights

Next to fenders, bicycle lights are perhaps the most maligned bicycle accessories. Like fenders, lights are not very common on bicycles sold and ridden in the U.S. In many other countries they are a prescribed accessory, and I know of at least one cyclist who got into serious trouble on a tour abroad because he thought lights were a waste of time. Of course, they are not. If you have ever seen an unlit cyclist appear out of nowhere in your car headlights or when riding your bike during darkness or at dusk, you will perhaps appreciate just how dangerous it can be to go without. The fact that you didn't run into him does not prove that it is safe to go without lights: the risk is infinitely greater without than it is with lights.

Many cyclists argue they never ride in the dark anyway. However, from experience I can report that just about everyone who told me that was not only lying, he was also playing with his life. Sooner or later during any tour, you will want to leave the place you are staying without being able to return before dark. Or your day's trip will take you longer than expected. In short, though you may not *plan* on using lights, you should have them available in case you do need them.

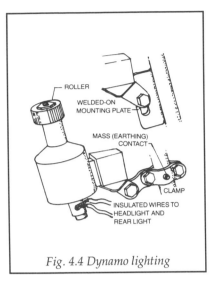

Fig. 4.4 Dynamo lighting

One generator that doesn't slip even in the rain: Swiss DT hub generator. Similar in concept to the old Sturmey-Archer Dyno-Hub, this one actually delivers enough power to light up the road.

Bicycle lights may be either batter- operated or powered by means of a generator, referred to as a dynamo in Britain. In recent years, lighting systems with a central battery have become popular. For bicycle touring they are not as suitable as generator-powered systems, because their rechargeable batteries need to be recharged regularly, which will be impossible on a camping trip and at best inconvenient in many other cases.

Generator-operated models are almost invariably permanently installed, while most regular battery-models may be simply removed from the bike. One advantage of the latter is that they will double for use off the bike as a flashlight, called a torch in Britain. The removability may be good or bad: bad if it's stolen when you do leave it on, good if you can avoid somebody messing around with it by taking it off yourself.

Although generator lights are not so easily stolen, they can be tampered with, and unfortunately often are. It may happen if you have to leave your bike for some time in a place that makes it clear you won't be back very soon, such as a public swimming pool. Even if the lights are not stolen or vandalized, they may get damaged, so it will be wise to check their operation regularly and to tighten all mechanical and electric connections.

A typical generator lighting set is depicted in Fig. 4.4. The generator is activated by means of a lever-operated spring-loaded mechanism that pushes a friction roller, connected with the generator's rotor, against the side or the tread of a tire, depending on the type used. Although some touring cyclists disagree, I find the roller generator quite satisfactory—with minor adaptations. This model generally provides significantly less physical resistance and causes less tire wear. However, due to its location under the bike, it tends to slip in wet whether even more than the conventional generator. The contact pressure between the roller and the tire can be increased by means of an elastic cord, pulling the roller towards the rear drop-out. On a regular generator, the resistance is least when the roller runs along the rim rather than the tire—the Swiss Nordlicht generator is available with a narrow rubber roller for this kind of use and other models can be adapted this way by replacing the roller by e.g. a toy car wheel with a narrow rubber tire.

On virtually all generator systems, the electric current is carried from the (single) generator contact to the contacts of front and rear lights and returns over the metal-to-metal contacts of the installation hardware and the bicycle frame. If the system malfunctions, it may be either a burnt out-bulb, a bulb that is not fully screwed into its fitting, a loose wiring or mass contact, a broken wire or simply the generator's roller slipping off the tire, which is most common in rainy weather. Keep the generator

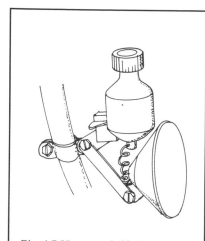

Fig. 4.5 Home-made block generator light.

The best place for your rear light: on the rear luggage rack.

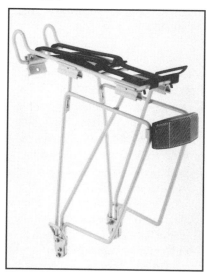

aligned, attach all the hardware and the wires properly, and check the whole system at least once a month.

It is possible to use an easily removable form of generator lighting. In that case, you will have to make do without a rear light, which is perhaps justified if you use a really big reflector or a flashing battery-powered light in the rear. Removable units are installed on the front fork and consist of a generator with light attached. Most of the commercially available models, referred to as block generators, are not very satisfactory. That's why I would suggest making your own, following the proposal by John Forester, illustrated in Fig. 4.5.

Personally, I prefer lights and reflectors that are always there over temporarily installed models, because they are available when I need them unexpectedly. Thus, I could ride without fear through dark tunnels along the Oregon coastline, while other cyclists, who either didn't have them or didn't stop to install their handy clip-on lights and reflectors, felt like members of a suicide squad. In cases like that, you should at least take the trouble to install the temporary goodies whenever there is a need for them.

The many possible trouble sources of most generator lighting systems, and the physical resistance caused by their mechanical inefficiency, are the reasons why many cyclists prefer battery lights. The batteries and the bulbs must match the light unit: some use a single flat 4.5 volt battery, other models two D-cells, still others two C-cells, and recently popular ones 4 AA cells. Make sure to get correctly rated bulbs for the batteries used, both in terms of voltage and wattage or amperage. In recent years many special lights, powered by a large central rechargeable battery have been introduced. In general, the larger the battery, the more powerful and longer lasting the light is likely to be. My objection is that when touring you may not have a chance to recharge your battery.

Don't assume that battery lights are free from problems, but there are indeed fewer potential causes of failures than systems with a generator. Whether generator- or battery-powered, take the appropriate spare bulbs along. I suggest using the krypton or halogen gas filled bulbs, the latter are brighter when new, while both types stay equally bright throughout their useful life-span, whereas regular bulbs dim to less than half their original and rated light output.

Furthermore, for a regular battery light, you will need at least one set of spare batteries. Normal carbon-zinc batteries produce a gradually decreasing electric output over the battery's life. Replace such batteries when the light begins to dim—don't wait until the thing is virtually dead. If you have to leave the bike out in the rain, you'd better remove the batteries and store them in a

Fig. 4.6 Tire gauge

dry place. This stops them from swelling up, becoming useless themselves and damaging the light unit to boot.

Although rechargeable systems are not suitable for long-distance touring, they are certainly *en vogue*, probably due to the high-tech appeal associated with their high price. Rechargeable NiCad (nickel-cadmium) batteries give a more constant output but go out quite suddenly when the charge is depleted, which happens much sooner than on a regular battery. NiCads have a limited shelf life, meaning they run out even when not used, over a period of about 3 weeks. So make sure the battery is charged regularly, or that you have a charged spare with you, since there is no warning when the light will go off. If you have a system with a central battery, you may also use a lead-acid gel battery, which has a longer shelf life than NiCads but must also be recharged regularly, in this case to protect it from damage that results if it is fully discharged.

In addition to lights, some reflectors are quite useful. But they can not completely replace lights, and some reflectors are of no protective benefit whatsoever. The current crop of international requirement that all bicycles must be equipped with a whole plethora of reflectors is a big step in the wrong direction. It originated with the notoriously incompetent American CPSC (Consumer Product Safety Commission), and was promptly followed by agencies in other countries, where this regulation actually was made legally binding to the cyclist. It gives the cyclist a false feeling of being adequately protected with the wrong equipment. Add to that the particular models prescribed show up brightly under certain obvious but irrelevant conditions, and you've been fooled. Only a big rear reflector is useful—even as a substitute for a rear light. It must be mounted where it will not be obstructed by luggage, for example at the back of the rear luggage rack. In the front only a light can protect you, and from the sides, no reflectors are of any use.

Pump and Tire Gauge

While traveling, you will need to keep your tires inflated properly. Don't count on having gas stations handily available to inflate your tires, and don't just guess at the pressure. For loaded touring, the tire pressure is important, both since it allows efficient performance and because it protects the tire and the tube against damage. If you are experienced enough to have developed a calibrated thumb, you may do without a tire gauge for checking the pressure, but nobody should go without a pump.

The pump should be a model suitable for developing an adequately high pressure. Depending on the tire design, that may be anywhere from 4–6 bar (60–90 psi) gauge pressure for road use. Be guided by the pressure quoted on the tire sidewalls as an absolute minimum for unloaded cycling on smooth roads. On

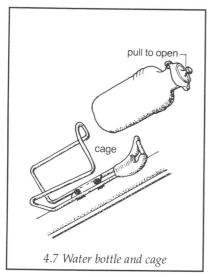

pull to open

cage

4.7 Water bottle and cage

rough roads you will need 15% more in the back, 5% more in the front. Loaded with luggage, you will need another 10% more on the loaded wheel. Tires on which it says, "inflate to 60 psi" can safely be inflated to 75 psi in the rear and 65–70 psi in the front. As a basic rule, narrower tires will require—and withstand—a higher inflation pressure than wider models of the same materials and design.

In the preceding chapter, I recommended getting tires with Presta valves (also referred to as French valves). Make sure both the pump and the gauge have connections that correspond to the type of valve used. Don't use a pump with a flexible hose connector, since the air trapped in the hose makes it impossible to reach an adequate pressure with a normal hand pump. For quick tire inflation at home you may keep a big stand pump, which has enough volume to work fine with a flexible hose connector.

Nowadays, pumps are mostly designed to clamp directly between the bike's top tube and bottom bracket along the seat tube. These are referred to as frame-fit pumps, and are available in several sizes to match a range of frame sizes. That works fine on a bike with only one water bottle installed. But if you carry two bottles, you should use a pump clamped between two pegs (or lacking pegs, between mushroom clips) installed along the bottom of the top tube. If the pump doesn't work properly, tighten the screwed nozzle and if necessary replace the underlying rubber grommet that seals around the valve, taking care to install it the right way round, so it doesn't leak even more afterwards.

Water Bottle and Cage

Elegant Tacx water bottle and clip

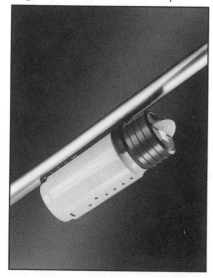

Here's another essential touring accessory, especially in hot weather. Of course, you can also stuff a properly closed bottle in your luggage, which has the advantage that it doesn't get as hot as it would exposed to the sun; but the frame-mounted water bottle is a lot more convenient. In case your bike lacks the bosses, most bottle cages are sold complete with a pair of rather crude clips to put around a frame tube. If you need to mount the thing that way, first stick a tire patch around the frame tube, as explained under *Clamps and Clips* in this chapter.

Bike water bottles are available in cheap and fancy versions. The more expensive bottles should have the kind of spout illustrated in Fig. 4.7, which is operated by pulling the central part out and closed off by pushing it back in. Don't drink by sucking at the spout: instead, hold the bottle inclined with the spout down one or two inches from your open mouth and squirt the water in by squeezing on the bottle.

There are some interesting bottle variants on the market these days. One of these actually squirts when held upright, due to an internal tube that runs from the spout to the bottom of the bottle. There are also Sigg aluminum bottles. No, they can't be squeezed, but they work quite well and have the advantage of being more hygienic and neutral in taste.

Finally, there are thermos bottles, insulated with a foam material. Another way to keep a cold drink of water cool is by wrapping a cloth (such as a sock) around it. Moisten this cloth occasionally by squirting some water out, so that evaporation will draw enough heat out of the bottle to keep the contents cool. Of course, that is only practical with water. You may also want a bottle with a more nourishing liquid, such as fruit juice. In winter, I use the insulated thermos bottle and keep a hot liquid in it.

Locks

The lock is your most essential accessory, even when touring. Always try to lock the bike to something solid when you have to leave it unattended.

Unfortunately, a good lock is an essential accessory for any kind of cycling. The very best lock is barely good enough to hold on to your bike in many parts of the world nowadays. Ideal are the cylindrical-link chains that look like snakes. Next best are the large U-locks. They may be installed on the bike by means of a bracket. Since that takes away bottle mounting options, I prefer to keep the lock at the top of one of my bike bags.

Don't just lock the bike onto itself, but secure it to some immovable object. Though the U-locks fit nicely around many street furnishings, you may also want to use a strong cable or chain with end loops or shackles big enough to fit the lock. This allows you to tie the bike up to something bigger. Select an object from which the lock cannot be lifted off: a chain around a parking meter is of little use if the cable can be slipped over the top. To help you stop the front wheel from rolling away, the Flick Stand, which clamps between down tube and front wheel, is useful—but not on a bike with fenders. Instead, lock the wheel by inserting something between the front brake lever to apply the front brake when the bike is parked.

Even with the best lock, you may not be able to completely protect your bike, equipment, accessories and luggage against vandalism and theft of individual items. The smartest thing to do is to be totally paranoid and suspect thieves and thugs everywhere and anytime. Never go anywhere without securing your gear. If at all possible, don't leave your equipment out of sight. When touring in a group, you may decide to take turns keeping an eye on things. At least keep the most valuable items in a bag that you always take with you when you're off the bike. Despite the horror stories told about other countries, the risk of theft and vandalism is probably greater in the U.S. than it is in any other country I have ever visited.

Warning Devices

When traveling on a narrow, winding mountain road, you may want to alert others to your presence for your own protection. In most European countries a hand-operated bell is prescribed, which is totally ineffective against anything big enough to endanger you. Instead, or in addition, you can use a compressed gas-powered sound horn that can be carried in your back pocket or installed on the handlebars. If you cycle on paths frequented by pedestrians, joggers, roller skaters, dog walkers and casual cyclists, you may prefer to use a bell as well, since it is less offensive, yet adequately audible under the circumstances.

Tools and Spares

Depending on a number of factors, you should carry some tools and spare parts. How many you need depends on the distance and the difficulty of the terrain, as well as the population and bike density of the region. In an area with plenty of gas stations and a bike shop every twenty miles, you do not need as many items as you should carry when crossing the desert. Here's a list of the essentials that should always be taken along on any longer trip away from home:

☐ A set of three tire levers (also known as tire irons).

☐ A tire patch kit, containing patches, rubber solution, chalk, sandpaper, talcum powder and a piece of canvas to mend a damaged tire casing.

☐ A small screwdriver with a 4 mm (³⁄₁₆ in.) wide blade.

☐ Crescent wrench (adjustable spanner), 6 or 8 inches long.

☐ Allen keys in whatever sizes correspond to the recessed hexagon bolts used on your bike.

☐ Crank extractor tool, especially the wrench part, which will be needed to tighten a loose crank.

☐ Spoke wrench (nipple spanner) to straighten a bent wheel.

☐ Chain rivet tool to take the chain apart or to join it up again.

☐ A pair of small pliers, such as needle-nose pliers with sharp cutters.

☐ Spare spokes of correct length, brake cable, spare tube, spare chain links and lighting parts. If you also take a spare tire, turn it into three loops, as shown in Fig. 4.8.

☐ Waterless hand cleaning paste.

☐ Rags to wipe your hands as well as protect or clean any messy parts before working on them.

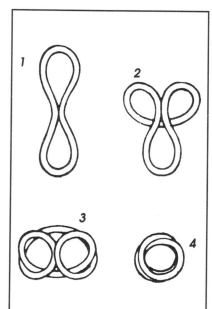

1. Fold in half to make a figure 8.
2. Fold one half inward so it meets center of first fold.
3. Draw the larger loop in to match the size of the two other loops.
4. Draw the three loops together and tie them into a tight circle.

Fig. 4.8 Wired-on tire folding method

As this is really only a very basic set, you may want to add quite a number of other items on longer trips. You may carry a small can of oil, to keep things like the chain and other moving parts lubricated and to prevent rust. And you can carry an assortment of various tools to take apart the components that may have to be overhauled on your bike. Establish by very conscientiously checking which tools in which sizes and how many of each are needed. Conversely, on a short trip in known terrain, you may feel adequately prepared with nothing more than a pump, a small screwdriver and the equipment needed to fix a flat.

Whenever you are buying tools, consider that under the primitive roadside repair conditions, you should have the best tools available. Get quality tools. That means expensive tools, exactly fitting the parts in question. Don't let terms like "economy tools" fool you: in the long run the best tools are much more economic than any cheap tool will ever be, since the former last forever, while the latter quickly wear out and may actually damage the bike's components.

Covers and Pouches

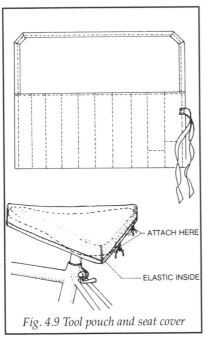

Fig. 4.9 Tool pouch and seat cover

ATTACH HERE

ELASTIC INSIDE

Don't just dump the tools in a side pocket of your bike bag, since they may get lost or they could damage other items that way. I suggest you carry them in a pouch that holds all the tools you ever plan to carry and has a few spare slots. If you can't buy one ready-made, it will be easy enough to sew your own. Be guided by Fig. 4.9, using a strong material such as denim from an old pair of blue jeans. Allow enough space between the various items to enable you to roll it all together when it is full. On shorter trips, when you do not need to take everything along, you may leave certain slots blank.

Other useful items in the same vein include covers for your equipment, to protect bike and luggage against the elements. I'd say the minimum is a cover for your saddle, certainly if it is either a real leather type or one of the leather-covered foam-padded ones so popular among tourists these days. Some of these items can be bought ready-made, but you can also sew your own using plastic-coated cloth. In addition, you may want to carry a waterproof bike cover—or you can again make your own. Simply take a sizable piece of sturdy plastic or coated nylon cloth and attach straps in several places. Either variety will serve you well in rainy regions, allowing you to cover and protect both bike and luggage when you are stopped. Besides, it will double as a ground sheet to sit on when the ground is damp.

CHAPTER 5

Luggage Carrying Equipment

To most people, bicycle touring means riding a heavily loaded machine. Although it will be possible to go on short trips with no more luggage than what fits in a small bag attached to the bike or carried on the back, most serious touring requires more luggage. This chapter is devoted to the equipment for carrying all kinds of luggage. In addition to the information found here, it will be smart to consider just what to take along and which items you may be able to do without. For this subject, you are referred to Chapter 13, *What to Take and How to Pack it*.

For heavily loaded cycling at speed, the best is barely good enough when it comes to luggage carrying equipment. That means you will need bags and racks that are strong and rigid enough not to sag, get damaged or come loose. It also means the bags should not sway during a fast descent, even on a rough road or in sharp curves. An additional important factor is the location of the racks, since that determines how the weight of the luggage will affect the bike's handling and steering.

This is one instance where mail order companies may be a useful source of information. Their catalogs often list many more different items in this area than your local bike shop can stock. Furthermore, the descriptive information given in these catalogs can be very useful, even if you end up buying the equipment at a regular bike shop, as I do myself whenever I have the choice.

Dividing the Load

Two methods of loading: bike bags and a luggage trailer.

The correct distribution of weight for carrying luggage on a bike has been established in computer analyses and confirmed by means of practical tests. The following is a summary of the main conclusions of these tests:

☐ Ideally, the weight should be concentrated close to the bike's mass center (also referred to as center of gravity).

☐ Preferably, loads should be stable relative to the bike's frame, rather than to the steering system.

☐ Anything mounted in the back should be as far forward as possible, while it need not be particularly low.

☐ Anything mounted on the front and attached to the steering system should be close to the center of the the steering axis at the height of the front wheel axle.

☐ Everything—whether rack or bag—should be attached so that it does not shift or sway as the bike is leaned over or when turning, accelerating, slowing down, climbing, descending or bouncing.

It is possible to check in practice whether the bike, its racks and the luggage attached are properly constructed and mounted, respectively. To do that, hold the loaded machine by the center of the handlebars, as shown in Fig. 5.1, and shake it. If the bike is well-constructed, the racks are well-built and mounted properly, and the bags are loaded and tied down correctly, there will be a minimum of noticeable sway propagated over the entire bike. Since the swaying effect is transmitted back to the point of the movement's origin, you will easily feel whether things are constructed, attached and loaded correctly.

The rules listed above can be translated into a number of practical recommendations as follows:

☐ Any bag or rack must be attached as rigidly to the bicycle's frame as possible, tying not only the top at two points, but also at least one point at the bottom.

☐ When carrying little luggage, take it in a bag that is attached as close as possible to the mass center, i.e. a saddle bag.

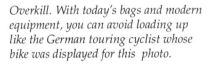

Overkill. With today's bags and modern equipment, you can avoid loading up like the German touring cyclist whose bike was displayed for this photo.

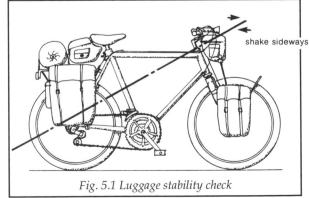

shake sideways

Fig. 5.1 Luggage stability check

☐ Racks must be constructed and attached very rigidly, requiring specifically a stiffener or brace to avoid lateral deflection.

☐ When loading a bike with bags and racks in the back, the load should be carried as far forward as possible. That means that the top of the rack may be used and that there is no sense installing the bags particularly low, since that would force a rearward installation to prevent interference with the heels while pedaling.

☐ To carry luggage in the front, it would be preferable to have a rack that attaches to the frame, rather than one attached to the steering system. The small-wheeled sprung Alex Moulton bikes from Britain are unique in offering this solution.

☐ If front bags are attached to the steering system, as is usually the case, they should be installed as low and as close to the wheel axle as possible.

The various possible ways of distributing the luggage over front and rear racks, with their corresponding effects on steering and balancing characteristics, have been investigated by Jim Blackburn, a major manufacturer of bicycle racks and other accessories. It was found that of the solutions shown in Fig. 5.2, the one in the middle detail (low in the front, high and forward in the rear) provided the best solution. Consequently, that is the loading technique I advise you to follow.

Luggage Racks

Heavy luggage and high speeds over longer distances form a tough test for any kind of equipment. Speed and the unevenness of the road surface, combined with the rider's alternating driving forces, translate into a combination of different cyclical loading changes that are likely to propagate along the bike, presenting serious steering and handling problems. Furthermore, this kind of thing may lead to a phenomenon known as fatigue failure.

Unlike the more familiar form of fatigue from which you or I may suffer at times, structural materials do not recover from the

Fig. 5.2 Methods of luggage distribution. The method shown in the center is preferable.

fatigue caused by frequently repeated high load changes. After a certain number of such loading cycles, the part will break, unless it is designed with enough safety margin to consider this kind of thing. Specifically, it can be observed that the higher loading values are more likely to be avoided when the vibrations are dampened by a rigid construction.

Consequently, there are a number of details to look for to make sure you are getting the best in racks. But the rack is not an independent structure: don't judge a rack by itself, but consider the rack mounted on a bicycle—preferably your own machine. Holding the bike, check how it responds to vertical and lateral forces applied by hand. This will give you a good idea of what will happen out on the road.

Any rack should be attached firmly in at least four points, preferably by means of sizable bolts with flat washers under the heads. The purpose of these washers is to reduce friction when tightening the bolts. Spring washers, which actually increase friction and resist turning, are not satisfactory. The attachments must be to points on the bike that are themselves firm and solid, and the stays of the racks should preferably be stiffened by means of braces.

The materials most suitable for racks are steel tubing, aluminum rod, and steel rod—in that order. If aluminum rod is used for the rack, as it usually is nowadays, it should be at least 7 mm thick, while steel rod should be at least 6 mm, even if that seems like a heavy solution, which is the reason aluminum is so widely used these days. Tubular steel is a light, strong and expensive solution, and requires diameters of 9 mm or more. For moderate loads, tubular aluminum material with a minimum diameter of 12 mm may be suitable.

The method of construction is as important as the materials used. Racks made of solid steel or aluminum should be welded, while tubular materials must be brazed. The difference between the two operations is that in welding the material is heated to such a high temperature that it melts and bonds together. Brazing, on the other hand is done at a lower temperature by melting a filler material of lower melting point to bond the parts. The thin walls of tubular members would be weakened excessively if welding were used. Light folding racks have pivot points where the stays attach to the platform. Check to make sure these are of a solid metal construction. Plastic joints are a no-no, whether rigid or pivoted.

Vertical load-bearing capacity and rigidity of a larger rack in the back can be assured only if twin stays in an inverse V-pattern are used at both ends. Even so, the greatest strength can only be expected if each set of stays is connected by means of a horizontal stiffener, which may be designed quite long, so it also helps to

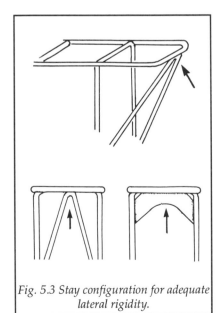

Fig. 5.3 Stay configuration for adequate lateral rigidity.

avoid sway of the bag once it is mounted. If only one pair of stays is used on a smaller rack for light luggage, they should be attached just beyond the midpoint of the platform along the rack's length.

Lateral rigidity can be best provided when the stays are triangulated laterally. This is a remarkably important criterion, since I have several times observed that otherwise lightly constructed racks with such lateral bracing held up much better than much heavier racks that lacked this kind of lateral stiffener. On one of my bikes, I use a set of very light aluminum racks with tubular stays by the Dutch Steco company and have had excellent experience with them, while earlier racks weighing three times as much have failed under similar conditions.

As we've seen, the rear rack should allow placing the load far forward, rather than bringing it as low as possible. Thus, the so-called low-rider racks are of no benefit in the rear. What is important, though, is that the rack should not only provide adequate support at the top, but also a vertical plane for the back of the bags to rest against lower down, to prevent swaying of the bags.

The primary criteria for the front rack are a low and centered mounting position, close to the steering and wheel axes, maximum rigidity, supported at the top and the bottom. The combination of adequate rigidity with a low-rider style is a bit tricky: weird looking constructions with big loops extending around and over the top of the front wheel turn out to be necessary in most cases.

To carry (some) luggage on top of the rack, a relatively wide and long flat top frame or platform is useful. In the front you should only put very light things on the top platform, if any at all. In the rear you will actually find this a fine place to carry such luggage as a small rigid suitcase which may contain quite heavy items. To prevent shifting of the load, which might interfere with the operation of the brakes, a stop should protrude from the top of the rack.

Types of Bags

Depending on your needs, specifically on the amount of luggage to be taken along, several different kinds of bicycle bags may be appropriate. Three basic types can be distinguished: bags that attach to the rider, models that attach directly to the bike and those that attach to luggage racks on the bike. The various kinds of bags will be described in some detail here, while you will be shown what to look for in materials and construction, whatever the type of bag selected, in the next section. In addition, the general remarks about the distribution of weight given under *Dividing the Load* at the beginning of this chapter should be borne in mind.

Personal Bags

Bags that are worn directly on the body are of three basic types: light backpacks (referred to as rucksacks in Britain), large backpacks with a separate or integral carrying frame, and belt packs, usually referred to as fanny packs in the U.S. None of these are the answer to your main luggage carrying problem. However, they can come in handy for short trips, for things that must be taken along when you leave the bike, or for temporary use, such as the groceries purchased shortly before a meal or before setting up camp.

The belt pack should have a really wide belt part and a stiff but flexible area that rests against the back, also supporting the bottom of the pack. It is at best suitable for carrying small items such as would be carried in a woman's handbag: money, documents, sunglasses, perhaps a camera and a bite to eat. Try it out in the store before buying, to make sure it is comfortable and will not slip around the waist when cycling.

Large backpacks with or without frame are to my mind not really suitable for bike touring. However, they do have the advantage of requiring no racks on the bike. A bike without racks is easier to transport in a car or on public transportation. I occasionally travel on trains and buses on which bikes were not accepted as accompanied luggage, and found a bike without racks and fenders could be dismantled and hidden in a light bag, while all the regular luggage could be carried in a backpack. If you choose a bag of this kind, make sure it has really wide padded straps and an additional waist strap to restrain its movement while cycling. This kind of bag should also be tried out for comfort before it is purchased.

A small and light backpack comes in very handy for provisional carrying tasks. I have one that weighs only half a pound and fits in the small side pocket of another bag. I use it to take things along when I leave the bike, or when I have groceries or other shopping that don't fit in the regular bike bags. It will only be comfortable to carry if you stiffen the back by means of a light, rigid board (I use a clipboard with the clip removed). When not in use, it easily slides inside another bag. Since the same board can be used as a writing support or as a tray when eating or preparing food, it need by no means be regarded as ballast.

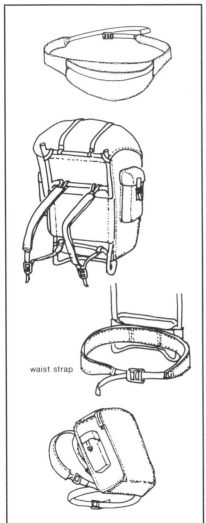

waist strap

Fig. 5.4 Types of bags carried on the body. From top to bottom: belt bag (fanny pack), large backpack with waist strap detail, small frameless backpack.

Bike-Mounted Bags

Bags carried directly on the bike are of three kinds: saddle bags, handlebar bags and frame bags. The saddle bag is so universally used in Britain that one wonders why it has not found its way to the U.S. in a comparable quality and variety. It is attached to the back of the saddle. That is no problem on a leather model with carrying eyelets, whereas other saddle types may require the installation of a special clamp.

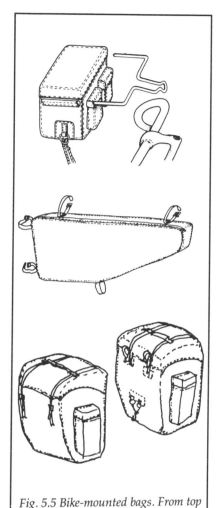

Fig. 5.5 Bike-mounted bags. From top to bottom: handlebar bag, frame bag, pannier bags.

Saddle bags exist in various sizes, ranging all the way from 10 liters, which is barely enough for the absolute essentials, to 30 liters (that's more than a cubic foot). The latter is big enough for a weekend trip if you don't go camping. A large saddle bag, especially if it is used on a bike with a relatively low saddle, should be supported by means of some kind of a rack or bracket to keep it off the rear wheel and the rear brake. It should have side pockets for small items and straps on the top to carry your rain gear. Before buying such a bag, look at it very critically and ascertain that it is properly supported and will neither interfere with your movements nor drag on the rear wheel or the brake.

It is also possible to install a handlebar bag, which is more widely available in the US, behind the seat post by means of a clamping bracket sold under the name Seat Post Thing. Handlebar bags are quite popular in the U.S. and France, although I would put them at the bottom of my list. They are suitable for carrying small items to which you want frequent access along the way, especially if the bag is of such a design that it can easily be removed from the bike, but not for anything heavy. The handlebar bag should be designed so that it is supported at the top by a bracket that fits on the handlebars, while the bottom of the bag is held down to the front fork-ends with bungee cords. A few external pockets and a transparent map compartment are helpful. Preferably it should open towards the rider. When buying this kind of bag, make sure it does not interfere with steering, braking or lighting. A special version of the handlebar bag is available to carry a camera and photographic accessories.

The frame bag is a rare bird indeed. Trapezoidally shaped and tied between the frame tubes, it must be packed compactly to avoid its swelling up to a thickness that interferes with the movement of your legs. World travelers, who have to carry as much as possible, may find a use for a bag like that, in addition to every other bag that can be mounted on the bike.

Pannier Bags Pannier bags are the kind hung on either side of a luggage rack. Available in a whole plethora of shapes and sizes, they are the mainstay of bicycle touring. So many manufacturers offer different bags of this kind, that it will be hard to find the best ones—although there are plenty to choose from.

Different sizes are intended for front and rear use, though you may find the small front bags quite suitable for the rear as well. It will be just as important to try the bags out on your bike and your racks as it will be to watch for all the details of construction and design, described under *Bag Details*. Each pannier bag should be attached by means of convenient hooks at two points close to the top and a bungee cord at the bottom clipped to, e.g., the drop-out or fork-end. A sizable outside pocket may be installed in the rear, while only a relatively flat pouch (or better still: two even smaller ones, side by side) would be suitable on the side of the bag that faces out when installed. Make sure the shape of the bag is such that adequate heel clearance remains on rear bags even when they are stuffed.

Combination bags are single pieces of luggage comprising three compartments: two panniers and a top compartment. They are hung over the luggage rack, and seem more practical than they really are. Hard to pack and even harder to install or to remove from the bike, the rather modest price is their only redeeming feature. There are also combination bags without the top compartment, which I find to be generally a lot more convenient, though still less so than separate panniers. One interesting model of the combination bag can be carried off the bike as a large backpack.

Rack-Top Bags Bags to fit on top of a luggage rack are recommended for use only in the rear. They may either be of the stuffsack variety or rectangular cases. My preference is for a small rigid suitcase, mounted sideways. In fact, what I use consists of two relatively rigid halves that can be extended in height almost infinitely in order to accept more or less. This is where I keep my food and cooking gear on a camping trip. It is tied to the top of the luggage rack by means of long webbing straps with buckles.

In general, either webbing straps or leather belts are more suitable to tie things onto the bike than bungee cords. The disadvantage of the latter is the fact that they stretch when the load shifts or gets unbalanced, which often leads to items shifting or even falling off the bike. Bungees also have hooks at their ends, which tend to get caught in the spokes, occasionally leading to falls and accidents.

Bag Details

In the present section we shall have a look at the details of construction of all the bags described above. We will be looking at materials of the bags and their attachments and at the tricky points such as design, supports, closures and reinforcements.

Wherever there is a chance of rain, the bags should either be water resistant themselves, or everything inside them must be wrapped in plastic. The best material against rain, oddly enough, is not some modern coated synthetic fabric, but old fashioned canvas or ducking, sewn with cotton yarn. In the rain, the natural fibers swell up, sealing both the pores in the fabric and the stitch holes. I have spent whole days in the rain with luggage carried in old fashioned canvas bags without problems, whereas a really rainproof synthetic bag is a very rare thing indeed.

Today, virtually all bags are made of coated synthetics, and there are ways to keep your gear at least reasonably dry in them.

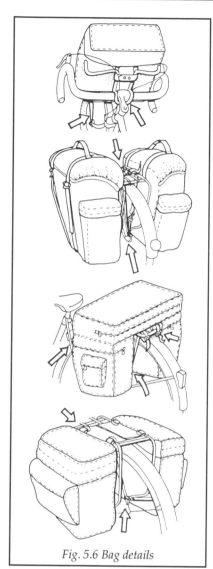

Fig. 5.6 Bag details

Look for bags made of a relatively heavy cloth: at least 500 g/m^2, or 14 oz./sq. yd., gives you a reliable material. Bags of this cloth really aren't that much heavier than models of lighter materials (since a lot of the weight goes into the mounting materials), but they are much more durable. To make bags of such materials reasonably water resistant, all the seams must be sealed with a special sealing compound bought at a backpacking supply store. This applies even to those models that are claimed to be sealed when sold. Don't forget the seams with which zippers are sewn in and the attachment stitchings of the straps.

On any synthetic bag, it may be a good idea to sear, or melt, the exposed edges where the cloth was cut at the seams (inside) to prevent them from fraying. This is no unnecessary luxury, since the material easily frays and comes undone at the seams if it is not prevented this way. Simply turn the bag inside out and melt the edge of the cloth by holding it over a candle flame. Move along as soon as the fibers begin to melt together—before they generate a nasty black smoke.

As for the design and construction details, look for bags with really big access openings, with a zipper or a drawstring closure that does not restrict the size of the bag at the entrance. The closure should run all around the top, and any zippers or other openings must be covered with a generously overlapping flap. Preferably, they should be sewn with double seams. Reinforcements should be sewn on in sensitive locations, such as the attachment points of straps, the ends of zippers, points of contact with the bike or the rack and all exposed corners.

The bags should have strong and simply operated means of attachment and closure. The closure flap should be held down by means of wide webbing straps with buckles. They allow the contents to be compressed, keeping the entire bag compact and preventing shifting or rattling, even if the bag is only half full. These straps should be separate from the devices with which the bag is mounted on the bike, so access to the contents does not affect the attachment to the bike, and conversely the bag's mounting system does not interfere with access. Additionally, there should be some kind of stiffener board in the back, to assure the bag retains its shape well enough not to interfere with the bicycle's moving parts. If not built in, you may install one yourself, using any lightweight water-resistant fiber board, cut to fit the back of the bag.

The top of any bag that hangs down by the side of a rack, from the saddle, or from any other point of the bike, should be held in two points. For rack-mounted bags, the preferable solution is by means of simple plastic-coated metal hooks at points close to the front and rear ends of the bag. Make sure these hooks do not hang loose on the rack and that the rack has the right

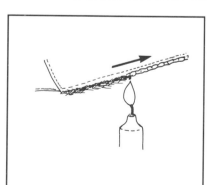

Fig. 5.7 Searing cut edges inside bag

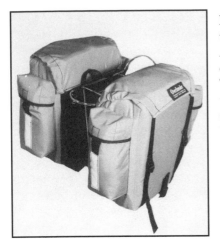

Excellent British pannier bags made by Carradice. These stand up to some rain.

length to accommodate them (if the hooks are made of metal, they can be bent into the right shape using two pairs of pliers). At the bottom, the bag must be held to a fixed point on the bike or the rack by means of a strap or a tightly stretched elastic cord. The attachment point of this strap must be higher on the bag than it is on the bike, so it tends to put tension on the bag. This strap should be secured so that it does not shift or come undone. But it must also be easily accessible and simple to attach.

Check the effectiveness of the mounting system by assuring the bags don't shift perceptibly when the bike is held in several positions. To do that, you have to statically simulate the effect of dynamic conditions that influence the bike and its luggage when riding, steering, climbing, descending, bouncing, braking and accelerating. That is done by holding the bike with heavily loaded bags in various orientations as follows:

☐ upside down;

☐ vertically up with front wheel off the ground;

☐ vertically up with rear wheel off the ground;

☐ horizontally to the left;

☐ horizontally to the right;

☐ from the handlebars, shaking the bike loaded with luggage as described previously and as illustrated in Fig. 5.1 on page 68.

Bicycle Trailers

Another bike trailer. This one does not project very far behind the bike.

An alternative to the conventional way of carrying luggage in bags mounted on the bike is the use of a trailer behind the bike. Several models are available, most with two wheels, and usually attached to the seatpost by means of a flexible coupling. There are also single-wheel models attached more rigidly; even side cars have been available. In general, the trailer should have a rigid but light frame and big wheels rolling on ball bearings and pneumatic tires. It will perform best if it has some kind of suspension built in. Their disadvantage is the difficulty they present if they have to be transported or stored, much more than any negative effect on bike handling.

CHAPTER 6

Clothing On and Off the Bike

Gore-Tex cycle clothing. Although this material is quite comfortable in moderate weather, it does leak in torrential rain, and in hot weather it becomes too hot.

In the present chapter we shall first look at conventional bicycle dress, followed by sections devoted to clothing for cycling under unfavorable weather conditions and things to take on a bike tour to wear when you are not cycling. Bicycle clothing is probably the most functional gear ever designed for any sport, and though there should be no need to ride around looking to all the world like a bicycle racer, it makes sense to aim at the same comfort that has been developed to accommodate racers.

This stuff has been designed the way it is to provide the freedom of movement, the control of temperature and humidity and the protection against chafing that allows a racer to continue non-stop for seven hours, covering 150 miles or more. That, I'm sure, will also be comfortable when touring half the distance at half the speed on a loaded machine.

In the first section of this chapter, I shall highlight the points that make the various items of bicycle clothing so suitable for their purpose. These will also be the things to watch out for when buying clothing that is not specifically designed for the purpose, to determine whether it will serve you anyway. You may refer to Fig. 6.1 for an idea of what a typical cycling outfit looks like. What you don't see there is the colors and the materials. Whereas traditional racing garb used to be rather drab looking woolen garments, today's cycling fashion is bright and garishly, relying heavily on synthetic fibers.

Shoes and Socks

The shoes are perhaps the single most important item that can make the difference between effective cycling and plodding along. Special cycling shoes consist of light leather uppers with a thin but very stiff sole, generally with a metal plate built in to achieve that sole stiffness. This helps distribute the pedaling force over a large area of the foot and prevents deformation where the toeclips hold the shoe to the pedal. Consequently, the pressure at any one point of the foot is within the comfortable range, and a more efficient transfer of energy from the legs to the bicycle drivetrain results.

Cycling shoes either have metal or plastic cleats to hold the feet in place on the pedals, or they are made to match a particular brand of clipless pedal. The stiff sole and secure connection to the pedal optimizes the effectiveness of pedaling. There is little doubt that either system allows more secure pedaling, especially on long trips where there is rarely a need to get off the

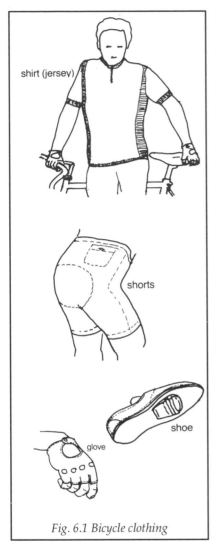

shirt (jersey)

shorts

shoe

glove

Fig. 6.1 Bicycle clothing

Shorts and Slacks

bike. However, these things make it nearly impossible to walk, and tricky enough to get on and off the bike.

When touring, you will probably want to be able to walk in reasonable comfort as well. That not only rules out many of those modern clipless systems, but also makes old fashioned cleats highly inconvenient. If you choose clipless pedals, make sure they are available with special shoes that allow walking. If you use regular pedals, you should either do without cleats or carry a spare pair of shoes easily accessible for getting around when off the bike. Depending on how much luggage you are prepared to carry, either solution is satisfactory for long cycling trips with few interruptions. If, on the other hand, you are touring around Europe, stopping frequently to inspect interesting sights, you will be much better off wearing shoes without cleats even when cycling.

In addition to the real things, compromise solutions in the form of walking/cycling shoes exist these days. They have stiff, slightly profiled plastic soles and well-ventilated uppers. This kind of shoe is probably the best solution for most touring purposes that involve getting off the bike frequently. The cloth uppers unfortunately cause your feet to get saturated in the rain—more about that under *Rain Gear* below.

Whatever kind of shoes you wear, they must have the right length and width not to hurt. Pull the shoelaces relatively tight in the middle part of the closure, so that the toes do not slip forward, getting pushed against the front of the shoe. Inside the shoes, choose cotton or wool socks that absorb perspiration. To be comfortable, they should be relatively thick, especially in the sole, and they should not have a knotty seam in the toe area. Tennis socks are generally very suitable. I suggest getting socks that are long and elastic enough to fit over your trouser legs when you wear regular street clothing, which keeps pant cuffs out of the chain.

Specific bicycle shorts are stretchable knitted garments with rather long, tight-fitting legs and a high waist. They generally stretch so elastically that they stay up without the need for a belt, though suspenders (braces to my British readers) may be required, depending on your body build. Sewn in the crotch area is a soft and smooth piece of real or synthetic chamois, which protects the skin against chafing and absorbs perspiration (this is one case where the substitute is preferable to the real thing, because the synthetic material used here is easier to clean and more c omfortable to wear than real chamois). Worn directly over the bare skin, they should be washed out daily. Consequently, you need at least two pairs and have to wash one pair out every night.

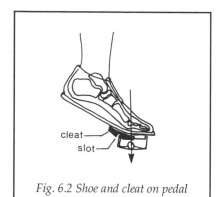

Fig. 6.2 Shoe and cleat on pedal

This laundry problem is reduced by selecting modern acrylic or polypropylene materials. Old fashioned woolen pants have the advantage that they regulate your body temperature better and get less smelly when they absorb perspiration. On the other hand, synthetics take up less moisture, dry a lot faster, and are much easier to wash. Being conservative, I still prefer woolen shorts.

One other way of minimizing the laundry problem is by wearing very light, stretchy seamless underpants underneath the cycling shorts. They are much easier to wash out, quicker to dry and perfectly comfortable to wear. If no other source can be found, most men may well succeed in getting something that fits among underwear intended for women.

In addition to ordinary bicycle shorts and long-legged versions of these same things (not just for cold weather, because covering your legs also protects you against sunburn), there are special bicycle touring shorts and slacks. These are based on the same materials and construction methods, but are tailored more to look like regular street clothing. They have convenient pockets and look a lot more civil. Alternately, you may wear any other pair of shorts or pants, providing you first establish whether they are comfortable when pedaling.

They can only be comfortable if they are smooth and soft. Stretchable materials are best and they should have no bulky seams. Slacks must be tight enough around the lower leg not to get caught in the chain. If they are not quite tight enough there, tuck the legs inside your socks or keep them together by means of elastic straps with a Velcro closure. Of course, you can also cycle in real racing shorts and put light slacks on over them when it is appropriate to dress up a little.

Shirts and Other Tops

The cycling shirt, or jersey, is a tight-fitting knitted garment with short sleeves, a very long bodice and pockets sewn on in the back. It absorbs perspiration, covers the parts of the torso that should be covered even when bending over, and doesn't flap in the wind. Similar shirts with long sleeves are designed for colder weather. Both long- and short-sleeved cycling shirts are available in wool and various synthetics.

Though modern materials and designs make some of these cycling garments remarkably fashionable, they're as unsuitable for visits to churches, theaters and restaurants as are conventional cycling shorts or swim suits. So you may wish to tuck the jersey inside your pants and slip into a dress shirt or jacket to wear over the top when you have to look a bit more respectable. You may consider this unreasonably old fashioned, but you will probably learn, as I did, that you enjoy the trip more if people do not take offense at your appearance.

When it gets cooler, you may either wear a regular long-sleeved cycling jersey or a thin, tightly fitting sweater over the top. Except in really cold weather, get a model that can be opened at the neck by means of a zipper. You may also wear a light wind-proof jacket over the top of your cycling shirt, providing it is made of a densely woven material that allows air and perspiration through. Special cold and wet weather gear will be discussed separately below.

Gloves

Even in warm weather, special cycling gloves are highly recommended, since they make the ride a lot more comfortable. This applies especially if you select a low riding posture, which places a rather high percentage of your weight on the handlebars. These gloves have leather insides and open knit top panels and have fingers cut off to a length of about an inch. The palm area should be padded. If you do not like to wear gloves, at least use foam handlebar sleeves instead of (or underneath) regular handlebar tape, since this also provides the kind of cushioning effect needed to prevent nerve damage in the area of the palms. For colder weather, special winter cycling gloves are available, as described below.

Head Protection

Back in the 60s and early 70s, head protection might at best have meant something to keep the rain off your head. Today you will have ample choice of real accident protection for your head. Even outside the U.S., the hard shell helmet, as it is generally called, is beginning to get established, although not in traditional cycling countries like England and France. I suggest you wear one—even if you go touring in countries where there is more chance of being ridiculed than of the thing saving your life. You may never need a helmet, but it will make all the difference if you ever should fall on your head. See Chapter 11 for more details on the safety aspect of head protection.

The helmet should be comfortable to wear, well ventilated, and attached so that it will not move out of place upon impact. Most of these important criteria are satisfied if it meets the American standard ANSI Z-90.4. So many makes and models are now available that nobody has to go without, whatever his preference in style and design. Some helmets can be combined with a shield or visor to keep the sun out of your eyes or the rain off your glasses.

There is one situation where a helmet becomes too uncomfortable to wear for most people. That happens on a steep climb in hot weather. This situation is characterized by a combination of profuse perspiration, due to the heat generated as the result of performing work close to your maximum output, with the slow speed that virtually precludes the natural ventilation induced by

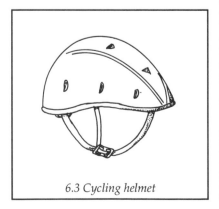

6.3 Cycling helmet

air movement. I simply take off the helmet in a case like that. Just don't forget to put it back on as soon as the descent begins.

Rain Gear

Yes, it is entirely possible to ride a bike in the rain—in the Pacific Northwest or my native Holland you'd never get very far if you stopped for every shower. Yet more people ride bikes there than anywhere else in the western world. Besides equipping the bike to keep the rain and spray off your body, the bike and the luggage, as explained in Chapter 4, you can make sure to have clothing that will see you through most rainstorms in reasonable comfort. Both this kind of clothing and the material described for cold weather cycling in the next section justify the investment in a couple of bicycle mail order catalogs. Most of these companies have a summer and a winter catalog, the latter one often containing lots of useful items, complete with worthwhile information on the properties of various materials and designs.

The big problem with most rain garments is that perfectly waterproof materials don't only keep rain out, but also keep perspiration in. Even if you are not usually aware of it, the cyclist is continuously perspiring as a result of performing the work necessary to propel his machine. Normally, this perspiration evaporates immediately as it is absorbed by the air passing along the body. When an impermeable barrier in the form of rubber- or plastic-coated fabric prevents this natural process, the moisture condenses on the inside of the barrier and very soon it penetrates every fiber between your body and the rain gear, until you are as dismally soaked as you would have been without rain wear.

The only satisfactory solution to this dilemma is the use of a special material that is just porous enough to pass water vapor, without allowing the passage of liquid water. One material that satisfies this criterion is Goretex, a trade name for a cloth consisting of woven fabric with a barrier layer of stretched PTFE, better known as Teflon. Another solution is provided by a material called Tenson, where the fibers are treated so that they expand enough to achieve the same effect when a certain humidity is exceeded. There are a few other materials and coatings that do the same after a fashion, varying widely in price, weight and appearance.

Although most garments made with these materials are awfully expensive and often garishly styled, I consider the investment absolutely essential in rainy regions at any time, and at least for off-season cycling in milder areas. Available are jackets, capes, coats, pants and suits, designed either specifically for cycling or for general use. Try a number of different models out in a cycling or backpacking store, to make sure you get a model that is not so generously cut as to be unsuitable for safe cycling.

Bike-A-Lite rainsuit. Note how the jacket back panel comes down very far—that's what it takes to keep water from running down your pants when you are leaning forward on the bike.

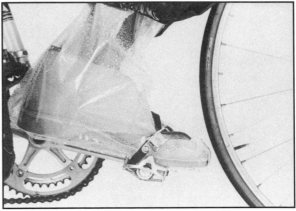

Left: Shimano SPD pedals and matching shoes—clipless cycling shoes with which you can actually walk. Right: Light plastic overshoes from VK International.

Personally, I find the rain cape is still the best solution, provided it is combined with spats. The latter are a kind of leggings that are open in the back. They may be either home-made or purchased from Custom Cycling Fitments (address listed in the Appendix), the only source I know in the U.S. The cape should preferably be a model without a built-in hood, since the hood restricts your peripheral vision, which is especially important when checking behind before turning off. The best thing to keep your head dry is a helmet without holes, or—for those who choose not to wear a helmet—a Sou'wester.

Finally, with regard to rain gear, the feet are a real problem. Cycling shoes are little use when it comes to keeping your feet dry, especially if a constant jet is being thrown up from the front wheel, as will happen when you have not installed a front fender with a mud flap. To ward off the rain from above, you may find good spats, with long beak-shaped extensions that reach over the tops of the shoes, quite effective. Another solution is to simply wear plastic bags around the socks, inside the shoes: not very elegant, but remarkably effective.

Cold Weather Wear

To be comfortable on the bike in cold weather, you will not need quite so much in the way of clothing as you would standing around watching a ball game. In the first place, the cycling activity generates enough heat to keep at least your trunk reasonably warm. In the second place, all that gear would hinder your movements. The heat is mainly generated in the trunk and the upper legs, so these parts will keep warm more easily, while the extremities of ears, hands and feet may need much thicker clothing.

Since the relatively high speed at which the cyclist proceeds causes high air velocities, excessive wind chill may ensue in many cases. That is especially critical during descents, when the speed is high and your energy output low. Besides, even in sum-

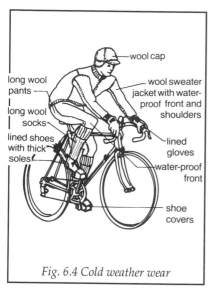

long wool pants

long wool socks

lined shoes with thick soles

wool cap

wool sweater jacket with water-proof front and shoulders

lined gloves

water-proof front

shoe covers

Fig. 6.4 Cold weather wear

mer it may get quite cold at high elevations. Consequently, bicycle touring in the mountains will cause additional problems, since you will be experiencing all the extremes. You'll be exposed to warm weather in the valleys and cold weather on the peaks, hard heat-producing cycling without significant wind cooling when climbing, and cold, fast air-cooled descents.

To arm yourself for cases like that, dress in layers that are easily put on and taken off. In addition, the wind must be kept out, for which a wind-proof outer layer is needed. That means a rather closely fitting, long jacket, made of very densely woven cloth that is permeable to water vapor, preferably in two-layer construction. This same kind of outer shell also protects you best in winter, when winds seem to cut right through the warmest woolen wear.

Underneath this outer layer, wear several relatively thin layers of warm materials. Quite close-fitting knitted or other very stretchable materials are ideal. For long underwear, polypropylene and silk are good solutions, since these materials are very light and not as hard on the skin as wool and most other synthetics. As for design, all these garments must be long, stretchable, close-fitting and easy to put on or take off. Zippers and other closures should be installed in such a way that there is a large enough overlap to keep the cold out, especially in the front.

Hands and feet cause greater problems, since the body's thermostat turns off the supply of heat-carrying blood to these extremities whenever the temperature of head and trunk is in danger of falling below the vital organs' required minimum operating temperature. Thick woolen socks inside special thick-soled and lined winter cycling shoes keep the feet comfortable. Add plastic bags, as described above for rain wear, if the combination of cold with rain or sleet occurs. In addition, you may use pedal covers to keep the feet comfortable under such conditions. Nylon-backed woolen gloves or relatively light lined leather models, such as cross-country skiing gloves, may suffice for the hands. Thick lined mittens may be needed when it gets even colder.

For the head, finally, a helmet without air scoops will be most comfortable. In very cold weather, you may have to wear a thin cap underneath the helmet to cover your ears and other exposed portions of your head. And if you elect not to wear a helmet, you can wear a knitted wool cap, as shown in the illustration.

Though hard to find, there are specific winter riding garments of the kind that are readily available in traditional cycling countries like France and England. If you should ever get there on your travels, don't forget to stock up on such useful things while you get the chance. These garments are integrated items that combine warm materials in a design specifically intended for cycling, with wind-breaking panels in the front of jacket and pants. In addition, there are special add-ons to normal cycling garments that can be put on or taken off easily—although they look awful. These are particularly convenient at times and in areas where significant temperature differences are encountered in the course of a day's ride.

Street Clothes

However effective bicycle clothing is, you probably want to look less conspicuous at certain times when touring for longer periods. That may be appropriate when looking for accommodations or when going for a meal, when sight-seeing or whenever you are off the bike. The easiest way to handle that is by wearing normal cycling gear, and carrying light wash-and-wear clothing that is wide enough to be worn over it.

Especially when traveling outside the U.S., it will help if you wear things that are relatively unobtrusive: no excessively bright colors or far-out designs. There should always be enough room in your bicycle bags to add a pair of slacks or a skirt, a shirt or a blouse, a pair of light dress shoes and perhaps a nylon raincoat. Select easily washable materials that don't suffer too much from storage in full panniers. Alternately, you may consider wearing less obtrusive cycling garments that are suitable off the bike as well.

Campsite Wear

When camping, you'll want to move about in reasonable comfort. I have found that a combination of cycling clothing with some of the more respectable items of dress described above serves my purposes adequately. An exception should be made for the feet, which need extra protection in wet or merely humid climates. Especially when first getting up in the morning, the ground will be wet, certainly if you are camping in a grassy area. Once your shoes and socks are wet, there is no way of being comfortable for a long time. A pair of light but high plastic overshoes will serve you well under those conditions. If it is not too cold, the smartest solution is perhaps to go barefoot until the grass is dry, keeping a towel handy near the entrance to the tent.

If you like to add more to your packing list for campsite wear—"après pitch," so to speak—you may consider warm-ups, a training suit to my British readers. These things are very easy to put on or take off, as the temperature dictates, and can be worn on top of other clothes. They even double as pajamas, allowing you to get up at night quickly and without embarrassment—whether to visit the bathroom or to check up when it sounds as though somebody is snooping around, ready to take off with your bike. Just how much more you take is up to you. But keep in mind that everything taken has to be carried the entire duration of the trip, even if you only use it once or twice.

CHAPTER 7

Selecting Camping Gear

This chapter may seem to be of interest only to those who plan to spend their nights out in nature while bicycle touring. Yet much of the information contained here will also prove useful to many others. Though you may not plan on camping out all the time, you may have to spend at least some nights under the open sky, and it will be infinitely more comfortable when you are adequately prepared to do that. Here you are introduced to the various kinds of camping equipment, while remarks on the practice of camping will be found in Chapter 18.

This is not a complete manual on the selection of camping equipment. Instead, I shall only cover those points that are essential to the bike camper, highlighting the different considerations that will be of importance when selecting materials and equipment. The most basic equipment needed to spend the night outside consists of nothing more than a sleeping bag and a ground sheet. Depending on the intensity of the camping experience desired, you may expand this list with tent and cooking gear.

Sources of Information

In addition to the information imparted here, you may find quite a lot of useful information relevant to this subject in the catalogs of some specialized camping and backpacking mail order companies. You may find that some of this information and some of the equipment recommended in the present chapter is not the

At the camp site. This is clearly not a KOA franchise. (photo Dieter Glokowski)

same as you have seen recommended in authoritative backpacking and camping manuals. This is because the touring cyclist has different problems and potentials than the mountaineer and hiker, not to mention the camper who carries his gear in the back of a car or pick-up truck.

To give an example, as a bicycle tourist, you can usually descend from great heights to milder, lower lying regions in a matter of an hour or so, while the backpacker might spend much more time at higher elevations. Similarly, you can more frequently obtain fresh stores of food than the backpacker. Compared to the car camper, on the other hand, you have to economize with respect to luggage volume and weight. You must plan ahead more, since you won't be able to go far out of your way to get food or other supplies before pitching your tent.

Sleeping Bags

Sleeping bags are available in many different designs, materials and quality levels. The sleeping bag selected for bicycle camping generally need not be quite as superb as what would be selected for backpacking. On the one hand, you will probably not camp at such high elevations as to need the ultimate in warmth. On the other hand, the risk of getting the bag wet are greater—not so much when camping as when carrying the gear.

Of the available filling materials, natural down is still the lightest and—even more important on the bike—the most compact. A down bag weighs about two thirds as much and packs in about half the space as a qualitatively comparable bag with synthetic filling. On the other hand, the down bag is invariably more expensive, more delicate and more sensitive to moisture than its synthetic counterparts. If you do select down, which remains my preference, you will have to take extreme precautions to keep the bag dry, for instance by keeping it in a fully closed plastic bag, in addition to its own pouch.

Both down and synthetic fillings come in a number of different qualities. In general, you get what you pay for. I suggest, rather than selecting one make in preference over another, you simply buy the most expensive bag of the chosen kind of material that meets your basic criteria, which will be outlined below. With down, you'll find that the more expensive bag has a softer quality down, which quickly recovers from the compacted to the lofted state once released from its pouch.

Loft refers to the thickness achieved by the non-compacted bag. When you put the bag flat down loosely, it will attain a certain thickness: that thickness is defined as the bag's loft. Since the bag's ability to keep you warm is primarily a function of the thickness of insulation, this loft is a simple guide to the warmth the bag offers. Use the lofting figures only as a basis for comparison between individual bags of the same material. Don't as-

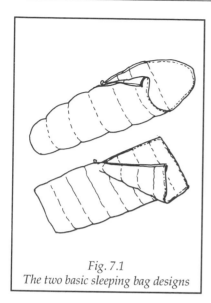

Fig. 7.1
The two basic sleeping bag designs

sume the thickest loft must necessarily give you the best bag for your purpose, since you will probably not be exposed to the extremes in low temperatures for which the high-loft bag is designed.

Nowadays, bags are often rated by their comfort range. Take the temperatures quoted by the manufacturers with a pinch of salt, though. A bag advertised with a comfort range from 60 to 15°F (18° to –9°C) probably does not give you the cozy comfort you may expect if the temperatures drop below freezing. In fact, my experience is that a comfort range to a minimum of 20°F (–7°C) is about right to handle most situations, even if it never freezes. When the temperature does stay high at night, you can always open the bag or lie on top of it. Don't choose too fancy a bag either: get one that is comfortable in summer, and sew a cover out of flannel cloth that can be used around the bag to upgrade it if you ever camp out during the colder time of the year.

The materials used for the outside are either polyamide, cotton or a combination of the two. Polyamide, usually simply referred to as nylon, which is its most common trade name, is invariably lighter, whereas cotton feels more comfortable, especially if you tend to develop allergies. When you first get into a bag, the nylon probably feels a little colder; however, after a very short time the nylon warms up. It also stays warmer throughout the night.

Furthermore, cotton takes up the moisture that is given off by the body, whereas it passes straight through the nylon. Consequently, the cotton often feels clammy in the mornings, whereas the nylon bag remains dry more easily. I like a bag that has cotton on one side and nylon on the other. I can use it whichever way round seems most comfortable for a particular situation: the nylon inside when it is cold or humid, the cotton inside when it is hot and dry.

Sleeping Bag Designs

The two basic sleeping bag designs are the square cut (or blanket) and mummy styles. The former is somewhat less space- and material-effective, and a little less warm than the latter. However, the square cut offers more room to spread out, can be opened up to serve as a blanket and is cheaper to make. On the whole, I think the square cut is an excellent design for bicycle use. Among the mummy designs, the preferred configuration should be one with a full-length zipper, so the bag may be opened when it gets too warm. Two matching bags with full-length zippers can usually be combined to form a bag for two. Either way, the zipper should be covered by a generous padded flap to keep the cold out when needed.

The cross section of the bag may be any one of the designs shown in Fig. 7.2. Sewn through is the simplest way to make a

Fig. 7.2 Sleeping bag cross sections: differentially cut and non-differentially cut.

sleeping bag. For a down bag, that may be good enough for temperatures down to about 40 °F (5 °C), if the bag is otherwise well constructed, and that is adequate for almost all summer and a good deal of spring and autumn use. If the bag has enough loft, the thin sections where the inner and outer layers are sewn together do not significantly detract from the warmth offered by the filling in the thicker sections.

A little more sophisticated is the straight box section design. These things are divided up into tubes, separated by walls, referred to as baffles. This allows a more even distribution of the filling material, leading to a slightly warmer bag with a given filling weight—at a correspondingly higher price, due to its more complex construction. The tubes may run either lengthwise or circumferentially. The former method generally allows a more consistent distribution of the filling, thus offering more durable comfort. The next step up is the slant baffle design, which theoretically results in an even warmer bag given the same amount of down. Finally, there is the overlapping baffle design, which is perhaps the ultimate (and most expensive) way of getting the most out of a given weight of filling.

Apart from the stitching or baffling method used, mummy bags may be either cut evenly or differentially. The different basic designs are represented in Fig. 7.3. Some manufacturers claim that a given amount of filling results in a warmer bag when the inside is cut smaller than the outside, while others claim that their bag is warmer because the inside is cut just as big as the outside. Then there are those who cut the bag differentially, yet recommend using it inside-out. I prefer a bag that is not differentially cut, but you are free to differ.

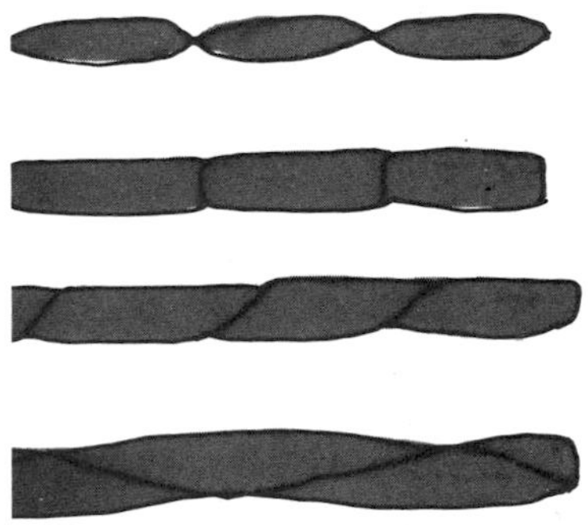

The closure and the hood of the bag are important details. To be warm enough, it should be possible to tighten the bag around the top at some point above the shoulders. A hood may not seem necessary at all times, but I've often found one loses so much heat through the head, that it had to be tucked in. In those situations, a sleeping bag with a close fitting hood is a fine solution. Essentially all mummy bags have some kind of hood, but not all are equally comfortable. Square cut bags generally have a very simple hood that can only be kept in place by means of a drawstring.

Fig. 7.3 Sleeping bag details

Sleeping Bag Care

Take good care of your sleeping bag. After the night, hang it out to air before packing it away. It dries quickest in wind and sunlight. Just don't keep nylon bags out in the sun more than necessary, since the ultraviolet rays eventually ruin the material. Especially cotton bags and down fillings should be dried and aired very thoroughly. To put the bag in its pouch, do not roll it up tightly, but literally stuff it into its pouch, starting at the foot

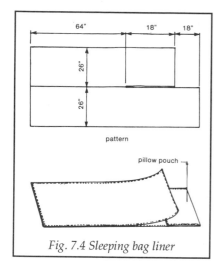

Fig. 7.4 Sleeping bag liner

Tents and Shelters

end. You will be able to limit the bag's packing size by taking in the pouch until it is just barely big enough to accept the bag, and then sew it up in that size. Just don't store the bag tightly packed over longer periods between trips, especially if it is damp or dirty. Instead, hang it up draped over a coat hanger, making sure it is thoroughly dry first.

It may be a good idea to use a liner or sheet bag inside the down- or synthetic-filled sleeping bag. The liner keeps the latter clean and can itself easily be washed. Fig. 7.4 shows how such a liner can be made, using any lightweight cotton, silk or synthetic material (if you're not allergic to it). The same liner can be used if you ever choose to stay in a youth hostel, where this design is prescribed for use under the blankets provided (except in countries like Germany, where many hostels demand you rent the peculiar mattress and blanket covers common there).

In many regions and at certain times, it is quite possible to go camping without a tent. The easiest method, and indeed one of the greatest ways to sleep, is directly under the stars, providing you can keep insects at bay and protect your bag against moisture from above and below. From below, the problem is solved with the help of a waterproof ground sheet. Alternately, you can make or purchase a protective sleeping bag cover. Make sure it is wide enough to allow you to turn around a little with the sleeping bag if you pitch the corners into the ground with tent pegs. The bottom should be of really waterproof material, such as rubber- or plastic-coated fabric. The top should be of water repellent material that allows water vapor to pass through, if it is to be comfortable at all. This extra sleeping bag cover will also keep

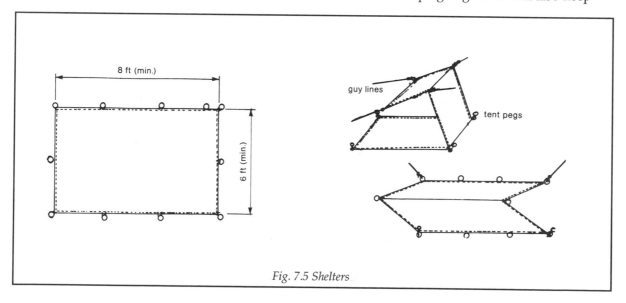

Fig. 7.5 Shelters

you quite a bit warmer: even a thin one adds at least 5°F (3°C) to the comfort range of your bag.

The next more sophisticated solution is to use a larger ground sheet that can be pitched up to cover the bag from below and above. This can also provide an adequate shelter against the wind, assuming the wind does not turn around during the night.

If you are camping in an area with mosquitoes or other bothersome insects, as is often the case in areas where cycling is good, you will want to sleep in a closed tent. You'll probably want to do the same whenever using an official camp site, where adequate privacy would not be possible without having your own four walls. The simplest tent can be no more than the previously shown ground sheet with a piece of mosquito netting sewn on. I have camped with such an item, weighing no more than two pounds, quite satisfactorily when traveling alone.

The next step up is a real tent, of which there are numerous basic designs and even more variants. The most relevant basic tent designs are illustrated in Fig. 7.6. Tents have either one or more internal poles or external rods or hoops to support them. Basically, a distinction can be made between tent designs with one or more central poles, and those suspended from an external support. In the latter, the cloth is tensioned by means of bent rods, as in an umbrella.

On the whole, the latter types are more space-efficient, since the walls and roof of the tent are naturally curved out instead of hanging inward, as is the case with the older tent designs. Among the various conventional tent designs with upright poles, the models with a wide opening, in which you sleep across the width, rather than in the length, are by far the most spacious and practical, although they are usually both more expensive and more sensitive to the wind.

If you will be camping in rocky or sandy areas, where tent pegs either do not penetrate or hold, dome and tunnel tent designs, characterized by their external rod supports, are preferable. In areas with frequent rain, the tent, whatever design it is in other respects, should at least allow plenty of height to sit upright. Under those circumstances, you may have to spend a lot of time inside the tent, where you will also have to cook and eat. Fig. 7.7 shows some of the ergonomic criteria for tent dimensions.

The ideal designs, especially for rainy weather or in a strong sun, are those with a very generously dimensioned, covered front porch. This allows you to live and work under cover at the entrance to the tent. Thus, your cooking gear will be outside the tent under the porch, while you can sit inside at the entrance. You will find this way of working much more enjoyable and efficient than either closing yourself off inside the tent or standing

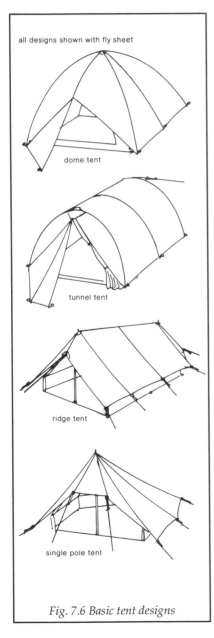

all designs shown with fly sheet

dome tent

tunnel tent

ridge tent

single pole tent

Fig. 7.6 Basic tent designs

outside. Chapter 18 contains some guidelines on how to "furnish" your camp.

Tent Materials

Cotton, nylon and polyester fibers are used to weave the cloth for tents. Nylon is generally the cheapest. Since it is very sensitive to ultraviolet light, it can not be recommended for the outside roof or the flysheet of a tent or its porch, where either polyester or cotton will last much longer. If the tent is of double-wall construction, consisting of an inner tent and a full-size flysheet, the inner tent may be of uncoated nylon or a very light cotton, while the flysheet should be of water-repellent material, but not nylon. The floor of any tent should be of rubber- or plastic-coated cloth, sewn to the tent proper. Only such truly waterproof materials keep out the moisture from the ground. Even in dry regions, the ground gives off moisture at night, when the air is colder than the ground.

Whatever the material, the most densely woven fabric, made with the finest and most even filament, will be of superior quality: light, strong and more impervious to water than more loosely woven cloth. This criterion is particularly important for flysheets and the roof section of single-wall tents. The ground sheet should be coated on the side facing down. Coated, really waterproof material can also be used for the flysheet, while the tent proper must allow air and water vapor to pass through.

For additional ventilation, a large window or even an entire door flap made of mosquito netting makes the tent more inhabitable and allows you to look out even when the tent is closed to insects. There should be an additional flap made of normal tent fabric to cover the mosquito netting, if necessary on account of the weather. Some very light tents are entirely made of mosquito netting don't offer much privacy unless they come with a wrap-around flysheet. They are suitable only for very mild climates.

As for the hardware, aluminum poles and pegs are stronger and lighter than fiberglass, while steel items are unnecessarily heavy.

The maximum size tent that can be carried on a bike is one that accommodates four people. Although most people prefer to

Fig. 7.7 Ergonomic criteria

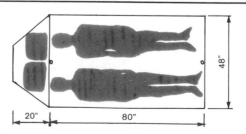

Length:	2 m	(6 ft. 6 in.)
Width:		
1 person:	90 cm	(3 ft.)
2 persons:	120 cm	(4 ft.)
3 pesons:	170 cm	(5 ft. 4 in.)
4 persons	220 cm(	7 ft. 4 in.)
Additional luggage space:		
1 person:	0.4 m²	(4 sq. ft.)
2 persons:	0.7 m²	(7 sq. ft.)
3 persons:	1.0 m² (	10 sq. ft.)
4 persons	1.3 m² (	13 sq. ft.)

Table 7-I Minimum tent dimensions

Sleeping Pad and Air Mattress

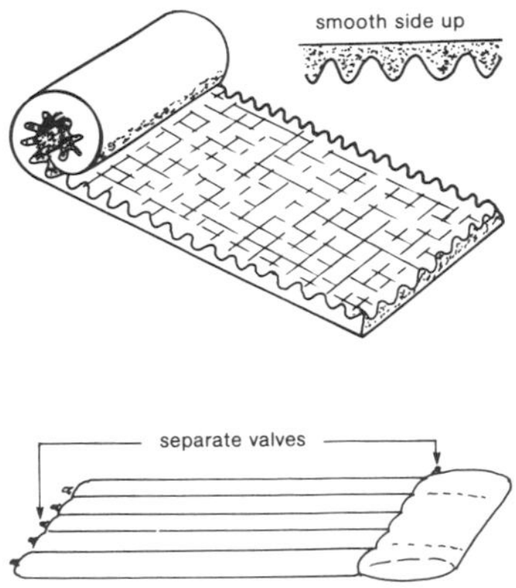

Fig. 7.8 Top: open cell pad. Bottom: air mattress with separate air chambers.

use several two-man tents instead of one larger tent, the latter solution offers more useful space and may be lighter to carry. In addition to the occupants, there must be room to keep the luggage—either in the tent itself or next to it, protected under the fly sheet. Depending on the number of persons the tent must accommodate, the floor plan should be dimensioned according to the sizes summarized in Table 7-I.

Even if you have a tent with a sewn-in groundsheet (which is customary these days), it will be a good idea to also take a separate groundsheet. It will serve to cover the bikes, your luggage or other items around the camp site. A small groundsheet also allows you to sit outside when the ground is wet.

Whether you sleep in a tent or not, the sleeping bag alone is not really adequate. If you use a down bag, the down gets compressed flat under your body weight, which reduces the comfort and insulating properties drastically. Synthetic materials do not compact quite as much, but even they may prove uncomfortable. A few manufacturers make bags that have down in the top and either synthetic filling or foam material in the bottom. But the most universal way to assure comfort and warmth is by means of a separate pad.

Three basically different types of foam pads are in use: open- and closed-cell foam and inflatable pads. Closed-cell foam, of which Ensolite is a familiar trade name, is hard to compact. Consequently, it does not get flattened underneath the sleeper, even though these pads are usually very thin. This material comes in different thicknesses, widths and lengths. For comfort, I consider the minimum required size to be 2 cm (¾ in.) thick, 55 cm (22 in.) wide and 120 cm (48 in.) long. Unfortunately, the insulating property goes hand in hand with a large package when rolled up, even though the weight is minimal.

The second type of pad is made of much less resilient open-cell foam of much greater thickness. Usually this is smooth on one side, while the other side has a pattern reminiscent of an egg carton. It should be at least 6 cm (2½ in.) thick. Length and width should be the same as the minimum dimensions for the closed-cell material. Though a full length pad is more comfortable, it may be too big to carry on the bike.

The third kind is a variant of the air mattress. The Therm-A-Rest pad differs from your everyday air mattress not only by being much lighter and thinner, but also by having a fine foam inside that prevents the air circulation that makes regular air mattresses so cold. Even the lightest air mattress is no lighter than either type of foam pad described above, but it can be packed up much more compactly, which is at least as important in cycle touring as the weight factor.

In addition to the mattress or pad, I carry a cushion made of open-cell foam. This is my one piece of extravagant luxury away from home, serving both as a pillow at night and as a cushion to sit on by day. Many campers pack their spare clothes and towels together, some rest their heads on their shoes or sleep on a rock, but I prefer to be comfortable. You will probably find, as I did, that it is easy enough to wriggle around long enough to get reasonably comfortable on your back or side when sleeping, but your head only gets the rest it deserves when it is supported on such a soft, smooth pillow.

Cooking Equipment

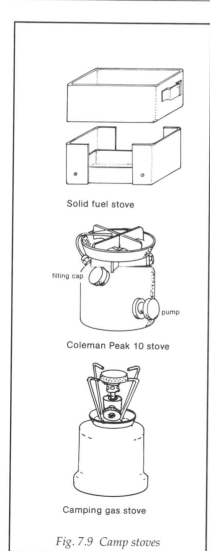

Solid fuel stove

Coleman Peak 10 stove

Camping gas stove

Fig. 7.9 Camp stoves

Build a wood fire to do your cooking whenever you get the opportunity. It adds greatly to the charm of outdoor living. But often you will not be able to do that. In many area of the U.S. it is strictly regulated, and in most of Europe it is prohibited, while firewood may be hard to find even where it is allowed. For that reason, I suggest you also carry a camping stove.

You will be well served with any of the various models intended for backpacking—what's light and small enough to be carried on the trail also serves its purpose for bicycle camping. Stoves that operate on several different types of fuel are available. The lightest and smallest burn solid alcohol tablets (such as Esbit). Slightly heavier are models that run on white gas (petrol in England), kerosene (paraffin oil) or pressurized propane gas.

If you travel alone and only rarely intend to use it, the solid alcohol stove is probably adequate, especially if your needs do not exceed the occasional cup of coffee, a boiled or fried egg and a warmed-up can of soup. This type of stove cannot be regulated and burns up its fuel rather fast. On the other hand, the fuel is light and convenient to carry. At a very modest price, you can get a set consisting of a stove, a miniature saucepan, a lid that also serves as a frying pan, and enough fuel to last one person for one or two weeks. This kind of fuel can be bought at most drugstores (chemists to my British readers), and on the bike you will pass enough stores to make this a very convenient type of stove.

There are numerous camp stoves designed to burn either white gas or kerosene, my favorite being the Coleman Peak 10. Whatever make and model, this is the most cost-efficient kind of stove, burning cheap fuel efficiently. The problem with both is the inconvenience of fuel resupply: it is hard to get it in quantities of less than a gallon at a time. Fine if your trip is of modest length, if your group is small or if you don't do much cooking: you can carry a liter (1 quart) of fuel in a special sealed metal or plastic bottle, available at backpacking stores. That will last one or two people about a week if you cook a full meal each day. On longer trips with several people, you may have to consider installing a large fuel can on one of the bikes. With the exception of the Peak 10, all kerosene-burning stoves must be pre-heated using methylated spirits or solid fuel. Don't forget to take a supply of the special fuel for that purpose.

Stoves powered by liquefied pressurized propane gas are convenient and clean. The fuel is quite expensive and rather heavy to carry, since you have to carry the cartridges as well as the fuel they contain. In Britain and on the European continent these stoves are convenient, since the fuel cartridges are readily obtainable. In the U.S., where their distribution is much poorer, you would need an unreasonably large supply of these awkward cartridges, certainly if you intend to cook frequently on a longer trip.

Other Camping Equipment

Depending on the intensity of the camping experience and the comfort desired, you may want to take more or less camping gear in addition to the items listed above. Generally, you'll want at least a nesting set of cooking pots, cup, plate, bread board (essentially a lap-top table, made of a 12 x 18 inch piece of fiberboard), cutlery, can and bottle openers, a foldable plastic water container and a similar wash basin. Furthermore, I suggest you take some form of lighting, wind screens for light and stove, and a number of storage containers, as well as strong, sealed bags to carry food and other supplies. Finally, you'll need dishwashing liquid, brush, scouring pad and dish towel to keep your pots clean. Most of the other items needed on a bicycle tour are the same whether you go camping or not.

For most of these things, you will find backpacking stores to have an astounding range of different types. You will also be able to improvise or make certain items yourself. Get things that are as light as possible and relatively insensitive to deformation. Select screw-on tops for large containers, plastic rather than metal, small and oval cross sections in preference to large round ones. You may also appreciate that the simplest items will be the easiest to carry and maintain. To give but one example, candles are more effective and convenient than a much heavier electric light.

In the Appendix, you will find a proposed packing list. Though you may find such a list helpful at first, the biggest secret to effective packing and camping is the art of leaving things home (or even in the store) selectively. Deciding what to buy and carry is even more important than selecting the lightest, smallest or best items. Before buying or packing anything, consider seriously whether you can improvise somehow without it, or whether something else may serve its purpose as well without the weight. For further suggestions on this subject, you are referred to Chapters 13 and 18, which deal with the practical aspects of packing and bicycle camping, respectively.

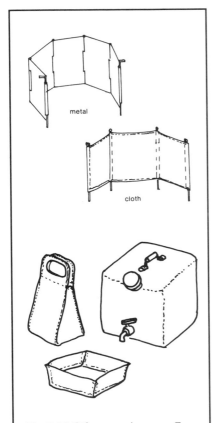

Fig. 7.10 Other camping gear. From top to bottom: windshields, water canister and wash basin.

Part II.

The Art of Bicycle Touring

CHAPTER 8

Bike Fit and Riding Style

The chapters of this second part of the book are primarily devoted to the skills and knowledge that are prerequisite to the safe and enjoyable practice of cycling. Some of this material may also be found in general bicycle books. However, here the practical background of touring is specifically considered. Many of the topics covered in these chapters are not considered at all in conventional general bicycle books.

This particular chapter will first help you arrive at the adjustments that are necessary to cycle in comfort. This is followed by practical advice on posture, riding style and the methods that allow you to cover significant distances on a loaded bicycle. Excluded from this material will be the subjects of gearing choice and pedaling rate, since these topics are covered comprehensively in the next chapter.

Riding Posture

Whether mountain bike or road touring bike, a comfortable riding position is the key to long-term comfort. (photo Renner)

To cycle long distances without exhausting, the conventional idea of a comfortable position may have to be reconsidered. Though bicycle racers have long known that they are most comfortable in a relatively low crouched position, most other cyclists—whatever kind of bike they ride—seem to feel that to be comfortable one has to sit upright. That may be fine if you travel only short distances in town or make minor excursions at low speed in easy terrain. However, the serious bicycle tourist has

Fig. 8.1 Riding postures seen from the front.

much more in common with the racer than he has with the occasional short-distance cyclist. The fact that you probably have luggage on board and difficult terrain to handle makes this even more important.

Fig. 8.1 shows the three basic kinds of riding postures for comparison: upright, inclined and fully crouched. If you are used to riding in the upright position, you may well be convinced this is the only comfortable way to ride a bike, but the first and most important step towards more comfortable riding is a different riding posture. In the lower position, your weight is divided more evenly over handlebars, saddle and pedals. This reduces the pressure on the buttocks, and it allows the relaxed fast pedaling technique so essential for long-duration power output. Thirdly, it enables greater restraining forces to bring more force to bear on the pedals when needed. Finally, it reduces the wind resistance, which is a major factor in cycling, especially when traveling fast or against the wind.

Hard to Learn? Strangely enough, many people to whom these advantages have been demonstrated nevertheless insist on riding in the upright position. They bring all sorts of arguments, ranging from, "That's only for racing" to, "That is terribly uncomfortable" or, "You couldn't cycle any distance that way." The undeniable fact is that they are fooling themselves. In reality, they are less comfortable, whatever they think, and have to do more work to proceed the same distance or to ride at the same speed. Get accustomed to the right posture early in your cycling career, and you'll be a more effective cyclist, one who gets more pleasure and less frustration out of the pursuit.

Even within the general range of comfortable positions, there are enough different variations to allow changes and variations. This makes it possible to adapt to different conditions and gives you the chance to vary your position from time to time. The latter helps avoid the numbing feeling when pressure is applied for a longer period in a certain position. The position of the hands may require some variation, certainly if you are not yet used to supporting a significant portion of your weight on your arms.

approx. 50°

Fig. 8.2 Relaxed riding posture seen from the side.

Bike Fit

The following sections will describe just how the saddle and the handlebars should be set to achieve the basic relaxed position that is shown in Fig. 8.2. This particular posture is worth looking into a little closer. Study the proportions, noting also that merely holding the handlebars in a different location allows adequate variation. This may be required to apply more force to the pedals or to reduce the wind resistance by lowering the front, or to get a better overview of the road or the scenery by raising the front by as little as perhaps 10 cm (4 in.) either way. The following description is based on the assumption that you have a drop-handlebar derailleur bicycle of the right size to match your physique and a crank length that equals one half the upper leg length, as described in Chapters 2 and 3, respectively.

Saddle Height

The height of the saddle, or rather the distance of its top relative to the pedals, is the most critical variable for effective cycling. It should be adjusted so that the leg can be stretched comfortably without completely straightening the knee joint, which would force excessive force and rotation on the joint. At the same time, the distance between the pedal at its highest point and the saddle must be such that the knee is not bent excessively. Once the former has been set, the correct crank length, as established above and in Chapter 3, assures that the latter condition is also satisfied.

Here I shall describe three methods of establishing the correct seat height. These are all good enough for preliminary set-up and the first thousand miles of cycling. Your ultimate seat position may require additional individual experimental fine-tuning, based on your subjective long-term comfort. On the other hand, in the vast majority of cases, each of these techniques will lead to a satisfactory seat position that is suitable for touring, without the need for subsequent fine-tuning.

109% Rule The first method is referred to as 109% rule. It was developed at Loughborough University in England and is illustrated in Fig. 8.3 To use it, first measure your inseam leg length by standing with your back against a wall with your legs straight, your feet about 5 cm (2 in.) apart, wearing thin soled shoes with flat heels. Make a pencil mark for the location of the crotch on the wall. This is easiest to do with the aid of a drawing triangle (oddly enough called a set square in Britain) or a rectangular board held upright and pushed up against the wall between your legs. Measure the vertical distance between this mark and the floor.

Now multiply that figure, be it in inches or in cm, by 1.09. That is presumed to be the optimal distance between the top of the saddle and the pedal axle when the pedal is down, crank in line with the seat tube. Measure it out and set the seat accordingly with the plane connecting front and back of the saddle cover horizontal. How the saddle is raised or lowered will be explained under *Saddle Adjustments,* below.

Trial and Error The second method seems less theoretical and is illustrated in Fig. 8.4. It is a trial-and-error method and is easy to carry out without help. You must again wear cycling shoes with flat heels. Place the bike next to a wall or post for support (I like to do it in

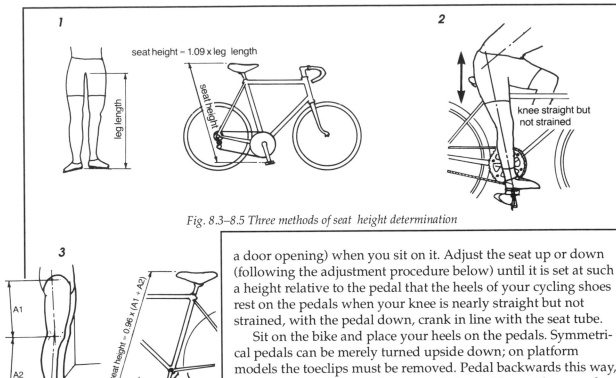

Fig. 8.3–8.5 Three methods of seat height determination

a door opening) when you sit on it. Adjust the seat up or down (following the adjustment procedure below) until it is set at such a height relative to the pedal that the heels of your cycling shoes rest on the pedals when your knee is nearly straight but not strained, with the pedal down, crank in line with the seat tube.

Sit on the bike and place your heels on the pedals. Symmetrical pedals can be merely turned upside down; on platform models the toeclips must be removed. Pedal backwards this way, making sure you do not have to rock from side to side to reach the pedals. Now raise the saddle 12 mm (½ in.) above this height. Tighten the saddle in this position. Note that the heels-on-pedals style only applies to adjusting the seat height, not to riding the bike, as will be described below.

Hodges Method The third method is illustrated in Fig. 8.5. It was developed by the American bicycle racing coach Mark Hodges. It is probably the most accurate method, applicable to touring cyclists as much as it is to racers. You will need a helper to measure your leg length and a calculator to figure out the correct saddle height. Stand barefoot upright with your back against a wall, your feet 15 cm (6 in.) apart. Now measure the distance from the floor over your ankle joint and your knee joint to the greater trochanter. That's the outwardmost bump on the femur, or hip, which coincides with the hip joint's center of rotation: when you raise your leg, this point should not move.

To establish the optimal seat height, measured between the top of the saddle near its center and the center of the pedal axle (crank pointing down in line with the seat tube), multiply the distance found above by 0.96. If appropriate, add an allowance for thick soles, thick cleats or unusually shaped pedals.

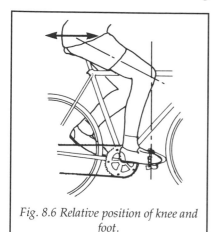

Fig. 8.6 Relative position of knee and foot.

Fine-tuning Even after using any of these methods, you may have to do some fine-tuning to achieve long-term comfort. Riders with disproportionately small feet may want to place the saddle a little lower, those with big feet perhaps slightly higher. No need to get carried away: raise or lower the seat in steps of 6 mm (¼ in.) at a time and try to get used to any position by riding several hundred miles or several days before attempting any change, which must again be in the order of about 6 mm to make any real difference.

When cycling, the ball of the foot (the second joint of the big toe) should be over the center of the pedal axle, with the heel raised so much that the knee is never straightened fully. Not all cyclists incline the foot equally as shown in Fig. 8.6. Consequently, the amount by which the saddle is moved relative to the point determined may vary a little for different riders—a matter of 6 mm (¼ in.) one way or the other.

Saddle Position and Angle

The normal preliminary saddle position is such that the seat post is roughly in the middle of the saddle. For optimal pedaling efficiency, adjust the saddle forward or backward after it has been set to the correct height, as explained in the preceding section. On any bike designed on conventional lines, sitting on the bike with your foot under the toeclip and the crank placed horizontally, the center of your knee joint should be vertically aligned with the spindle of the forward pedal. You can locate the center of your knee joint at the bony protrusion just behind the knee cap.

The angle of the saddle relative to the horizontal plane should initially be set so as to keep the line that connects the highest points at the front and the back level. After the handlebars have been set to the correct height, it may be necessary to modify this angle to prevent slipping back and forth. This too may not become apparent until after some miles of cycling. Adjusting procedures for both forward position and angle are outlined below.

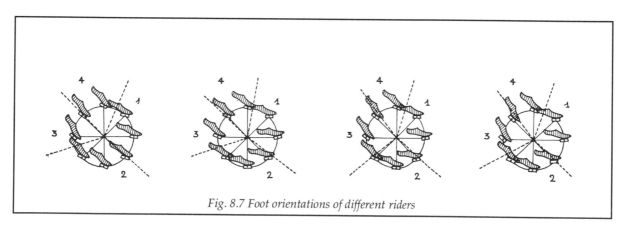

Fig. 8.7 Foot orientations of different riders

Saddle Adjustments

To do the actual mechanical adjusting work on the saddle, first take a close look at the way it is installed on the bike. Adjust the saddle height by loosening the binder bolt behind the seat lug, raising or lowering the saddle with the attached seat post in a twisting motion, and then tightening the binder bolt again at the required height, making sure it is straight.

To change the forward position, undo the adjustment bolts (only one bolt on some models) on the seatpost. These bolts are usually reached from under the saddle cover, though they can be reached from below or the side on some models. Once loosened, push the saddle until the desired position is reached; then tighten the bolts, making sure the saddle is held at the desired angle relative to the horizontal plane.

Handlebar Height and Position

Even for bicycle touring, the highest point of the handlebars should always be lower than the top of the saddle to ride efficiently. Just how low will be determined by the shape of the handlebars and the rider's physiognomy. It depends on the relative distribution of body weight as well as on torso height, and the upper and lower arm length. That's why only experiments can tell what will eventually be right for any particular rider. Here I shall merely tell you how to determine the initial position for a frame size check, followed by the adjustment for a relaxed initial riding style. After about a thousand miles of cycling, you should be able to fine-tune the handlebar height and stem length to match your needs perfectly.

The following description is again based on the use of a correctly dimensioned frame, as outlined in Chapter 2. In order to make sure the handlebars are not too high, first check whether the fully crouched position can be achieved. Place the handlebars in their lowest possible position and, sitting on the saddle, hold them in the lowest part of the bend (below the brake levers). With the lower arms horizontal and the elbows at a slightly acute angle, the upper body should now lie almost horizontally. This is the fully crouched or "full tuck" position. It may be necessary to choose a longer or shorter handlebar stem for comfort in this position. If this full tuck is not possible with any handlebar stem available, you probably need a smaller or (more rarely) a larger frame.

To set the handlebars for a relaxed initial riding style, without sacrificing the advantages of the full tuck when conditions call for it, proceed as follows. First set the top of the bars about 3 cm (1¼ in.) lower than the saddle. Sit on the bike and reach forward for the part of the bends between the straight top and the brake lever attachments. In this position your shoulders should be about midway between seat and hands. The arms should feel neither stretched nor heavily loaded and they should be parallel.

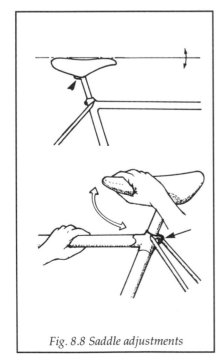

Fig. 8.8 Saddle adjustments

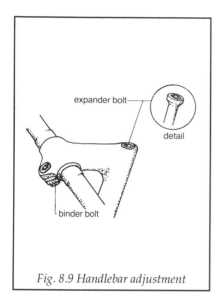

Fig. 8.9 Handlebar adjustment

If they don't satisfy the last criterion, your handlebar bend is too wide or too narrow; if you can not find a relaxed position, you will need a longer or shorter stem. If you have a particularly long combination of lower arms and torso in relation to your leg length, you may not be comfortable even with a long stem. In that case, a slightly larger frame, which has a longer top tube as well as a longer seat tube, may be in order. Conversely, long legs combined with short arms and torso may require you use a shorter frame to achieve the right top tube length. In extreme cases of either variety, the right top tube length just cannot be achieved with a bike that fits in height. In this case, you may need a custom-built frame with the desired dimensions of seat tube and top tube. This would be the ultimate solution, although it is probably not quite so critical that you can't make do with a stock frame.

Finally, grab the handlebar bend at the ends, leaning forward on them while seated. The handlebar angle relative to the horizontal plane should be such that the hands don't tend to slip either into the bend or off towards the ends in this position. If you initially have difficulties achieving this position, you may start off with the handlebars somewhat higher. In that case, the ends must also point down slightly. Lower and level them out as you develop the style that allows you to ride with the lower handlebar position after some practice.

Handlebar Adjustments

To vary the height of the handlebars, first straddle the front wheel, facing the bike. Undo the expander bolt, which is recessed in the top of the stem. If the stem does not come loose immediately, you may have to lift the handlebars to lift the wheel off the ground, then tap on the head of the expander bolt with a hammer. This will loosen the internal clamping device. Now raise or lower the handlebar stem as required. Tighten the expander bolt again, while holding the handlebars straight in the desired position.

To change the angle of the handlebar ends with respect to the horizontal plane, undo the binder bolt that clamps the handlebar bend in the front of the stem. Twist the handlebar bend until it is at the desired angle, and then tighten the binder bolt again, holding the bar centered. To install a longer stem or a different bar design, you are referred to any bicycle maintenance book or your friendly bike store. The correct handlebar position often puts more strain on the hands than beginning cyclists find comfortable, especially when rough road surfaces induce vibrations. Minimize this problem by always keeping your arms slightly bent, never holding them in a cramped position. If you still experience discomfort, you can try cushioned foam sleeves (such as Grab-On) instead of normal handlebar tape.

Adjusting Special Bikes

If you use a mountain bike for touring, most of the adjustments described above also apply as long as you ride on the road. Since most bicycle touring will be done on the road, whatever kind of bike is used, the only real difference is that the flat mountain bike handlebars do not allow the lower position for the full tuck. Consequently, I suggest you set the saddle and the handlebars so that the relaxed position described above is possible when holding the flat bars at the ends.

Once you do start riding off-road, especially in mountainous terrain, you may want to lower the saddle or to put it further back to cycle down a steep incline. Since the variation in geometry from one make and model to the next is quite significant, you may have to do a bit of experimenting to find the optimal positions for such special uses. Certainly the saddle adjustment is much easier for experimenting and frequent change, with a quick-release binder bolt and sometimes an additional quick-release bolt to hold the saddle to the seatpost, as installed on virtually all mountain bikes.

Besides the users of off-road bikes, two other groups of cyclists also encounter different fitting problems: tandem riders and children. Chapter 20 is devoted to the subject of touring with children, while advice for tandem riders will be found in Chapter 21.

Basic Bike Handling

Once saddle and handlebars are adjusted correctly, it will be time to take to the road on your bike. In case you are not yet familiar with the derailleur bicycle and the rest of your equipment, here's just a suggestion for getting on and off the bike. All other riding and handling techniques involve long learning processes that will be treated in separate chapters, but the simple act of starting the bike should be mastered immediately. Easy though this may seem, it is worth practicing, if only to avoid embarrassing or dangerous mishaps, especially when cycling with others or in traffic.

Of course, most cyclists are not entirely new to the game: you too may feel you've been cycling long enough to do without any additional advice or practice. It still does not hurt to follow the procedures described below seriously and consciously, so you become more efficient at handling the bike when touring. Your first experience will probably be on a bike without luggage, but it is a good idea to also load the bike with luggage and practice handling it that way before your first serious tour. When cycling with packs, take care to find the loaded bike's mass center, from which it is easiest to balance. Also note that getting on and off a loaded bike may require special precautions, depending on the extent to which the bags protrude.

Left: Quality bikes come in an adequate range of sizes: Here a 48 cm and a 65 cm model.
Right: Although still common in Britain, the mixte bike frame is not used much in the U.S. these days.

Before you start off, make sure your shoelaces are tied and tucked in, or short enough not to run the risk of getting caught in the chain. Make sure the bike is set in a low gear, with the chain on the middle chainwheel (or the smaller one on a machine with only two chainwheels) and an intermediate or big sprocket. The bike should have been checked to make sure it will be operating properly and that the tires are well inflated.

Start off at the side of the road, after having checked to make sure no traffic is following closely behind. Straddle the top tube by swinging the appropriate leg either over the handlebars, the top tube, or the saddle. Hold the handlebars with both hands at the top of the bend. Tap against the pedal with the toe of your starting foot to turn it around. This brings the toeclip on top, after which you can immediately place your foot under the toeclip. In case you use shoes with cleats, place the slot of the cleat over the ridge of the pedal. Pedal backward until the pedal is in the top position. Pull the toestrap, but not quite so tight as to cut off circulation in your foot, then pedal back three quarters of a revolution to bring the pedal to two o'clock, just above the horizontally forward position.

Safe Stopping and Slowing Down

Look behind you to make sure the road is clear, then check ahead to establish which course you'll want to follow. Place your weight on the pedal, leaning lightly on the handlebars. Put the other foot on its pedal as soon as it is in the top position. The first few revolutions will be cycled with this second pedal upside down, either standing up or seated. When you have gained some momentum, tap your toe against the back of the free pedal to turn it over, and right away push your foot in under the toeclip. Pedal a few more strokes, then pull the loose toestrap taut, securing the second foot to its pedal as well.

To slow down, whether just to stop or to get off the bike, first look behind you again to make sure you are not getting in the

Decending rapidly is a skill apart (photo Renner)

way of cyclists or motorists following. Aim for the position where you will want to stop. Change into a lower gear, appropriate for starting off again later. Push against the buckle of the toestrap for whichever foot you want to have free first, meanwhile pulling your foot up and back to loosen it when that pedal is up. When using cycling shoes with cleats, the strap must be just loose enough to raise your foot to clear the pedal with the cleat.

Slow down by braking gently, using mainly the front brake to stop. When you have come to a standstill, or just before that point, make sure the pedal with the loosened strap is up, then pull your foot up and out. Place it on the ground, leaning over slightly in that same direction, while moving forward off the saddle to straddle the seat tube. Now you are in the right position to dismount or start again.

If you want to get off the bike at this point, bring your other foot up, pedaling backwards, and loosen the buckle of the toestrap to release your foot. Now you're ready to get off the bike. However, under most circumstances you will find that especially a loaded machine is most easily controlled when you remain on the bike, straddling the top tube. I suggest you only dismount completely if it is really necessary.

CHAPTER 9

Selecting and Using the Gears

Modern touring bicycles as sold in the U.S. and Britain are invariably equipped with derailleur gearing. Nowadays, 21-speed systems are generally used for genuine touring machines, although systems with fewer gears may be quite adequate for many touring purposes. The most common systems have 3 chainrings, combined with 7 sprockets, or cogs, allowing 21 different combinations. To change gear, the chain is shifted onto any chosen combination of chainring and sprocket with the aid of two derailleur mechanisms.

The derailleur method of gearing allows minute adaptations of the gear ratio to the cyclist's potential on the one hand, and the terrain, wind resistance and road conditions on the other hand. All that is mere theory, because in reality the majority of people, including most beginning touring cyclists, plod along in the wrong gear for the workload. Indeed, learning to select the right gear may well provide the biggest single step towards improved cycling speed and endurance. That's the subject of the present chapter.

There is a sound theory behind the principle of gear selection. Interesting though this theory is, there is no need to wait to apply the technique until you thoroughly understand the underlying theory. That's why I shall only outline the correct use of gearing to the extent you will need it as a touring cyclist at this point.

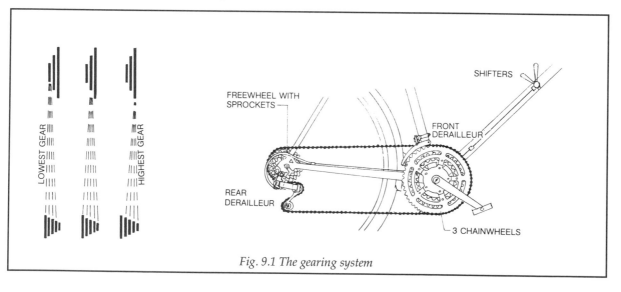

LOWEST GEAR   HIGHEST GEAR

SHIFTERS

FREEWHEEL WITH
SPROCKETS

FRONT
DERAILLEUR

REAR
DERAILLEUR

3 CHAINWHEELS

Fig. 9.1 The gearing system

The Derailleur System

Fig. 9.1 shows and names the mechanical components of the derailleur system. The chain runs over two or three chainrings mounted on the RH crank, and any one of 6, 7 or 8 sprockets, or cogs, mounted on a freewheel block at the rear wheel. As long as you are pedaling forward, the chain can be moved from one chainring to another by means of the front derailleur, or changer, and from one sprocket to another by means of the rear derailleur.

Because the various chainrings and sprockets have different numbers of teeth, the ratio between pedaling speed and the speed with which the rear wheel—and with it the whole bike—is driven changes whenever a different combination is selected. Bigger chainrings in the front and smaller sprockets in the rear result in higher gears, smaller chainrings and bigger sprockets give lower gears. Higher gears are selected when cycling is easy, so the available output allows a high riding speed. Select a lower gear when higher resistances must be overcome, such as riding uphill or against a headwind, or when starting off from a standstill.

Each derailleur is controlled by means of a shift lever, usually mounted at the handlebar ends or on the frame's down tube. Modern racing bikes are often equipped with shifters integrated in the brake levers, and although these are indeed very convenient, they are very expensive and in my opinion too sensitive for serious touring use. Mountain bikes, with their flat bars, allow the use of thumb shifters, mounted directly on the handlebars, within easy reach from the handgrips, or more recently also twist grips.

Make sure derailleurs and levers match and that both are suitable for touring use. They will be if they are intended for gears that are relatively widely spaced. The bike shop is the place to find out what is suitable hardware for your bike.

Most shifts are made with the rear derailleur, while the front changer is primarily used to move from one general range of gears to the other. With the usual 21-speed set-up, all the gears in the high range are reached by means of shifts of the rear derailleur, while the front derailleur remains on the largest chainring. All the intermediate gears are reached by shifts of the rear derailleur, after the front derailleur has been moved once to engage the intermediate chainring. All the gears in the low range are again selected with the rear derailleur, once the front derailleur is used to put the chain on the smallest chainring.

Although it is also possible to select chainring and sprocket sizes in such a way that intermediate gears between rear derailleur shifts are always reached with a front changer shift, the above method simplifies the gear selection procedure considerably. This is certainly so for the typical touring bike set-up with 21-speed gearing. Intermediate gears may have to be engaged by

Long-cage derailleur. The long cage allows shifting over a wide range of different chainring and sprocket sizes.

means of double shifting on systems with 12, 14 or 16 speeds, on which only two chainrings are installed on the RH crank.

The rear derailleur is controlled from the RH shift lever. To put the chain on a different sprocket in the rear, move the RH shift lever, while pedaling forward with reduced force. Pull the lever back to change to a larger sprocket, which results in a lower gear; push it forward to reach a smaller sprocket, resulting in a higher gear.

The LH shift lever controls the front derailleur, or changer, which simply shoves the cage through which the chain runs to the left or the right, moving the chain onto the smaller or the bigger chainring. Pulling the lever back engages the bigger chainring for the higher gear range on most models; pushing it forward engages the smaller chainring, to obtain the lower gearing range.

The Need for Gears

The reason for gearing lies in the possibility it provides to pedal at an efficient rate with comfortable force under a wide range of different conditions and riding speeds. If the combination of chainring and sprocket size were fixed, as it is on a single-speed bicycle, any given pedaling speed invariably corresponds to a certain riding speed. The rear wheel will be turning at a speed that can be simply calculated by multiplying the pedaling rate with the quotient of chainring and sprocket size (expressed in terms of the numbers of teeth):

$$v_{wheel} = v_{pedal} \times T_{front} \div T_{rear}$$

where:

v_{wheel} = wheel rotating speed (RPM)

v_{pedal} = pedaling rate (RPM)

T_{front} = number of teeth, chainring

T_{rear} = number of teeth, sprocket

The actual riding speed depends on this wheel rotating speed and the effective wheel diameter. The effective diameter of a nominal 700 mm wheel is about 680 mm. This results in a riding speed in MPH that can be determined by multiplying the wheel speed in RPM by 0.08. These two calculations can be combined to find the riding speed in MPH directly from the pedaling rate and the chainring and sprocket sizes as follows:

$$MPH = 0.08 \times v_{pedal} \times T_{front} \div T_{rear}$$

where:

MPH = riding speed in MPH and the other symbols are as defined above. To express riding speed in km/h, use the following formula instead:

Another way to shift: Grip-shift controls mounted on the handlebar ends.

$$km/h = 0.125 \times v_{pedal} \times T_{front} \div T_{rear}$$

To give an example, assume you are pedaling at a rate of 80 RPM on a bike geared with a 42-tooth chainring and a 21-tooth rear sprocket. Your riding speed, expressed in MPH and km/h respectively, will be:

$$0.08 \times 80 \times 42 : 21 = 13 \text{ MPH}$$

$$0.125 \times 80 \times 42 : 21 = 20 \text{ km/h}$$

Depending on the prevailing terrain conditions, that may be too easy or too hard for optimum endurance performance. If you are riding up a steep incline, this speed may require a very high pedal force, which may well be too exhausting and damaging to muscles, joints and tendons. On a level road the same speed will be reached so easily that you don't feel any significant resistance. That may be acceptable for cruising, but not for serious touring if you have to cover a greater distance in a reasonable time.

The derailleur gearing system allows you to choose the combination of chainring and sprocket sizes that enables you to operate effectively at your chosen pedaling rate for optimal performance. You may of course also vary the pedaling rate, which would appear to have the same effect as selecting another gear. Indeed, with any given gear, pedaling slower reduces riding speed and therefore demands less power, whereas a higher pedaling rate increases road speed, requiring more power.

However, power output is not the sole, nor indeed the most important, criterion. Performing work at a given level of power output may tax the body differently, depending on the associated forces and speeds of movements. It has been found that to cycle longer distances effectively, without tiring or hurting excessively, the pedal force must be kept down by pedaling at a rate well above what seems natural to the beginning cyclist.

Whereas the beginner tends to plod along at 40–60 RPM, efficient long-distance cycling requires pedaling rates of 80 RPM and more, while racers generally pedal even faster. That doesn't come overnight, because the cyclist first has to learn to move his legs that fast, but it is an essential requirement for efficient bicycle touring. Much of your early cycling practice should therefore be aimed at mastering the art of pedaling faster. That must be done in a rather low gear to ensure that training intensity is limited by the factor to be developed, namely muscle speed, rather than by power output or muscle strength.

Gearing Practice

Once you know that high gears mean big chainrings and small sprockets, it's time to get some practice riding in high and low gears. First do it "dry": the bike supported with the rear wheel off the ground. Turn the cranks by hand and use the shift levers

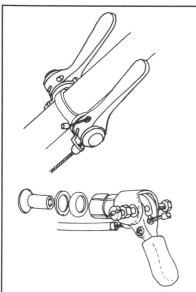

Fig. 9.2 Shifter types: downtube shifter (top), and bar-end shifter (bottom).

to change up and down, front and rear, until you have developed a good idea of the combinations reached in all conceivable shift lever positions. Listen for rubbing and crunching noises as you shift, realizing a shift has not been executed properly until the noises have subsided.

Now take to the road. Select a stretch of quiet road, where you can experiment around with your gears without risk of being run into the ground by a closely following vehicle or get in the way of other cyclists. Start off in a low gear and shift the rear derailleur up in steps. Then shift to another chainring and change down through the gears with the rear derailleur, followed by the third chainring, assuming a 18- or 21-speed system.

Reduce the pedal force, still pedaling forward as you shift. Especially the front derailleur will not shift as smoothly as it did when the cranks were turned by hand. You will notice that the noises become more severe and that some changes just don't take place as you had intended. To execute a correct change, you may have to overshift slightly first: push the lever a little beyond the correct position to affect a definite change and then back until the chain is quiet again. Get a feel for each gear and try to imagine which gear you should select for given conditions. Practice shifting until it goes smoothly and naturally.

Occasionally, it may be necessary to fine-tune the front derailleur setting after a change with the rear derailleur. That will be the case when the chain is twisted at an angle that causes it to rub against the side of the front derailleur cage. Some people never learn, quite simply because they don't take the trouble to practice consciously. Others take that trouble and learn to shift predictably and smoothly within a week. Half an hour of intensive practice each day during one week, and the continued attention required to do it right during regular riding, is all it takes to become an expert very quickly.

Since about 1986, virtually all bicycles sold have been equipped with indexed gearing, on which a ratchet in the lever eliminates the need for fine-tuning while shifting. For the serious touring cyclist this is less of a blessing than it would at first appear, because these mechanisms do get out of tune with wear and damage. Whereas a conventional friction shifter will always work, the indexed ones will always miss once they are out of synch. For that reason it is important to get a model with a supplementary lever or knob with which the shifter can be put into the friction mode.

Gear Designation

Just how high or low any given gear is may be expressed by giving the respective numbers of teeth on chainring and sprocket engaged in the particular gear. However, this is not a very good measure. It may not be immediately clear that a combination designated 42 X 16 (that should be read as 42 ÷ 16) has the same effect as one designated 52 X 21 (actually 52 ÷ 21) , though they really do result in the same ratio, as can be verified mathematically. It will be clear that it becomes nearly impossible to compare gears on bikes with different wheel sizes this way.

To allow a direct comparison between the gearing effects of different gears and bikes, two methods are in use, referred to as gear number and development, respectively, and illustrated in Fig. 9.3. Gear number is a somewhat archaic method, used mainly in the English-speaking world. It is the equivalent wheel size in inches of a directly driven wheel that corresponds to any given combination of wheel size, chainring and sprocket. It is determined by multiplying the quotient of chainring and sprocket sizes with the wheel diameter in inches:

$$gear = D_{wheel} \times T_{front} \div T_{rear}$$

where:

gear = gear number in inches

D_{wheel} = wheel diameter in inches

T_{front} = number of teeth, chainring

T_{rear} = number of teeth, sprocket

Returning to the example for a bike with nominal 700 mm or 27-inch wheels, geared with a 42-tooth chainring and a 21-tooth sprocket, the gear number would be:

27 x 42 ÷ 21 = 54 in

This is the customary, though rather quaint method used in the English-speaking world to define bicycle gearing. The rest of the world expresses the gear in terms of development. That is the distance in meters covered in one crank revolution. Development is calculated as follows:

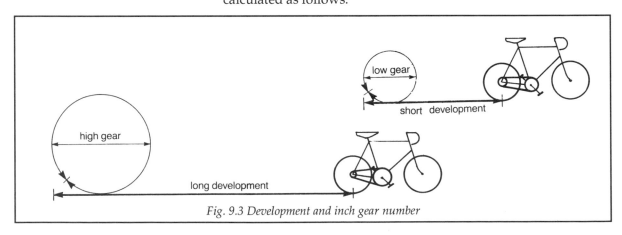

Fig. 9.3 Development and inch gear number

Dev. = 3.14 x d_{wheel} x T_{front} ÷ T_{rear}

where:

Dev. = development in meters

d_{wheel} = wheel size in m

T_{front} = number of teeth, chainring

T_{rear} = number of teeth, sprocket

The development for the same example would be:

3.14 x 0.680 x 42 ÷ 21 = 4.27, rounded off to 4.30 m

In practice, you are not expected to figure this kind of thing out yourself. Instead you may refer to the tables in the Appendix. Just remember that a high gear is expressed by a high gear number or a long development. For touring purposes, very low gears in terms of gear number are in the upper twenties and the thirties (around 2.20–3.20 m in terms of development). High gears are those above 80 in. (development of more than 6.40 m).

Gear Selection

Possibly the biggest problem for the beginning cyclist is to determine which is the right one out of the bewildering array of available gears. To generalize for most touring conditions, I would say it's whichever gear allows you to maximize your pedaling rate without diminishing your capacity to do effective work.

Perhaps you start off with the ability to pedal no faster than 60 RPM. That'll be too low once you have had some riding practice, but for now that may be your limit. So the right gear is the one in which you can reach that rate at any time, preferably exceeding it. Count it out with the aid of a wristwatch frequently until you develop a feel for your pedaling speed. If you find yourself pedaling slower, change down into a slightly lower gear, to increase the pedaling rate at the same riding speed. If you're pedaling faster, keep it up until you feel you are indeed spinning too lightly, and only then change into a slightly higher gear to increase road speed at the same pedaling rate.

Gradually, you will develop the capacity to pedal faster. As that happens, increase the limiting pedaling rate along with your ability, moving up from 60 to 70, 80 and eventually even higher pedaling rates. When riding with others, don't be guided by their gearing selection, since they may be stronger or weaker, or may have developed their ability to pedal fast more or less than you have.

It should not take too long before you learn to judge the right gear in advance, without the need to count out the pedal revolutions. You will not only know to change down into a lower gear when the direction of the road changes to expose you to a headwind or when you reach an incline, you will also learn to judge just how far to change down—and up again when the conditions become more favorable. Change gear consciously and frequently in small steps, and you will soon enough master the trick.

Derailleur Care and Adjustment

For optimum operation of the derailleur system, several things should be regularly checked and adjusted if necessary. The derailleurs themselves, as well as the chain and the various sprockets, chainrings and control cables, must be kept clean and lightly lubricated. The cables must be just taut when the shift levers are pushed forward and the derailleurs engage the appropriate gear. The tension screw on the shift levers must be kept tightened to give positive shifting without excessive tightness or slack.

If the derailleurs do not shift properly, the problem can usually be eliminated by adjusting the cable tension, referring to Fig. 9.4. Set the front derailleur in the lowest gear (smallest chainring) and adjust the cable at the front derailleur until it is just taut. Similarly, adjust the rear derailleur while it is set for the highest gear (smallest sprocket)

When the chain gets shifted beyond the biggest or smallest chainring or sprocket, or when certain combinations cannot be reached, the derailleurs themselves must be adjusted. For this purpose they are equipped with set-stop screws, which can be adjusted with a small screwdriver. If necessary, place the chain back on the sprocket or chainring, and select a gear which combines a small chainring with a small sprocket. To adjust the front or rear derailleur, proceed as follows:

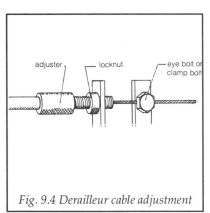

Fig. 9.4 Derailleur cable adjustment

1. Establish where the problem lies: front or rear derailleur, shifted too far or not far enough, on the inside or the outside.

2. Determine which of the set-stop screws governs movement limitation in the appropriate direction. On many models these screws are marked with an H and L for high and low gear, respectively. If not, establish yourself which is the appropriate screw by observing what happens at the ends of the screws as you shift towards the extreme gears. The high range set-stop screw is the one towards which an internal protrusion moves as you shift into the highest gear with the appropriate derailleur shift lever.

3. Unscrew the set-stop screw slightly (perhaps half a turn at a time) to increase the range if the extreme gear could not be reached. Tighten it if the chain was shifted beyond the last sprocket.

4. Check all possible gear combinations to establish whether the system works properly now, and fine-tune the adjustment, if necessary.

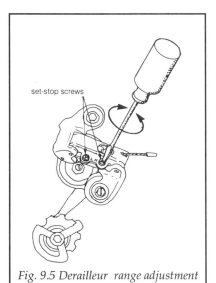

Fig. 9.5 Derailleur range adjustment

Selecting Chainrings and Sprockets

All of the preceding is fine, assuming you are satisfied with the combination of gears available on the bike as it is purchased. However, you may determine that you need lower or higher, more or fewer gears than what is installed as standard. Or you may want to determine the gearing range yourself for a bicycle that is custom-built or adapted specifically for you. In either of these cases, you will want a convenient system of establishing the sizes of chainrings and sprockets needed to meet your needs.

To aid the selection process, you may find the graph in Fig. 9.6 useful, even if it looks a little bewildering at first. Here I shall explain how to use it to determine the optimal sizes of sprockets and chainrings for any derailleur system.

First, decide what will be the maximum and minimum gears you want to have available. To do that, you need some experience. If you want to change your existing set-up, you'll have to establish which of the gears you now have are unnecessarily high or low for the conditions you will encounter or, alternately, which additional higher and lower gears you'll require. If you do not have the experience to decide that yet, ask for advice in a good bike shop or be guided by Table 9-I.

Once the range has been established, decide on likely combinations of chainring and sprocket for the extreme gears with the aid of a gear table, such as the one found in the Appendix. Keep in mind that the normal smallest sprocket has 14 teeth for a freewheel block with five sprockets, or 13 teeth for models with six sprockets. Thus, in order to get a top gear of 100 inches, a 14-tooth sprocket should be combined with a largest chainring that has about 50 teeth. Alternately, the same gear can be achieved

Fig. 9.6 Selection chart for chainrings and sprockets.

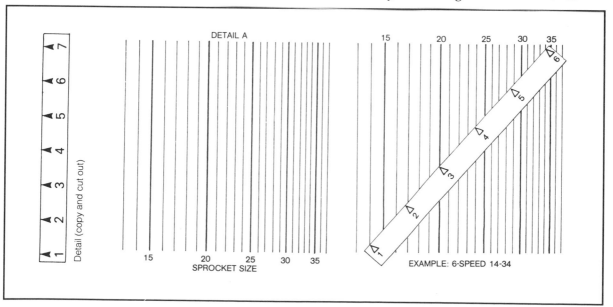

Terrain type	Gear range (in.)
mainly level no wind:	45–95
mainly level, wind:	40–100
hilly:	35–105
very hilly	30–105
mountainous	25–100
off-road	25–90

Table 9-I. Recommended gearing ranges.

with a smallest sprocket of 13 teeth and a large chainring of 47 teeth. Other maximum and minimum combinations can be established from the gear table.

Next, consider over how many gears this range is be divided up: 12, 14, 16, 18, 21 or 24. When using a system with three chainrings, you will probably have a smallest chainring that has 20 teeth less than the biggest. From the gear table, check what will be the size of the largest sprocket required to arrive at the desired lowest gear when such a smallest chainring is used. In our case, the use of a smallest chainring with 50 – 20 = 30 teeth would require a largest sprocket with 34 teeth to get a 25-inch lowest gear. This is a really low gear for hard climbing, and suggested here as an example only. Decide for yourself what your lowest gear should be, to determine which sprockets you need.

Now establish the optimum distribution of sprocket sizes within the range that was determined this way (in the case of the present example: seven steps from 14 to 34 teeth). This is where Details A and B of the graph come in. Cut out a copy of Detail B and place it on top of Detail A with the first arrow on the line corresponding to the smallest sprocket, and the fifth, sixth, seventh or eighth arrow (depending on the number of sprockets on the freewheel) on the line corresponding to the largest sprocket. In the illustrated example this is shown for the case of a 6-speed freewheel ranging from 14 to 34 teeth, resulting in sprockets of 14-16-19-22-25-29-34 teeth.

The ideal sizes of the intermediate sprockets can be read off opposite the arrows marked with the intermediate numbers. You may have noticed that the resulting distribution of sprocket sizes gives values that are closer together at the low end (high gears) than at the high end (low gears). This results in steps between subsequent gears that feel gradual, because they represent equal percentage differences relative to the respective preceding gears.

Finally, we shall determine the ideal size for the intermediate chainring. This is done with Detail C and some simple arithmetic. From the appropriate scale of Detail C, you can tell what the approximate percentage step between sprockets is. This is determined on the basis of the size of the largest sprocket, e.g. 19 percent in the case of our example. The best middle chainring size will be one that differs half this much from the largest one. Thus, in our case, it should be 9.5% smaller than 50 teeth, which is calculated as 45 teeth.

CHAPTER 10

Bike Handling Skills

In the present chapter we will take a closer look at the skills needed to cycle effectively and safely. Though other cyclists—be they racers or commuters—also have to master similar skills, there are some special aspects to consider for bicycle touring. Handling a bicycle with luggage is a different matter altogether from dealing with the same bike unloaded. In addition, the touring cyclist will probably be forced to cycle under more adverse conditions from time to time. Finally, some of your touring may be on poorly paved roads or even off-road altogether. All these situations require special attention with regard to handling skills.

The first section of this chapter will deal with learning to ride the bicycle competently, with proper control over the steering and braking mechanisms. This will help you cycle with minimal effort and maximum confidence. In the next section you will be introduced to the peculiarities of effective riding techniques for touring. Although an understanding of the theoretical background is helpful, I shall concentrate as much as possible on the practical aspects, making you practice what you learn. If you should be more than superficially interested in the material covered here, you are referred to John Forester's excellent manual *Effective Cycling*. Better yet, you may follow a practical course on the subject, by contacting the LAW (League of American Wheelmen) at the address given in the Appendix.

With this much luggage on the bike, you need to have pretty good bike handling skills. (photo Dan Gindling)

The Steering Principle

A bicycle is not steered most effectively by merely turning the handlebars and following the front wheel, as is the case for any two-track vehicle, such as a car. Though bicycles and other single-track vehicles indeed follow the front wheel, they also require the rider to lean his vehicle into a curve to balance it at the same time.

If you merely were to turn the handlebars, the lower part of the bike would start running away from its previous course in the direction in which the front wheel is then pointed. Meanwhile, the mass of the rider, perched high up on the bike, would continue following the original course due to inertia. Thus, the center of gravity would not be in line with the supporting bike, and the rider would come crashing to the ground. Due to the effect of centrifugal force, the tendency to throw the rider off towards the outside of the curve increases with higher speeds, requiring a more pronounced lean toward the inside of the curve the faster you are going.

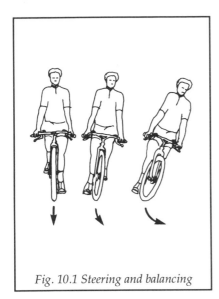

Fig. 10.1 Steering and balancing

It is possible to steer by turning the handlebars, and then correct lean and steering to regain balance afterwards. The more effective technique for riding a curve at speed is based on placing the bike at the appropriate angle, where the centrifugal force is offset by a shift of the mass center to the inside, *before* turning off. Two methods may be used, depending on the amount of time and room available to carry out the maneuver. I refer to these two methods as the natural and the forced turn, respectively. To understand either, we should first take a look at the intricacies of balancing the bike when riding a straight line, after which the two methods of turning can be explained.

Bicycle Balance

What keeps a bicycle, or any other single-track vehicle, going without falling over is the inertia of its moving mass. Rolling a narrow hoop will show that it is an unstable balance: once the thing starts to lean either left or right, it will just go down further and further until it hits the ground. That's because the mass is no longer supported vertically in line with the force. Try it with a bicycle wheel if you like. If the bike's front wheel could not be steered and the rider couldn't move sideways, he'd come down the same way very soon.

On the bicycle, the rider feels when the vehicle starts to lean over. Theoretically, there are two ways out of the predicament: either move the rider back over the center of the bike or move the bike back under the rider. In practice, the latter method is used most effectively, especially at higher speeds. When the bike begins leaning to the side, the rider oversteers the front wheel a little in the same direction, which places the bike back in such a position that balance is restored. In fact, this point will be passed, so the bike starts leaning over the other way, and so on.

This entire sequence of movements is relatively easy to notice when you are cycling slowly. When standing still, the balancing motions are so extreme that only a highly skilled cyclist can keep control. The faster the bicycle, the less perceptible (though equally important and therefore harder to master) are the steering corrections required to retain balance. To get an understanding of this whole process, I suggest you practice riding a straight line at a low speed. Then do it at a higher speed, and see whether you agree with the explanation.

Clearly, both riding a straight line and staying upright with the bike are merely illusions. In reality, the bike is always in disequilibrium, following a more or less curved track. The combination of bike and rider leans alternately one way and the other. At higher speeds the curves are longer and gentler, while the amount of lean can be perceptible; at lower speeds the curves are shorter and sharper, with less pronounced lean angles for any given deviation.

The Natural Turn

Under normal circumstances, the rider knows well ahead where to turn off, and there is enough room to follow a generously wide curve. This is the situation of the natural turn. It makes use of the lean that results from normal straight path steering corrections. To turn to the right naturally, you simply wait until the bike is leaning over that way, while the left turn is initiated when the bike is leaning to the left.

Instead of turning the handlebars to that same side, as would be done to get back in balance to ride straight, you just leave the handlebars alone for a while. This causes the bike to lean over more and more in the direction of the turn. Only when the lean is quite significant do you steer in the same direction, but not as abruptly as you would do to get back up straight. Instead, you fine-tune the ratio of lean and steering deflection to ride the curve out.

When the turn is completed, you will still be leaning over in the direction of the turn, and you would ride a circle without some other corrective action on your part. You get back on the straight course by steering further into the curve than the amount of lean demands to maintain your balance. This puts your mass center back right above the bike or even further over, allowing you to resume the slightly curving course with which you approximate the straight line.

Unconsciously, you probably learned to do this when you were a kid, but never realized that you were doing all this. You could perhaps continue to ride a bicycle forever without understanding the theory. However, to keep control over the bike in the demanding situations encountered while touring in difficult terrain with a loaded machine, you will be much better off if you

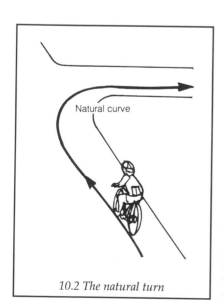

Natural curve

10.2 The natural turn

have the theoretical knowledge and have learned to ride a calculated course, making use of this information. Get a feel for it by riding around an empty parking lot many times, leaning this way and that, following straight lines and making turns, until it is both second nature and something you can do consciously, knowing the relevant limitations.

While you are practicing this technique, as well as when riding at other times, note that speed, curve radius, lean and load are all closely correlated. A sharper turn requires more lean at any given speed. At a higher speed, any given curve requires much greater lean angles than the same curve radius at a lower speed. Finally, the loaded bike tends to lean more than an unloaded machine.

The Forced Turn

You will often be confronted with situations that don't allow you to wait until you are conveniently leaning the appropriate way to make a gradual turn. Deficiencies in the road surface or the presence of other traffic in the road may force you into a narrow predetermined path, with only a few inches to deviate sideways. Or a sudden obstacle may force you to divert suddenly. Finally, you may have to get around a curve that is too sharp to be taken naturally at your current riding speed.

These situations require the second method of turning, which I call the forced turn. In this case, the turn must be initiated quickly, regardless which way the bike happens to be leaning at the time. You have to force the bike to lean over in the appropriate direction and at the right angle consistent with the direction and radius of the turn. And it has to be done quickly.

Do that by sharply steering away from the turn just before you get there. You and the bike will immediately start to lean over in the direction of the turn. You would risk a disastrous crash, as your bike moves away precipitously from the mass center, if you were to continue in a straight line. You have very quickly achieved a considerable lean angle in the direction of the turn. This must be compensated by steering quite abruptly in the same direction. Since this is the direction of the turn, you are set up just right to make a sharp turn. Once completed, steer back into the turn just a little more, to get the lean for regaining the roughly straight course, as explained for the natural turn.

The forced turn technique must also be practiced intensely and consciously, since it by no means comes naturally. Initiating a left turn by steering right will probably require the beginning cyclist to overcome all sorts of reasonable inhibitions and demands lots of practice. Take your bike to a grassy area or an empty parking lot a few days in a row, wearing protective clothing in case you fall: helmet, gloves, jacket and long pants.

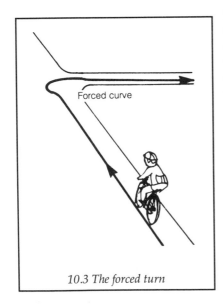

10.3 The forced turn

Practice and experiment until you've mastered the trick, and refresh your skill from time to time, until this instant turning technique has become second nature. Figures 10.2 and 10.3 allow a comparison between the paths taken in the natural and the forced turn, respectively. The latter technique will not only be helpful when taking a tight turn, but is of equal benefit when you need to temporarily divert from your straight course for one reason or the other. In a subsequent section of this chapter you will be shown how to apply it to the difficult task of avoiding a sudden obstacle.

Braking Techniques

The touring cyclist often has to use the brakes, though not always to make a panic stop. In fact, the sensible cyclist should hardly ever have to brake to a standstill. Instead, you will be using the brakes to control and regulate your speed. That may be necessary under touring conditions just as frequently as it is when riding in town or when racing, since the loaded bike and the sometimes imperfect roads may dictate sudden changes in riding speed to remain safely in control of the bike.

Effective braking means that you can ride up fast, close to the turn or the obstacle which requires the reduced speed, brake to reach the lower speed quickly, and accelerate immediately afterwards. So you will be using the brakes to get down in speed from 20 to 10 MPH to take a turn, or from 20 to 18 MPH to avoid running into the person ahead of you. Or you may have to get down from 30 to 10 MPH to handle a switchback, or hairpin curve, on a steep descent. To do that effectively without risk requires an understanding of braking physics. Though at times you may have to reduce speed quickly, you should also develop a feel for gradual speed reduction to prevent skidding and loss of control. In fact, most cyclists are more often in danger due to braking too vigorously than due to insufficient stopping power.

Braking amounts to deceleration or speed reduction, which can only take place gradually. The rate of deceleration can be measured and is expressed in m/sec^2. A deceleration of $1 \, m/sec^2$ means that after each second of braking the traveling speed is $1 \, m/sec$ less than it was at the beginning of that second. A speed of 30 MPH corresponds to 13 m/sec. To get down to standstill would take 13 sec, if the braking deceleration is $1 \, m/sec^2$; it would take 4 seconds to reach 9 m/sec or 20 MPH. At a higher rate of deceleration it would take less time (and a shorter distance) to get down to the desired speed.

The modern bicycle has remarkably effective brakes, providing it's not raining. A modest force on the brake lever can cause a deceleration of $4–5 \, m/sec^2$ with just one brake. Applying both brakes, the effect is even more dramatic, enabling you to slow

A situation like this usually requires a combination of braking and steering. And in the rain, your brakes will be less effective than in dry weather.

10.4 Weight transfer resulting from braking

down from 30 to 15 MPH within one second. There are some limitations to braking that have to be considered, though.

In the first place, rain has a negative effect on the rim brake's performance, as the build-up of water on the rims reduces the friction between brake block and rim drastically. This applies especially if the bike is equipped with ordinary rubber brake blocks, as offered by most manufacturers as standard equipment. With any rubber brake blocks, I measured a reduction from 4.5 to 1.5 m/sec^2 for a given hand-lever force (and to half that figure for bicycles with chrome-plated steel rims, which should therefore not be used, even on the cheap bicycles on which they are installed). Lately, some special brake block materials and ceramic rim finishes have been introduced that are less sensitive to rain.

The second restriction is associated with a change in the distribution of weight between the wheels as a result of braking. Because the mass center of the rider is quite high above the road, and its horizontal distance to the front wheel axle comparatively small, the bicycle has a tendency to tip forward in response to deceleration. Weight is transferred from the rear to the front of the bike, as illustrated in Fig. 10.4. When the deceleration reaches about 3.5 m/sec^2, the weight on the rear wheel is no longer enough to provide traction, even when the rear wheel is loaded down with luggage. Braking harder than that with the rear brake makes the rear wheel skid, resulting in loss of control.

In a typical riding posture, the rear wheel actually starts to lift off the ground when a deceleration of about 6.5 m/sec^2 is reached, whether using both brakes together or the front brake alone. Consequently, no conventional bicycle can ever be decelerated beyond this limit, regardless of the kind, number and quality of the brakes. This is a very high deceleration, which you should not often reach, but it is good to realize there is such a limit and that it can not be avoided by using the rear brake either alone or in addition to the front brake, but only by braking less vigorously. During a sudden speed reduction, or panic stop, such high decelerations may be reached. On a downslope, the effect will be even more pronounced, since it raises the rider even higher relative to the front wheel. In all such cases, reduce the toppling-over effect by shifting your body weight back and down as much as possible: sit far back and hold the upper body horizontally.

Since about twice as great a deceleration is possible with the front brake as with the one in the rear, the former should be preferably used under most conditions. In most circumstances short of a panic stop, you can brake very effectively using the front brake alone. When both brakes are used simultaneously, the one in the front can be applied quite a bit harder than the one in the rear. If you notice the rear brake is less effective when the

10.5 Body position in panic stop

lever is applied with the same force, it will be time to check, and if necessary adjust, lubricate or replace the brake cable.

Of course, most braking is not done abruptly. Gradual braking must also be practiced. In particular when the road is slick, in curves or when others are following closely behind, gradual deceleration and the ability to control the braking force within narrow limits is of vital importance. Practice braking consciously with utmost attention to the complex relationship between initial speed, brake lever force and deceleration, to become fully competent at handling the bike when slowing down under all conceivable circumstances.

Braking becomes a different kettle of fish in hilly terrain. On a steep downhill, the slope not only increases the tendency to tip forward, it also induces an accelerating effect, which must be overcome by the brakes merely to keep the speed constant. A 20% slope, which is admittedly rarely encountered, induces an acceleration of about 2 m/sec^2. Obviously, you will encounter big problems in wet weather on such a downhill stretch if you don't keep your speed down to start with. So it will be necessary to reduce the speed by gradual, intermittent braking. This will help wipe most of the water from the rims, retaining braking efficiency a little better. This way, the brakes are not overtaxed when you do have to reduce the speed suddenly, as may be required to handle an unexpected obstacle or a sharp turn.

Effective braking must be practiced to achieve complete control of the bicycle under normal and difficult cycling conditions. In particular, the dramatic difference between the bike's behavior when braking on the straight and in a curve must be experienced to be appreciated. Again, this is a matter for conscious practice in a place without traffic. Include braking in your regular practice sessions during the first weeks of cycling preparation. Even after you have been riding for some time, you may be well advised to repeat this kind of practice from time to time. It will pay off when touring.

Basic Riding Techniques

Riding a bicycle with total confidence requires hands-on experience. That might be considered a good reason to ride lots of miles before you go on your first tour. But some of the associated skills can be learned faster and more thoroughly when you understand the principles that are applied. Building up on the information about posture, gearing, steering and braking provided in the preceding sections, you will be shown here what to do in various typical riding situations. The many miles of experience will come soon enough when you start touring. However, the handling practice is gained more effectively when applying these techniques consciously.

Getting up to Speed

Although bicycle touring is not a matter of speed alone, you should still learn to reach an acceptable speed quickly and smoothly in order to ride enjoyably and effectively. In Chapter 8 you were shown how to get on the bike and start off smoothly. The next trick is to reach the ultimate riding speed quickly and efficiently. The idea is to waste as little time and energy as possible during this process of getting up to speed. That is tricky, because acceleration demands disproportionately high levels of power and consumes energy correspondingly. And the faster it's done, the more demanding it is.

Clearly, you have to strike a balance here. Accelerating faster than necessary wastes energy that will be sorely needed later. Done too slowly, it may become a plodding affair. It will be your decision to find the right balance between speed and power, but the way to reach it is easy to describe: start in a low gear and increase speed gradually but rapidly. Don't ride in fast and slow spurts but a gradual build-up of speed.

Either keep pedaling faster and faster in the low gear, changing up only as you reach a significant speed, or be prepared to do some short duration hard work, standing on the pedals, pulling on the upstroke, as well as pushing on the downstroke. As soon as speed is reached, sit on the saddle and select a good gear for spinning at a comfortable but high pedaling rate.

Maintaining a Constant Speed

With a small measuring device called accelerometer one can follow the changes in riding speed of a cyclist traveling at speed. It has been found that the most effective riders tend to be those whose speed varies least over time. Not only does a good cyclist ride the same number of miles one hour as the next, he travels as many yards one minute as the next, as many feet with one crank revolution as the next, and indeed ideally as many inches during each section within any revolution. If you slow down during one short section, it will take disproportionately more time and energy to make up for the loss.

Pay attention to this at all times while cycling. As long as the external conditions don't change drastically, you should make every effort to keep a constant speed and movement. Gauge your speed by comparing it to that of your companions, or use your watch, counting out pedal revolutions and milestones when cycling alone.

Accelerating

However efficient a constant speed may be, sometimes you will still want to accelerate to a higher speed. This may be necessary to catch up with riders ahead, so you can take advantage of the wind-breaking effect by riding immediately behind them, or to avoid getting dropped behind. In traffic, you may have to accelerate in situations like getting across an intersection before the light changes or to avoid running into another vehicle.

As with getting up to speed in the first place, it is most efficient to increase the speed as gradually as possible. Unless you are already spinning at your highest possible rate, you will find accelerating by increasing the pedaling rate more effective than by increasing pedal force in a higher gear. In other words, as long as you can spin faster, it is best to shift down into a slightly lower gear and increase the pedaling rate vigorously. Once you are gathering momentum and are getting close to your maximum spinning speed, shift up and continue to gain speed in the higher gear.

Riding Against the Wind

At higher speeds or whenever there is a head wind, the effect of air drag on the power needed to cycle is quite significant. Economize on your effort by avoiding the wind resistance as much as possible. Keep your profile low when cycling against the wind. Especially when riding alone, try to seek out sheltered parts of the road wherever you can, without exposing yourself to danger from other traffic.

When you ride in a group, try to exploit the wind shelter effect of riding immediately behind another rider, or staggered appropriately when there is a cross wind. This technique is referred to as drafting in the U.S., pacing in Britain. Figures 10.6 and 10.7 show the resulting configurations for situations without and with cross wind, respectively.

Hill Climbing

Climbing uphill by bike is not just another skill that can be learned equally well by all, it also requires a certain physique for greatest effectiveness. With some conscious effort, everybody's climbing skills can be improved up to a point; yet some riders are born climbers, while others may have to go uphill slowly all their lives. What it takes is a high power to weight ratio. To put it differently, you need a big heart and voluminous lungs relative to your total body mass. In general, a low body weight will be advantageous. Just the same, it is an ability that can be learned and developed well enough by the average rider to at least handle all hills you encounter, even if you will never go up as fast as a born climber.

Again, a regular motion is most efficient, and that is best mastered by staying seated in a rather low gear. For a hilly tour, you should take the trouble to equip the bike with wider ratio gearing than for level riding. Just what sizes of sprockets should be installed is up to you, but I'd say 90% of all beginners tend to pick gear ratios that are too high (or, to put it differently, sprockets that are too small). There should be nothing embarrassing about a rear sprocket with 34 teeth and a chainwheel with 36 or even fewer teeth for mountainous terrain. Many touring bikes, and particularly mountain bikes, are equipped with such extreme gears, which are low enough to tackle almost any hill without having to get up from the saddle.

Climbing out of the Saddle

When the lowest available gear is too high to allow a smoothly spinning leg motion, it is time to shift to another technique. Some riders try to increase the length of the power stroke by means of some hefty ankle twisting, really pushing the leg around at this point. That is an unnecessarily tiring technique, requiring long muscle work phases and short recovery periods. A better method of high gear, low pedaling speed climbing is referred to as honking in Britain, and seems to be a mystery to most American cyclists.

Honking makes use of the rider's body weight to push down the pedals, whereas the body is pulled up after each stroke very quickly by standing up. In this mode, the muscle work is done each time the body is raised, rather than when pushing the pedal down and around. To do it effectively, hold the tops of the brake handle mounts in the front of the handlebars. You can either take quick snappy steps or throw your weight from side to side in a swinging motion, as illustrated in Fig. 10.8. I suggest you practice honking as well as spinning: the one in a high gear at pedaling speeds below 55 RPM, the other in a low gear at 65 RPM or more. Avoid pedaling rates of 55–65 RPM by choosing the your gears to stay within either the one range or the other.

Fig. 10.7 Drafting with cross wind

Avoiding Obstacles

Oftentimes, you will be confronted with some kind of obstacle right in your path. This may be anything from a pothole or a broken branch to a discarded can or bottle. Even when traveling at speed and with little room to maneuver, you can learn to avoid running into such things by using the technique of the forced turn described in a preceding section. This maneuver is illustrated in Fig. 10.9.

As soon as you perceive the obstacle ahead of you, decide whether to pass it on the left or the right. Ride straight up to it and then, before you reach it, briefly but decisively steer into the direction opposite to that of your chosen avoidance (to the right if you want to pass on the left). This makes the bike lean over towards the other side (to the left in this case). Now steer in that direction just as quickly, which will result in a very sharp forced turn. As soon as you've passed the obstacle, oversteer a little more, to cause a lean that helps you put the bike back on its proper course.

This too is something to practice in an empty parking lot, wearing a helmet and two long sleeved shirts (the double layer of fabric is much easier on the skin, since the one layer will just

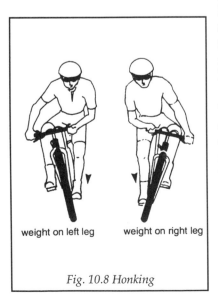

weight on left leg   weight on right leg

Fig. 10.8 Honking

slip off the other, rather than removing chunks of your flesh). Mark phony obstacles with chalk or place foam pads or sponges on the ground, and practice passing them abruptly on both sides until you've mastered the trick.

Jumping the Bike

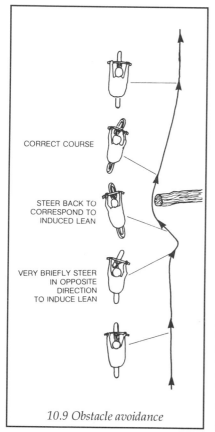

CORRECT COURSE

STEER BACK TO
CORRESPOND TO
INDUCED LEAN

VERY BRIEFLY STEER
IN OPPOSITE
DIRECTION
TO INDUCE LEAN

10.9 Obstacle avoidance

Another useful technique for hard riding situations is the skill of making first the front, then the rear wheel jump over or through an obstacle. You may have to do that when there is an un-avoidable obstacle ahead of you. It's a matter of shifting your weight back or forth to lift the appropriate wheel off the ground. To jump up, first throw your weight backwards, while pulling up on the handlebars to unload while lifting the front wheel. At the same time accelerate vigorously, by pushing hard on the for-ward pedal. With some practice, you'll soon be able to lift the front end of the bike at least a foot up in the air.

Next, try to do the same with the rear wheel, throwing your weight forward while pulling up your legs and bottom at the same time. This is harder, but it can also be mastered. Finally, practice coordinating the two shifts, so that you first lift the front and then, as soon as you've reached the highest point, start rais-ing the back. After some time, you should be able to actually make the bike fly: lift both wheels in such short sequence that the rear wheel comes off the ground well before the front wheel comes down.

One variant of this technique is the art of jumping up side-ways, which may be needed to handle obstacles like curbs, ridges and tracks that run nearly parallel to the road. To do this, the bike has to be forced to move sideways in a short and snappy diver-sion just preceding the jump. Do that by combining the diversion technique described above under Avoiding Obstacles with the jump.

Get close to the ridge you want to jump, riding parallel to it. Then briefly steer away from the ridge. This immediately causes the bike to lean towards the obstacle. Now catch yourself by

10.10 Jumping the bike

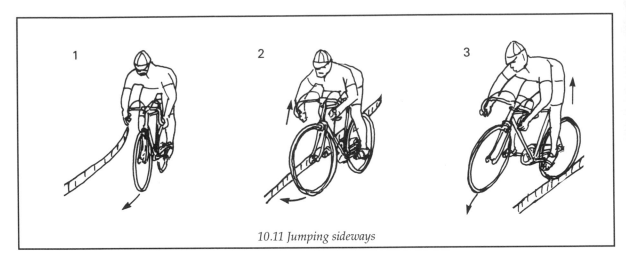

10.11 Jumping sideways

steering sharply in that same direction, lifting the front wheel when you are close to the obstacle, immediately followed by the rear wheel. Practice is all it takes, and the empty parking lot with a chalk line as a substitute ridge will be the best place to do that.

Sometimes, you will have to ride through a big pothole or other depression in the road surface. To do that with minimal risk to bike and rider, you can use something akin to the jumping technique. Enter the depression with your weight near the front of the bike. Then unload the front wheel by throwing your weight back and pulling up the handlebars just before the front wheel hits the lowest point of the depression. Finally, ride up the other side and pull up the rear, while shifting your weight to the front of the bike to climb back out. This technique is particularly useful when cycling off-road. In open terrain, select your route through the depression so as to avoid too abrupt a drop and subsequent climb.

CHAPTER 11

Safety and Health

Bicycle touring is not an entirely riskless undertaking. Neither are many other pursuits, but what probably scares off potential cyclists most is the danger of being involved in a collision with a motor vehicle. Yes, that chance exists in bicycle touring, as it does when crossing the street in front of your own house. Actually, this is but one of several kinds of possible injury causes in cycling. You can learn to avoid most of the risks and minimize the impact of these and other injuries or other health hazards. That is the subject of the present chapter.

Considering the various risks, ranging from those to your own body and equipment to the harm or loss you may cause others, it may be smart to take out some kind of insurance. Personal liability insurance is perhaps the most important of these. In addition, you may want to make sure you have adequate health insurance to cover the dangers of the road as well as whatever may happen to you while traveling, especially if you go abroad.

Although that will seem obvious to most Americans, it may be news to others. If you are used to a society like the British or Canadian, where a National Health Service takes care of your health needs, you may be astonished what a little health care can cost you abroad—and that many of those who administer such services expect to be paid on the spot when dealing with a

Don't overexert yourself. If it gets too tough, just get off and walk. (photo Renner)

foreign traveler. Finally, you may like to take out a travel insurance, making sure your bike and other equipment is covered.

In addition, it would be a good idea to learn how to deal with accidents, injuries, sickness and other health-related emergencies yourself. Do you really know what to do when you are bleeding, when you think you may have broken something, when one of your companions faints or is seriously hurt? Take a first aid course to be prepared for dealing with the unanticipated. That is a lot smarter than shutting your eyes, hoping nothing serious will happen. Even if you are spared yourself, you may be able to save someone else's life. If you can't for some reason take a first aid course, at least read up on the subject—appropriate literature is included in the Bibliography.

The Risks of Cycling

Quite a lot of research has been done on the subject of bicycle accidents and injuries. Some of these studies were specifically oriented to bicycle touring, such as the survey by Jerrold Kaplan of the injuries reported during the first year of the Bikecentennial program. Other reports are largely based on either day-to-day cycling experiences typical in an urban environment or on the accidents reported by club cyclists, racers or students. To summarize the available evidence in a nutshell, the majority of bicycle accidents are attributable to a very limited number of typical mistakes, most of which can be either avoided or counteracted by intelligent cycling techniques.

Of course, accidents, collisions and falls are not the only forms of injury to the cyclist, even though they are the most obvious. When talking to experienced cyclists, you will soon find out that other forms of injury are often of more concern in those circles. Saddle sores and torn tendons, inflamed knees and numb hands rank higher than broken collarbones and cracked skulls in their conversation about injuries, even though they get their share of broken bones too. We will take a look at both categories.

Perhaps the most important lesson to learn from the investigations dealing with the safety of touring cyclists concerns the correlation between risk and trip length. Put simply, the likelihood of getting hurt—be it as a result of a traffic accident or a fall—increases dramatically after a daily distance of 70 road miles. That applies especially to cyclists carrying luggage and handling difficult terrain, and most dramatically to inexperienced riders. Hence the following advice: If you are new to bike touring, keep your daily distance down to no more than 110 km (70 miles) on the road, or 7 hours of cycling overall, to minimize the risk. (Ten miles an hour may seem a low mileage, but it is a realistic average for bicycle tour planning to allow for stops.)

Another significant finding is that the more experienced cyclists have markedly fewer accidents, and can go longer distances before being exposed to the greater risk. This is one good argument for trying to gain experience and skills as quickly as possible. Following the advice contained in the preceding chapters not only increases the joy, satisfaction and effectiveness of your cycling, it also drastically reduces the risk to which you are exposed when touring.

Traffic Hazards

In the Bikecentennial survey of long distance touring cyclists, only two fatal accidents occurred. Indeed, fatal accidents are only a small percentage of all injuries, though numerous serious accidents do occur. Although the majority of all injured cyclists themselves are largely to blame for their injuries, there always will be some accidents that are directly attributable to bullying and inconsiderate motorists.

Unfortunately, this type of accident forms a high proportion of those that experienced cyclists encounter. These riders have learned to handle their machines rationally and safely in traffic, thus virtually eliminating their risk concerning the more common kind of accidents to which the less competent are exposed. Having practically eliminated the latter, they are just as vulnerable to the remaining irrational dangers of the road.

The only defense against inconsiderate road users is not to provoke them. Give in, even if that seems highly unfair. It's an unequal battle and sometimes it's just smarter not to insist on justice. You will encounter fewer of these particular risks if you avoid the kind of situations where they are most likely: Sunday afternoons and late evenings, when boisterous drunks are many on the road. Oddly enough, these accidents are also more likely on relatively lightly traveled roads near smaller towns. Although I realize that busy roads near big cities do not make the ideal bicycle touring environment, you may try to avoid the quiet roads near smaller towns at high-risk times.

Regular Accidents

Most accidents, of course, are not of this type. They simply happen while two people make a mistake each: one initiates a wrong move, and the other fails to react in such a way that a collision is avoided. Keep that in mind when cycling. Remain alert for the possible mistakes others may make, and try to avoid doing the unexpected or unconsidered yourself as much as humanly possible. Anticipate not only the predictable, but also the unexpected: the motorist looming behind the next corner or intersection, the dog appearing from a driveway, or the cyclist suddenly crossing your path in the dark without lights.

The latter subject deserves special attention, but the only way to arm yourself is to make sure you do not cycle out after dark without lights yourself, so at least *you* can be seen. Proper lighting on the bike is needed in addition to the curiously ineffective

131

array of reflectors that is increasingly prescribed by law in various countries. The gravest danger of reflectors lies in the inappropriate impression they transmit of your visibility. A bright light in the front and a big rear light or reflector facing back are essential, while all the other goodies won't do a thing that the former wouldn't do more effectively.

Most accidents occur in daylight, even though the relative risk is greater at night. Whether by day or at night, cycle with all your senses alert. In general, ride your bike as you would drive your car, always verifying whether the road ahead of you is clear, and taking particular care to select your path wisely at junctions and intersections. As a relatively slow vehicle, you must look behind you, to ascertain that nobody is following closely, before you move over into another traffic lane or away from your previous path.

Bicycles as Vehicles

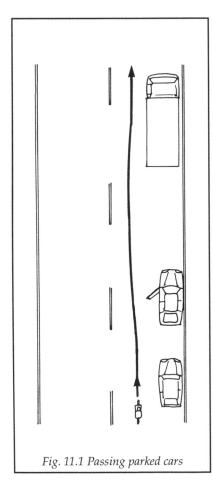

Fig. 11.1 Passing parked cars

Forget anything you ever heard about bikes being different from motor vehicles. As a wheeled vehicle, your bike answers to the same laws of physics as does a car. Adhere to the most basic rules of traffic you learned to handle a car while ridinging a bike as well, and you'll be safe. No doubt the worst advice ever given to cyclists in many parts of the U.S. is to ride on the side of the road where a pedestrian would go, namely facing traffic. On a bike you *are* the traffic, and you belong on the same side as all other vehicles traveling the same way.

The rules of the road as applied to motor vehicles are based on a system that has gradually evolved. This system works the way it does because it is logical. If it is dangerous for motorists to do certain things, then it will be at least as dangerous on a bike. This applies equally when traveling abroad, although it will be smart to prepare for the peculiar kind of laws that have been instituted in some societies which discriminatorily relegate bicycles to an inferior (and invariably more dangerous) place on the road.

In general, whatever you may be inclined to think, the most dangerous societies are those where cyclists are offered many separate bicycle paths and where different laws apply to cyclists than to other road users. France, Italy and England are wonderful cycling countries, whereas Holland, Belgium, Germany and Denmark are high-risk societies to rational cyclists.

Thus, for example, in Denmark the cyclist is expected to carry out the most dangerous maneuver when turning left, turning from the RH side of the road, crossing the path of all traffic continuing straight or turning right. I cannot possibly give you full instructions on the kinds of superhuman skills you have to master in order to satisfy such peculiarities of the laws in every country. Get this information from the host country's motoring organization, touring club or tourist office before leaving.

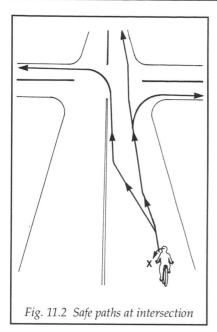

Fig. 11.2 Safe paths at intersection

In any traffic system, don't hug the curb but claim your place on the road. Your place is about 1.80 m (6 ft.) to the right of the centerline of the path normally taken by cars on a wide road. Keep at least 90 cm (3 ft.) away from the inside edge, even if the road is too narrow to stay clear to the right of the normal path of motor vehicles. Don't dart in and out around parked vehicles and other obstructions along the side of the road. When making a turn, adhere to the method outlined in Fig. 11.2 (assuming RH traffic). Thus, to go straight at an intersection, make sure you will not be overtaken by vehicles turning across your path. To turn right, get close to the RH edge. To turn left, choose a path near the center of the road or the middle of a traffic lane marked for that direction well before the actual intersection, after having established that you will not be cutting across the path of vehicles following closely behind.

Excessive attention is often paid to hand signals in traffic education for cyclists. Yes, you should signal your intention before you do things like diverting, turning off or slowing down. That applies particularly when cycling with others in a group, where the first person also should point out and audibly identify obstacles or hazards in the road. But avoid the dangerous habit of assuming a hand signal will ward off danger. Your hand is not a magic wand, and if somebody is following so closely that you can signal to him your intention of turning across his path, you should not do that. Instead, wait until your maneuver does not interfere with traffic following closely behind.

The most feared type of bicycle accident is the one that involves being hit from behind. These accidents do happen, and both the fatal accidents that occurred during the Bikecentennial survey were of this type. Though there is hardly any defense possible to ward them off, it is worth considering that they are characterized by a number of common factors. They invariably occur on otherwise deserted roads, where the attention of motorist and cyclist alike are at a low, since both feel perfectly secure.

Inconspicuous clothing, a low sun, blinding one or both participants, and a lack of the cyclist's awareness, due to tiredness at the end of a long day, are also common features. It may be smart to increase your conspicuity. Wearing bright colors, such as yellow, pink, orange or bright green, may well help others spot you in time to avoid this type of accident.

Falls and Collisions

Whether or not a motor vehicle is involved, virtually every injury to the cyclist in all falls and collisions results from the impact when the cyclist falls off the bike. He either hits the road surface, an object on or along the road, the colliding vehicle or the bike itself. The same skills necessary to prevent traffic accidents involving cars will keep you from experiencing most of the other types of falls and collisions. Be watchful, consider the effects of your own actions, and use the technical skills described in the preceding chapter to divert when the situation becomes threatening. Four types of falls and collisions can be distinguished: stopping, diverting, skidding and loss-of-control. Here I shall first describe these accidents, followed by a few hints about preventing and treating the typical injuries that may result.

Stopping Accidents   In a stopping accident, the bicycle runs into an obstacle that halts its progress. Depending on your speed, the impact can be very serious. As the bicycle itself is stopped, inertia keeps you going forward, throwing you against or over the handlebars. The kinetic energy of the moving mass will be dissipated very suddenly, often in an unfortunate location. Your genitals may hit the handlebar stem or your skull may crash onto either the road surface or the object with which the bike collided.

The way to guard yourself against these accidents is to look and think ahead, so you don't run into any obstacles. If necessary, control your speed to allow handling the unexpected when a potential danger may be looming up behind the next corner. Learn to apply the diverting technique described in the Chapter 10. The way to minimize the impact of the most serious form of stopping accident is by wearing an energy-absorbing helmet, which will be discussed more fully below.

Diverting Accidents   A diverting type accident occurs when the front wheel is pushed sideways by an external force, while you are not leaning in the same direction to regain balance. Typical causes are railway tracks, cracks in the road surface, the edge of the road, or touching another rider's rear wheel with your front wheel. The effect is that you fall sideways and hit the road or some obstacle by the side of the road. Depending how unexpectedly it happened, you may be able to break the fall by stretching out an arm, which seems to be an automatic reflex in this situation.

Characteristic injuries range from abrasions and lacerations of the hands and the sides of arms and legs to bruised hips and sprained or broken wrists. More serious cases, usually incurred at higher speeds, may involve broken collarbones and injuries to the face or the side of the skull. The impact of the lesser injuries can be minimized by wearing padded gloves and double layers of clothing with long sleeves or legs. Wearing a helmet will minimize damage to the side of the head, especially at elevated speeds.

Diverting accidents can often be avoided if you are careful and alert. Keep an eye out for the typical danger situations. Don't overlap wheels with other riders, don't approach surface ridges at a shallow angle. A last-second diversion can often be made along the lines of the diverting technique described in Chapter 10. In the case of a ridge in the road surface, use the technique of sideways jumping, also described there. When your front wheel touches the rear wheel of another rider, or if your handlebars are pushed over by an outside force, you may sometimes save the day if you react by immediately leaning in the direction into which you were diverted, and then steer to regain control.

Skidding Accidents   When the bicycle keeps going or goes in an unintended direction, despite your efforts to brake or steer, it will be due to skidding between the tires and the road surface. This kind of thing happens more frequently when the road is slick on account of moisture, frost, loose sand or fallen leaves. Especially under these conditions, sudden diversions or movements, hard braking and excessive lean when cornering may all cause skidding either forward or sideways.

Skidding accidents typically also cause you to fall sideways, resulting in abrasions, lacerations or more rarely fractures. Avoid them by checking the road surface ahead and avoiding sudden steering or braking maneuvers and excessive leaning in curves. Cross slick patches, ranging from wet or greasy asphalt or railway tracks, or sand or leaves on the road to the white lines used as road markings, with the bicycle upright. Achieve that by carrying out the requisite steering and balancing actions *before* you reach such danger spots.

If you cannot avoid it, once you feel you are entering a skid, try to move your weight towards the back of the bike as much as possible, sliding back on the saddle and stretching your arms. Follow the bike, rather than trying to force it back. Finally, don't do what seems an obvious reaction to the less experienced, namely getting off the saddle to straddle the top tube with one leg dangling. As with so many cycling techniques, skidding can also be practiced in a relatively safe environment on an empty parking lot.

Loss-of-Control Accidents   At higher speeds, especially in a steep descent, loss of control accidents sometimes occur. In this case, you just can't steer the bike the way you intend to go. This happens when you find yourself having to steer in one direction at a time when you are leaning the other way, or when braking for speed control initiates unexpected oscillations. Often this situation develops into a collision or a fall along the lines of either one of the accident types described above.

Prevention is only possible with experience: don't go faster than the speed at which you feel in control. The more you ride in various situations, the more you will develop a feel for what is a safe speed, when to brake and how to steer to maintain control over the bike. Once the situation sets in, try to keep your cool. Don't panic. Follow the bike, rather than forcing it over. The worst thing you can do is to tense up and get off the saddle. Stay in touch with handlebars, seat and pedals, and steer in the direction of your lean. This way, you may well get out of it without falling or colliding, though your nerves may have suffered.

How to Treat Injuries

In the following sections, you will be shown how to handle the most common types of injuries resulting from falls and other bicycle accidents. More detailed instructions can be found in any first aid manual. When there is any reason to suspect the injury is serious, do only the minimum to stay out of danger yourself and get medical assistance as soon as possible.

Abrasions

Abrasions, referred to as road rash in club cycling circles, are the most common cycling injury resulting from any kind of fall. They usually heal relatively fast, although they can be quite painful. Wash out the wound with water and soap, and remove any particles of road dirt to prevent infection. There may be a risk of tetanus if the wound draws blood. If you have been immunized against tetanus, get a tetanus shot within 24 hours only if your last one was more than two years ago.

If you have never been immunized before, get a full immunization, consisting of two shots within 24 hours, followed by two more after two weeks and six months, respectively. Apply a dressing only if the location is covered by clothing, since the wound will heal faster when exposed to the air. Avoid the formation of a scab by treating the wound with an antibacterial salve. See a doctor if any signs of infection occur, such as swelling, itching or fever.

Sprained Limbs

In case of a fall, your tendency to stick out an arm to break the impact may result in a sprained or even a fractured wrist. In other accident situations this can also happen to the knee or the ankle. Spraining is really nothing but damage to the ligaments that surround and hold the various parts of a joint together. Typical symptoms are a local sensation of heat, itching and swelling.

Whenever possible, keep the area cold with an ice bag. If you feel a stinging pain or if fever develops, get medical advice, because it may actually be a fracture that was at first incorrectly diagnosed as a sprain. This may be the case when the fracture takes the form of a simple "clean" crack without superficially visible deformation of the bone.

Fractures

Typical cycling fractures are those of the wrist and the collarbone, both caused when falling: the one when extending the arm to break the fall, the other when you don't have time to do that. You or medical personnel may not at first notice a clean fracture as described above: there may be one without any outward sign.

If there is a stinging pain when the part is moved or touched, I suggest you get an X-ray to make sure, even if a fracture is not immediately obvious. You'll need medical help to set and bandage the fractured location, and you must give up cycling until it is healed, which will take about five weeks. Sad if that happens during a bicycle tour, but better than continuing in agony.

Head Injury   If you fall on your head in any kind of fall or collision, the impact may smash your brain against the inside of your skull, followed by the reverse action as it bounces back. The human brain can usually withstand this kind of treatment without lasting damage if the resulting deceleration does not exceed about 300 G, or 3000 m/sec. Look at it this way: the head probably falls to the ground from a height of 1.5 m (5 ft.). This results in a speed of 5 m/sec at the time of impact. To keep the deceleration down below 3000 m/sec., this speed must be reduced to zero in no less than 0.002 sec.

Neither your skull, nor the object with which you collide is likely to deform gradually enough to achieve even that kind of deceleration. That's why energy-absorbing helmets with thick crushable foam shells were developed. Neither flexible nor hard materials will do the trick by themselves. It's not a bad idea to have a hard outer shell cover to distribute the load of a point impact, and it is nice to get some comfort inside from a soft flexible liner, but the crushing of about 2 cm (¾ in.) of seemingly brittle foam is essential to absorb the shock. The minimum requirement for a safe helmet is the American standard ANSI Z-90.4.

On the other hand, I do want to warn against putting excessive faith in the helmet. Outside the U.S., Canada and New Zealand, few cyclists if any ever wear a helmet, and anyone who has ever ventured out on the roads of Germany or Italy can confirm that is not because the motorists are more considerate elsewhere. Yet no more cyclists suffer fatal or serious injuries there than here. Even in the U.S., neither the fatal nor the serious accident rate has gone down since the introduction of the cycling helmet. There is a good reason to assume that the theory of risk compensation gets its confirmation here: people tend to optimize the relationship between risk and convenience at a fixed level. Those who wear a helmet accept carrying a sweat bucket, while those who do not wear one accept riding more carefully; both seem to end up with the same overall risk. I still recommend wearing a helmet of course, but I do not think any of us should sit in judgment of those who prefer to arrive at the same risk via a different route, and clearly riding unencumbered is just as legitimate a desire as is riding at the margin of risk.

Most of all, I fear the recent trend to demand compulsory helmet legislation, or for that matter the level of peer pressure that has now been reached within cycling groups in the U.S. that have effectively had the same effect. If I have the freedom to wear or not wear a helmet, I shall wear one whenever I consider the risk is high enough to warrant it, but if you start pushing me around, I'll consider my freedom more important. The less that gets regulated and forced upon the cyclist, the better it is for cycling in the long run.

Other Health Problems

The remaining part of this chapter will be devoted to the health hazards of cycling that have nothing to do with falling off the bike. We will look at the most common complaints and discuss some methods of prevention, as well as possible cures. This brief description cannot cover the entire field. Nor should most of the issues discussed here be generalized too lightly. The same symptoms may have different causes in different cases; conversely, the same cure may not work for two superficially similar problems. Yet in most cases the following remarks will apply.

Saddle Sores

Though beginning cyclists may at first feel uncomfortable on the bike seat, they have no idea what kind of agony real seat problems can bring. In bicycle touring, much more than in racing, you have the opportunity to avoid the most serious seat problems by taking it easy for one or two days when symptoms start to develop. Racers—and long-distance touring cyclists in a hurry—often have a much harder time of it. What happens during the many hours in the saddle is that the combined effect of perspiration, pressure and chafing causes cracks in the skin where bacteria can enter. The result can be anything from a mild inflammation to the most painful boils.

There is of course little chance of these things healing as long as you continue riding vigorously. As soon as any pressure is applied, when you sit on the saddle, things will get worse. Prevention and early relief are the methods to combat saddle sores. The clue to both is hygiene. Wash and dry both your crotch and your cycling shorts after every day's ride. Many cyclists also treat the affected areas with rubbing alcohol, which both disinfects and increases the skin's resistance to chafing, or with talcum powder, which prevents further damage.

You'll need at least two pairs of shorts on a longer tour or when going on frequent day rides, so you can always rely on a clean, dry pair when you go out. Wash them out, taking particular care to get the chamois clean, and hang them out to dry thoroughly, preferably outside, where the sun's ultraviolet rays may act to kill any remaining bacteria. Treat the chamois with either talcum powder or a special treatment for that purpose. I prefer to use a water-soluble cream, such as Noxema, since it is easier to wash out.

The quality of your saddle and your riding position may also affect the development of crotch problems. If early symptoms appear in the form of redness or soreness, consider getting a softer saddle, sitting further to the back of your saddle, or lowering the handlebars a little to reduce the pressure on the seat. If the problem gets out of hand, take a rest from cycling until the sores have fully healed. In the meantime, consider another touring activity, such as hiking or sightseeing.

Knee Problems   Because the cycling movement does not apply the high impacting shock loads on the legs that are associated with running, it's surprising that knee problems are so prevalent. They are mainly concentrated with two groups of cyclists: beginners and very strong, muscular riders. In both cases, the cause seems to be pushing too high a gear. This places excessive forces on the knee joint, resulting in damage to the membranes that separate the moving portions of the joint and the ligaments holding the bits and pieces together. In cold weather the problems get aggravated, so it will be wise to wear long pants whenever the temperature is below 18°C (65°F), especially if fast descents are involved.

Prevent excessive forces on the knee joint by gearing so low that you can spin lightly under all conditions, especially avoiding climbing in the saddle with pedaling speeds below 60 RPM. Equip your bicycle with the kind of gear ratios that allow you to do that, and choose a lower gear whenever necessary. Once the problem has developed, either giving up cycling or riding loosely in low gears will aid the healing process. I suggest you continue cycling in very low gears, spinning freely. That will probably prepare you to get back into shape, while forcing you to avoid the high gears that caused the problem in the first place.

Tendonitis   This is an inflammation of the Achilles tendon, which attaches the big muscle of the lower leg, the gastrocnemius, to the heel bone. It is an important tendon in cycling, since the pedaling force can not be applied to the foot without it. It sometimes gets damaged or torn under the same kind of conditions as described above for knee injuries: cycling with too much force in too high a gear. The problem is aggravated by low temperatures, which explains why it generally develops in the early season.

To avoid tendonitis, wear long woolen socks whenever the temperature is below 18°C (65°F). It may also help to wear shoes that come up quite high, maximizing the support they provide.

Get used to riding with a supple movement in a low gear, which seems to be the clue to preventing many cycling complaints. Healing requires rest, followed by a return to cycling with minimum pedal force in a low gear.

Numbness Especially beginning cyclists, not yet used to riding longer distances, sometimes develop a loss of feeling in certain areas of contact with the bike. The most typical location is the hands, but it also occurs in the feet and the crotch. This is caused by excessive and unvaried prolonged pressure on the nerves and blood vessels. The effects are usually relieved with rest, though they have at times been felt for several days.

Once the problem develops, get relief by changing your position frequently, moving your hands from one part of the handlebars to the other, or moving from one area of the seat to the other if your crotch is affected. To prevent numbness in the various locations, use well-padded gloves, foam handlebar covers, a soft saddle in a slightly higher position, or thick-soled shoes with cushioned inner soles, laced loosely at the bottom but tightly higher up, depending on the location of the numbness.

Backache Many riders complain of pain in the back, the lower neck and the shoulders, especially early in the season. These are probably attributable to insufficient training of the muscles in those locations. It is largely the result of unfamiliar isometric muscle work, keeping still in a forward bent position. This condition may also be partly caused or aggravated by low temperatures, so it is wise to wear warm bicycle clothing in cool weather.

To avoid the early-season reconditioning complaints, the best remedy is not to interrupt cycling in winter. Even two longer rides a week at a moderate pace, or extended use of a home trainer with a proper low riding position, will do the trick. Alternately, you may start off in the new season with a slightly higher handlebar position and once more a low gear. Sleeping on a firm mattress and keeping warm also seems to either help alleviate or prevent the problem.

Sinus and Bronchial Complaints Especially in the cooler periods, many cyclists develop breathing problems, originating either in the sinuses or the bronchi. The same may happen when a rider used to cycling at sea level gets into the mountains, where the cold air in a fast descent can be very unsettling. It's generally attributable to undercooling, the only solution being to dress warmer and to cycle slowly enough to allow breathing through the nose.

After a demanding climb in cool weather, do not strip off warm clothing, open your shirt, or drink excessive quantities of cold liquids—even if you sweat profusely. All these things cause more rapid cooling than your body may be able to handle. You will cool off gradually and without impairing your health if you merely reduce your output and allow the sweat to evaporate naturally through the fibers of your bicycle clothing. This works best if you wear clothing that contains a high percentage of wool.

Sunburn When bike touring, you will be exposed to the sun for many hours at a stretch. Unless you have a naturally high resistance to ultraviolet light, exposed parts of the body are likely to suffer sunburn. To prevent it, use a suntan lotion with a protection factor of 15 or more. This means that only one fifteenth of the ultraviolet rays reach the skin. Even more effective is zinc oxide-based protection, applied in selected locations such as the nose, the ears and the neck.

Sunburn is just that: a burn, and that means it should be treated like any other burn. Cold water and perhaps a light dressing such as baby oil are all you can do, apart from waiting for it to heal. In really severe cases, sunburn can be serious enough to justify professional medical care. There are substances that suppress the pain, but there is little chance of healing a burn quickly with any kind of treatment.

Overtraining Although this phenomenon is more commonly associated with the pursuit of bicycle racing, it can occur among ambitious touring cyclists as well. While it is not usually recognized as a cycling injury, it should be treated as one. There are certain symptoms associated with overtraining and there are real hazards in ignoring these. It is simply a matter of having pushed your body beyond its present limits by cycling too far and too fast.

On marathon tours, such as the Race Across America, even highly trained cyclists, like Sue Notorangelo, can suffer form overtraining. (photo Dave Nelson)

Two types of overtraining syndromes may be distinguished, referred to as sympathicotonous and parasympathicotonous conditions, respectively. Beginning cyclists, preparing for great feats or participating in tours for which they are not adequately prepared, are most likely to suffer from the sympathicotonous condition. It is due to inadequate preparation: too rapid an increase of workload from one week to the next. The symptoms include excessive nervousness, tension and perspiration, as well as a rapid pulse. The treatment is relatively easy, since all you have to do is slow down for one week, and only increase your workload very gradually.

More experienced riders sometimes suffer from the parasympathicotonous condition. This is caused by an excessive total workload, often exceeding the body's capacity to take in food for a prolonged period. Symptoms include listlessness, weight loss and what seems like incurable tiredness. Here too, the answer lies in a reduction of the workload, though a doctor must definitely be consulted if the feeling of fatigue persists for several days, despite a drastic reduction in workload.

The morning pulse is a convenient indicator that can warn you of either type of overtraining condition. If it increases more than it usually does between lying in bed and just after getting up, you'd better take it easy for a day. Perhaps equally useful is to ask yourself how you are feeling in general. If you have difficulty sleeping and tire more than usual, if you feel listless, have a poor appetite, perspire more than usual or feel unjustified anxiety, it will be time to suspect overtraining. Go see a physician if a couple of days' relative rest does not solve the problem.

CHAPTER 12

Cycling in Any Weather

Yes, I also prefer to ride when the weather is nice. On the other hand, you can't always pick the weather, and bicycle touring must not be limited to warm and sunny days. All seasons have their particular and characteristic charm. Once you learn to cope with bad weather spells, you will probably also find many more opportunities to enjoy the fair weather periods in between.

I grew up in a climate where sunshine and "real" summer weather are very rare indeed, yet we never hesitated about taking the bike. The first group ride I organized in California, many years later, was a different experience altogether. At seven in the morning the phone rang, with a prospective participant suggesting I call off the ride, since the forecast included a twenty percent chance of rain. Only three of our group of twelve finally showed up and had a wonderful ride. Not a drop of rain fell, but even if it had rained for a while, we would still have had a fine day's ride.

The moral is twofold: don't let uncertainty about the weather stop you from cycling, and prepare well enough to cope with poorer weather, if necessary. If you are adequately dressed, equipped and prepared, cycling can be enjoyable in almost any weather. Even if we agree that bicycle touring is better in favorable weather, and even if you do feel a little miserable at times, a ride in bad weather can still be a lot more enjoyable than

Masochist's delight: The Iditabike tour takes you clear across Alaska in winter. (photo Renner)

sitting at home under the same conditions. I have also included some useful references on instant weather forecasting in the Bibliography, which may prove useful to make the most of the good spells, as well as to prepare for whatever weather is coming up.

On a longer tour, when good and bad days follow one another, you may be able to restrict actual touring to the better days if time allows. Or you may have to ride whatever the weather, if your time is more restricted. In a nutshell people with long vacations, like students, teachers and the independently wealthy, can perhaps afford to pick their cycling weather, while the rest of us will just have to keep cycling. Yet you may establish soon that with the right preparation, riding a bike in supposedly inclement weather is actually better than you thought, even if you could have afforded to postpone the trip.

Hanging around a campsite or a motel on a rainy day is not necessarily that much fun either. You'll also find that sightseeing in a strange city is better done on days with favorable weather. Once you're cycling, you can keep reasonably warm and dry, but getting on and off the bike, going in and out of buildings, changing from rain gear into regular clothing, may well make such a sightseeing day more miserable than it would have been on the bike.

Then there are times of the year or parts of the world for which supposedly bad weather is the order of the day. Of course, it all depends on what you're used to. If you've lived in the American Southwest all your life, you may find it hard to imagine that people two thousand miles north cycle at all, where it even rains in summer, and where it gets pretty cool in the off-season. And what to think of those poor souls who grow up in places like Britain, where even the summers are nippy, and rain can be expected in any season? I suggest you learn to handle any kind of weather, in order to experience bicycle touring as intensely and as frequently as possible. You will probably most enjoy some of the rides in the kind of weather you would at first not have considered suitable.

Four things have to be kept in mind to handle unfavorable weather conditions, which will all be discussed in some detail below:

☐ clothing

☐ other equipment

☐ riding style

☐ touring technique.

Clothing for Touring

I shall be brief on the subject of clothing, since it was covered in Chapter 6. The secret is to consciously choose the kind of clothing that suits all the various types of weather you can reasonably expect to encounter on any one ride. In summer that will include some different things than at other times of the year, and on an extensive tour you will want to be prepared for more changeable conditions than you have to be on a one-day trip.

Also consider the difference of elevation in this respect. I shall not forget two exceptional tours in my own experience that showed me the importance of that. The first time was when I was seventeen years old and rode my trusty three-speed from my native city of Rotterdam all the way to the Swiss Alps. At 3000 m (9000 feet) above sea level, I had to put on every fiber I could find and stuff old newspapers under my cycling shirt as well. Even so, I caught an awful cold on the descent.

The second such experience was twenty years later on the Hawaiian island of Maui. All the way up to the top of Mount Haleakala it was warm and pleasant, as it would be the next day for the descent. Only, the night was a little rough, with temperatures around freezing. Equipped with only sheet sleeping bags for the night, we hid under old newspapers and cuddled up as closely as we could, without feeling even remotely comfortable. Still, experiences like this are perhaps the spice of bicycle touring: you tend to remember with some fondness even the little mishaps. As long as your health or safety is not seriously threatened, the charm of coping with the unexpected is undeniable.

When packing your gear, decide what range of temperatures and what kind of precipitation you are likely to encounter. Dress for the most immediate, but in such a way that you can convert to another kind of predictable weather without great ado. If rain is likely, make sure the rain gear is easily accessible, and if the temperatures may change, make sure you can accommodate by simply putting on or removing subsequent layers of clothing, rather than being forced to take items off before you can put other items on. Dressing in layers, with the coolest and lightest closest to the skin, will be best in changeable weather.

On the other hand, if the weather is expected to be and remain cold, you'll find it advantageous to wear warm woolen garments closest to the skin. If additional warm and long underwear is required, remember that your physical activity places specific requirements on your underwear that do not apply to those who are more inactive. Light but slightly bulky fabrics that are flexible and close fitting will be ideal, polypropylene scoring highest when it comes to long underwear.

Not only cold and rain, but even extremely hot or dry weather has to be considered specially. Though it may seem nice to wear as little as possible, keep in mind that you will be out on the bike in the direct sunlight for quite some time. Besides, especially in hilly terrain, sections of great exertion, where your effort

When you cross mountain passes, even in hot regions, be prepared for dramatic changes in temperatures. (Dieter Glokowski photo)

keeps you very hot, may be followed by downhill or windy sections, on which your body may get undercooled due to wind chill, even if the air temperature is quite high.

Certainly at higher elevations, I suggest covering up your tender skin. If you haven't a naturally high resistance to ultraviolet rays, wear the kind of cycling clothing that regulates the body's temperature and use an effective sunscreen. Refer to Chapter 11, *Safety and Health*, for some additional comments on protection against sunburn. To keep covered enough in the sun, you may wear relatively light cotton items with long sleeves and a helmet.

To provide the best temperature control effect, wool is definitely the best material, especially if it is closely knit of a relatively thin, soft and stretchable fiber. Your companions will also be pleased to note that wool does not smell nearly' as offensive as most synthetics and cotton once it is or has been soaked with perspiration.

Other Equipment

Cycling in cold or rainy weather is best done on a bike that is equipped with those conditions in mind. That applies even if you encounter such weather only occasionally. On the other hand, the use of removable gadgets, or even some inconvenience in doing without optimal equipment, may be appropriate in some cases. I shall leave it up to you to decide how much suffering you want to put up with. Similarly, it will be a matter of your own inventiveness to produce the handy quick-release attachments and improvised weather protection gadgets that some technically inclined people find a challenge to invent and construct. As for regular equipment to withstand the elements, that will be described in this section.

The bike itself must be equipped properly. As far as most components are concerned, that means getting high quality gear. To give an example, high quality bearings, as used on the most expensive hubs, bottom brackets and headsets, are much better sealed and more resistant to water than superficially similar items sold for half the price.

Three particularly important major items are brakes, tires and lights. All caliper brakes of reasonable quality work admirably well if used in conjunction with the right brake blocks and wheel rims, provided they are adjusted properly. Even though heavy loads and bad roads may suggest the use of presumably stronger steel rims, only aluminum rims provide an adequate coefficient of friction in conjunction with most brake block materials.

The brake blocks should be of any material that provides adequate friction even when wet. Though synthetic materials are widely advertised as being superior in the rain, only one type really lives up to its promise, namely the sintered material first used by Modolo in their D-0015 brake blocks and now available from several manufacturers. And contrary to popular prejudice, longer or larger brake blocks do not provide better braking action than short ones—neither wet nor dry. If your bike should have steel rims (though no longer installed on quality bikes in the U.S., still used in Britain), make sure they are not chrome-plated but stainless and are used in conjunction with special brake blocks intended for use on steel rims.

Tires for touring in wet or cold weather should probably have a more chunky tread profile than the skinny thin things recommended for easiest cycling. Even on a wet road, perfectly smooth tires, such as the recently popular slicks, provide adequate grip for propulsion and braking, as long as the road is not slick, and as long as you are going straight. However, a little snow, ice, mud or fallen leaves on the road, which is hard to avoid in the rain, can be handled much better if the tire has a well-defined tread profile. And to maintain traction in curves, you will find a roughened or profiled tread area wrapped relatively far around the tire's circumference to provide much more predictable road holding properties.

In wet and cold times of the year, you will probably more often find the need for lighting on your bike. This subject was covered in Chapter 4. Just make sure lights and reflectors are properly installed and maintained, and switch on your light whenever other road user's visibility may be impaired enough to justify lighting. In wet and snowy weather, a generator may more easily slip off the tire, and a battery may get soaked and ruined; so check up on these components more frequently. Proper adjustment, the use of a rubber cap over a generator wheel and removing batteries when not in use will prevent the most serious problems.

Other equipment-related points include a more frequent need for bike maintenance and the installation of some auxiliaries that may not otherwise rate very high. Lubrication is the major consideration here: cables, bearings and especially the chain will need regular cleaning, followed by lubrication, using a waxy spray can lubricant, oil or grease. Among special equipment, fenders or mudguards rate high, as does a mud flap at the end of the forward one, to keep the water off your body and out of your luggage. In weather that is both wet and cold, a pair of shoe covers on the pedals are very worthwhile.

Riding Style

In cold, windy and rainy weather, you may benefit from an appropriate riding style. Try to become aware of the effect any particular condition may have on your bike's behavior. In the rain you'll want to ride so as to stay as comfortable as possible, while retaining maximum stability and balance. In cold weather you'll

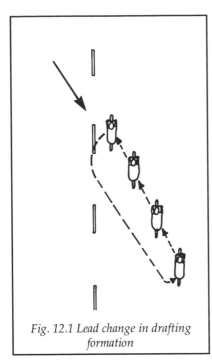

Fig. 12.1 Lead change in drafting formation

want to avoid exposing yourself too much and— when temperatures get down to freezing—you should make sure you don't skid on ice or snow. In very windy weather it will make sense to minimize your exposure to the wind, so as to reduce wind resistance and minimize the negative effect of the wind on your bike's balancing. The latter applies particularly in the case of a strong side wind, especially if the wind or its effect varies strongly during the ride.

To avoid spills on wet, muddy or icy roads, you should try to adjust your center of gravity far back, unloading the front end of the bike. The more weight you transfer from the front wheel to the back, the less likely a sudden move will be to result in a skidding or diverting type of disturbance, as described in Chapter 11. For the same reason, try to avoid excessive lean in corners: ride a natural, rather than a forced curve whenever possible. Read through the explanation in Chapter 10 again and practice the techniques recommended there on dry and wet roads to become really competent and confident.

In windy situations, it will generally pay off to keep your upper body low, in order to minimize wind resistance. When riding in a group, try to stay in some such formation that minimizes the individual riders' total exposure to the wind. That's done by riding directly in line closely behind each other when the wind comes from straight ahead. In the case of a side wind, fan out the group into a staggered formation as shown in Chapter 10. Either way, the strongest rider should maximize his time in the front, while the weaker ones should be granted maximum shelter. If all are more or less equally strong, take turns at the front. Lead changes are carried out as shown in Fig. 12.1.

Touring Techniques

Special touring techniques may be called for in inclement weather, although some people manage to solve all their problems by merely wearing appropriate clothing and having a properly equipped bike. One of the things to keep in mind is the long-term chilling effect, due to relative air movement, even if the temperatures do not seem quite so low. Keep your extremities warm and comfortable: feet, hands and head.

Additionally, there is the luggage, spare clothing and any camping gear to consider. Whenever the weather is or may become sub-optimal, you should have packed everything in such a way that vital items remain dry and are accessible without getting wet—including especially those things on which you have to rely later to keep you dry, warm and comfortable. That's a matter of packing and wrapping your equipment and luggage with due thought and consideration. It is not possible to give you precise guidelines on how to do it, but a warning to consider these points should suffice the intelligent rider.

Even if it is not raining, you may get wet in other ways. (photo Dieter Glokowski)

The way you plan the overall tour or the day's ride is also critical. In certain kinds of weather, you won't be able to cover big distances between stops. At other times, getting off the bike frequently may actually make the ride more uncomfortable. In an enduring rain, you will probably find it beneficial to attack the day as much as possible in just one or two long continuous stretches. By the time you are changed and getting about off the bike, you will be grateful if you don't have to start all over again after the interruption.

On the other hand, in particularly cold weather you should probably ride several shorter sections. Try to find a warm and sheltered place and something warm to eat or drink between these stages. Don't return to the bike until you feel comfortable. Though I shall probably never enjoy cold weather, I have at times covered quite significant distances this way without getting really miserable. Some people actually enjoy a brisk ride in the cold, being able to cover quite impressive distances without either harm or discomfort.

Even camping can be done with some success in temperatures around or below freezing. It will be a matter of adequate clothing and overnight equipment, as well as technique. Don't do it until you have experienced camping under easier weather conditions first. Until you can make yourself really comfortable in and around a tent in summer, there's little hope of your being at ease doing the same in winter. Make sure tent, sleeping bag and cooking gear are up to the task, and don't hesitate to transfer to a motel or some other form of solid housing if it gets too cold, wet or miserable.

In this context, I suggest there should be no compulsion to combine bicycle touring with life under canvas. Hotels, motels, hostels and the like save you from carrying a lot of gear, and they are fine places to spend the night. Riding a less loaded bike will pay off in winter even more than it does in summer. Throughout this book I have included references to camping, since there is both a significant interest and a corresponding need for accurate information. Besides, it is a field in which I myself have a lot of experience. Just the same, I regard a night under a solid roof, in a ready-made bed and with a private bathroom a blessing every cyclist should grant himself from time to time. That applies especially when the weather is less than perfect for a night under the stars.

CHAPTER 13

What to Take and How to Pack It

We now reach perhaps the most neglected subject in the field, the one thing that cannot be solved with either money or direct instruction alone. How to select the items you take along, and how to stash them inside the bags or on the bike, is indeed so inadequately known and considered that it is reasonable to devote an entire chapter to what is in other books usually covered in a few lines. In addition to this chapter, you are referred to the packing list in the Appendix, but the basis of sensible packing is the thought that goes into it, which is covered here.

Consider for a moment that my parents went bicycle touring in the late 20s with forty-pound bikes, in an age when aluminum, lightweight synthetic fibers, wash-and-wear clothing, plastic cups, containers or bottles and freeze-dried food were all equally unknown. Even so, they carried everything they needed without much suffering. Compare that with today's situation, with bikes weighing barely more than half as much and a nearly unlimited choice of specially designed lightweight gear available. Yet most of today's touring cyclists are loaded up to the point of approaching the limit of material endurance, if not personal bodily collapse. Today, more than ever before, you should be able to travel light if you pack it right.

Even if you have to carry a lot of gear, because of isolated terrain, it can all be packed away neatly. (photo Dan Gindling)

Packing Smartly

The secret, it seems, lies not so much in the quality of the equipment, but more in the selectiveness of the cyclist who packs it on the bike. What to leave at home is more important than what to buy. And knowing how to pack what you do choose to take along is at least as important as deciding which bags are bought and how they are installed on the bike.

Of course, choosing the right luggage racks and bags is still important, and you are once more referred to Chapter 5, where this subject was covered. In the same chapter you will find solid advice on the distribution of weight and the attachment of bags to the bike. I do suggest you go over those remarks once more after you have covered the material presented here, before you set out on your first serious tour.

What to Take

As in virtually all other bicycle touring manuals, you will find a number of suggested packing lists in this book, contained in the Appendix. But such lists must be used with great caution. Neither I nor anyone else can know just what you will need on a particular tour over a given distance at a certain time with a specific purpose in mind. And those are only the most basic variables. Your personal interests and your limitations, both physical and material, are additional and less tangible factors that affect what you should pack and carry.

Eventually, you yourself will have to compose the list of things to take, even if it is only by modifying one of the suggested packing lists found in this book or elsewhere. Whether you use a pre-printed list or one you thought up yourself, you will find it necessary to revise that list as you go along. You will probably find certain things inadequate, missing or incomplete, other items unnecessary, superfluous, too big or small, or expendable altogether. Many more items will turn out to be useful in some situations, in certain areas, at particular times only. And finally, there will be some items that you may never use, yet should not be left behind because your life or health may depend on them in extreme situations.

Essentials, to which you need access along the way and which you need to take with you when away from the bike, can be carried in a handelbar bag.

It is not my job to tell you just what these things are, certainly when it comes to the hard-core emergency supplies. I can merely suggest you consider such factors. Some people carry enough medicines to put an elephant out of his misery, others will feel totally secure with a copy of the Bible or some other work on religion or philosophy. And like so many other supplies, their importance varies with the different factors, ranging from the time of the year and the duration of the trip to the terrain encountered and the degree of your accumulated experience.

It will be easiest to keep track of the things you pack with the aid of simple 4½ x 6-inch notebooks. Make one of these up for each touring season, to take notes before and during your trips.

A second notebook is used for packing lists and other pre-tour notes, and is kept at home. I find my packing list gets longer and longer from year to year, yet I seem to be taking less and less as time and experience progress. That is due to the selective remarks about the usefulness of particular items and the desirability of others. Also see the remarks about record-keeping in in Chapter 23, *Keeping a Record of Your Tour.*

Over the years the packing list not only grows in length, it also expands in depth and detail, as remarks about the particular items are inserted. After each tour, the smartest thing to do is to unpack at least as systematically as you had packed before you left. Make four distinct piles:

1. Items you couldn't have done without whatever the situation.

2. Things you will only need under certain situations, or on particular tours.

3. Items you used on this tour, though they could be replaced by others that would also serve an additional purpose or that are smaller, lighter or otherwise more suitable.

4. Ballast, i.e. things you carried for no useful purpose or could have left at home with impunity whatever the situation.

In addition, by way of a fifth category, your notebook, in which you can write down those items you really missed and had not packed but would have liked to have along. At the same time, update the notebook to shorten or expand the list, as may be appropriate on the basis of your findings regarding the four piles of gear.

Saving Weight

Not only the nature, but also the number of these items is of significance. To give but one example, I have since my early youth limited the number of shoes, socks and undies to the absolute minimum. Whatever the duration of the tour, I take the stuff on my body when I leave home, and just one set of spare socks, undies and tops. When I started touring again with other people many years later, my companions always rejected this technique, carrying one or two pairs of additional shoes and enough other clothes to last a week without washing.

Whereas I cycled lightly packed and only spent a few minutes washing the day's socks and underwear at night, the others had loaded themselves up and were forever rummaging in their bags to separate the clean from the dirty from the not quite so dirty. Finally they finished up doing a major laundry operation, and the next day had to carry a week's supply of wet clothes around with them, that could not be dried conveniently. It took my companions one trip to limit the number of shoes they carried, and another one before they reduced their underwear supplies, until finally, after several years, they had learned how much more convenient it is to travel as lightly as I do.

The dictum of traveling light if possible should be paramount. Be selective in the materials you take, even if the particular kind of thing is very important to you. Thus, an avid photographer may be tempted to take a full stock of camera equipment, complete with several camera bodies, lenses, tripod and flash—nothing but the best. That makes sense if photography is the specific objective of the trip. If, on the other hand, you go for the bike ride, even the keenest photographer will find that he can get by admirably with just one small camera. I know one accomplished photographer who never takes more than a pocket tripod and an old Rollei 35 S, to take photos that were accepted for the covers of major pictorial periodicals.

You are of course free to take what you want. If you are like everybody else, you'll probably also learn to limit yourself to taking only the essential quantities after a few years of conscientious note taking and shaving off your packing list. On the other hand, you can take my advice right off on your first trip and be at least two years ahead of the others. Remember, though, that if you feel like chucking the whole bike touring business after your first trip, since you find it all too much of a burden, because of the laundry and the packing and carrying, you can return to this chapter and learn how to make life easier.

Different Loads for Different Trips

Many factors affect the number and type of items you should take along on a tour. I suggest you start off with some simple trips where you don't need to take too much along and where it doesn't matter very much if you do forget something that seems essential. Clearly, if you stay in hotels and eat in restaurants, you will need less than when camping, providing you are in a part of the world where restaurants and hotels are close enough to avoid hunger marathons and long rides in the dark to find accommodations.

If you cycle near towns and on weekdays, you will find it easier to purchase certain things along the way. In most European countries, where shops and most other facilities are closed evenings, Sundays and one or two afternoons each week, this can be particularly problematic. But even in regions with more liberal closing hours, I recommend starting with a simple day trip on a Saturday, followed by some midweek or weekend trips with overnight stays. If you start the latter on a Friday, you will have had the first night's experience to suggest what else you need while most shops are still open. The advice not to undertake your early trips in the outback is just as valid in Europe as it is in the U.S. or Canada, even if towns and shops are so much closer together in the Old World, where you rarely have to worry about being really stranded far away from civilization.

Take not only the right kind of clothing and overnight or other camping gear, but also the most elementary supplies for the maintenance of your bike and your own body, as well as adequate aids to orientation. A trip without a map is as frustrating as one without food or the appropriate clothing may be. And being stranded because you lack the tools or the pump to carry out a minor repair can turn a perfectly pleasant trip into a nightmare. Once more, it's up to you to decide what to take and what to leave at home, but try to systematically think of everything that may be needed.

Conversely, remember that the problem of taking too much may be just as serious. Before packing each item, consider what will happen if you don't take it. Leave anything home if its absence will not significantly detract from the enjoyment of the trip. Sounds simple, but it takes an astonishing amount of self-discipline to execute. Also take the weights of the various items into consideration. Compare the weights of several similar items, and choose the lightest consistent with the purpose. As you pack and decide, keep updating your packing list, so you are saved the same decision-making process for the next trip.

The Art of Packing

In addition to the remarks pertaining to the selection of bags and their attachment and distribution, as covered in Chapter 5, Luggage Carrying Equipment, you may benefit from some basic hints on how to fill these bags and how to attach the various pieces of luggage to the bike. That's what we'll cover in the present section.

The first thing to keep in mind is that whatever has to come out first or fastest must be most easily accessible: somewhere near the outside. That means these items must be packed last and preferably in outside pockets or even outside the bags altogether. Thus, your money and essential documents should be so easily accessible that you can immediately grab them and carry them on your body whenever you leave the bike.

Similarly, rain gear or a sweater and jacket in rainy or cold climes, or sunglasses and sun lotion in sunny regions, your camera, the current map and your notebook, should all be very easily accessible. These items must be located, accessed and used without getting off the bike. For most of these instant access items, you will find a handlebar bag most convenient. Personally, I don't like even the best handlebar bags, carrying the same kind of things divided over the pockets in my clothing, the saddle bag and a small pack on the front luggage rack. Rain gear should be strapped to the outside of the saddle bag or a pannier

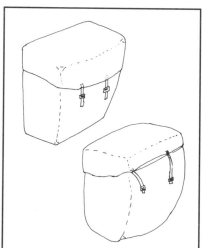

Fig. 13.1 Comparison of a well packed bag (top) and a poorly packed one.

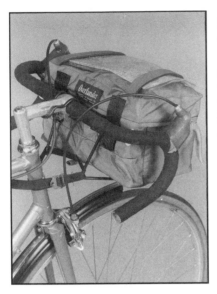

Neat looking small panniers from Eclipse.

bag, so it is both easy to reach and will not make the contents of the bag wet when you put it back.

But let's look at the sequence of packing, rather than only considering the most urgent items. The first thing to go in should be the last thing you'll need: spare laundry, sleeping bag, future supplies. Whether you pack big things first or last, often recommended in some apparently logical order, should solely be determined by the answer to the question of when you'll need to gain access to the various items. A big package like the tent is not best kept underneath a lot of small items, if that means you have to unpack all these things before you can set up camp.

Similarly, consider what is most sensitive to damage or to getting wet. A sleeping bag is a nice big package that can be conveniently removed in one piece, but if you have to do that in order to reach something more immediately needed, it may be getting wet in the rain or it may get torn if it is manhandled too much. Again, I can't prescribe a secret sole correct method. Instead, you will have to take my remarks and suggestions to heart, thinking and deciding for yourself.

Items that belong together are best kept together. That applies even if it means that one side of the bike will perhaps be loaded noticeably heavier than the other. Thus, the cooking gear and food, heavy though they are, are best put in one bag, while sleeping bag and sleeping gear, generally much lighter in weight, should go in another bag. That saves wild rummaging and searching, whereas the laterally unequal weight distribution does not affect the bicycle's stability. In fact, it prevents oscillations that are more likely to occur when the bike is packed equally heavy on both sides.

Tying Things Down

Items that are attached outside the bags or directly to the bike, as well as some of the bags that do not have their own integral means of attachment, are generally best held with webbing straps or leather belts. Either of these is far preferable to the inexplicably popular elastic bungee or shock cords. Since straps retain their length even when force is applied to them, they do not encourage sagging and slipping of the luggage. When using leather belts, treat them with the same waterproofing also used on leather saddles, such as Proofide or neat's foot oil. Webbing straps must have the kind of buckles that do not slip, yet are easy to tighten or loosen: try them out before you buy.

Food and other supplies bought along the way on your tour may be carried in rather provisional bags for a short time. I like to use an additional light backpack for this purpose. In the back of it I place a solid light fiberboard (such as a clip board with the clip removed), which maintains the bag's shape. This prevents hard and bulky items, such as cans of food, from causing excessive discomfort. If you have a few spare straps or belts, you may also be able to attach this bag to the bike over the top of another bag temporarily. Whatever you do, make sure everything is secured adequately and safely, so you neither loose anything, nor risk the bag's getting caught in the bike's moving parts or brakes, nor interfering with your movements.

The Inside Package

Finally, consider the question of packaging the items that go inside the bike bags. Their size and shape, as well as the form of protection they offer, are all significant. Wherever hard and non-deformable items are concerned, you'll find two smaller packages easier to store than one large item. So, though the soft and deformable package containing the sleeping bag is no problem to stack in one piece inside a bag, your camp stove fuel, beverages and other supplies are best divided up over several smaller containers.

When packing the various bags, consider the final shape they should take on when full. Their ultimate shape is more or less defined by the way they are sewn: never spherical but relatively long, flat and even. They are designed that way to remain compact and to interfere minimally with bike, rider and other objects, while protecting the contents optimally. Try to achieve that by stuffing the contents in such a way that the intended final shape is approached. Roll together the items that go inside in packages that each do not exceed the width of the bag. Put smaller and narrower items in last, stuffing them into the ends, filling up the length of the bag. If the packed bag takes on an almost spherical shape, as shown in the lower detail, you've gone about it the wrong way. This would make it hard to close the bag properly and may cause damage to bag and contents.

As far as the shape is concerned, long and narrow packages are more easily stashed than bulky items of the same volume. In addition, flat packages are handier than more nearly round or square cross sections. Thus, bottles should be long and of oval cross section, rather than short and round. You will not always get an opportunity to determine the shape of things to pack yourself, but in many cases you do have the choice when buying packaging materials. No need to keep things in the packages in which they are sold in the first place. You can easily get appropriate bottles and other containers from a backpacking or other outdoor supplies store.

Containers

Special items need special forms of packaging. All printed and written materials must be kept flat and dry. Thus, maps (excepting the current one, which should be kept handy), books and writing paper are best kept in a flat rigid case or binder. These are made of cardboard and fabric, and wrapped in a plastic bag

They packed everything away neatly. But where is the pump?

to keep them dry. Since maps, books and writing paper are not all the same size, you may have to make several of these, keeping items of similar size together. Put these cases in such a place that they are not bent or damaged by other things in the same bag.

The weight of packaging materials is as important a factor as is their size. With regard to the latter, make sure you don't waste space in your luggage on empty or unnecessary packaging. Estimate or even measure out how much of any one supply you will need for the duration of a particular trip, then take a container to match just that volume whenever possible. As concerns weight, choose the lightest materials and the lightest construction consistent with the amount of abuse received. The conscientious use of household scales, capable of weighing anything up to about 2 kg (4–5 lbs.) is highly recommended when it comes to selecting the packaging, as it is when comparing several items serving the same purpose. Mark each container with its volume and weight, using an indelible marking pen, for future reference. Use a different color marker to indicate the contents.

You may be able to scrounge quite suitable packaging materials for many purposes. I find an ample supply of bottles and boxes among the annual household consumption of supposedly one-way packaging materials. These things range from swivel-top shampoo bottles, useful for drinks and other liquids, to photographic film cans, suitable for keeping salt and matches dry, to simple plastic bags and sheets used to wrap moisture-sensitive items.

Easily spilled items, such as flour and sugar, may not be adequately protected by a plastic bag alone, though a rigid canister is not very space-efficient. The optimal protection of things like that is provided by a double bag, made up by sewing a cloth bag with drawstring closure around a plastic bag. Knives, forks and spoons should be stored and kept together in a pouch. If you can't buy a suitable pouch, make your own, sewn from any sturdy fabric, as shown in Fig. 13.2. This protects the other items in your luggage, while keeping the utensils together.

Carrying Your Bike

Carrying your gear is not only a problem while touring, but also when getting to your starting point and back home again. In the U.S. most bicycle touring seems to require some travel by plane, and that's where the bicycle itself is even more awkward than the gear you have to carry. Here are some basic considerations, while more detailed information is available in an annually updated booklet on airline travel for cyclists available from the League of American Wheelmen.

There are elegant and strong packing cases on the market these days, but what do you do with an expensive 4 x 3 x 2 foot plastic case, while you are cycling around the countryside? So if you can't package it that way, the safest way to put the bike on a plane is undisguised. Turn the handlebars in line with the bike and reverse the pedals (pointing in), perhaps with something wrapped around the frame tubes to protect the paintwork. That way everybody can see it's a bike, and not some anonymous cardboard box that can be thrown about and may end up at the bottom of a pile, covered by much heavier articles.

The problem is that most airlines don't accept bikes that way. They insist you put it in a box, and if you're lucky there is at least one airline desk that sells such things. Depending on the size of the box, you may have to partially dismantle the bike. And at the

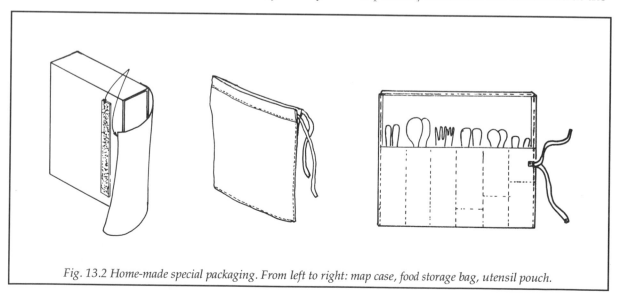

Fig. 13.2 Home-made special packaging. From left to right: map case, food storage bag, utensil pouch.

These Rhode Gear bags strap together neatly.

other end you'll be stuck with a box you can't carry around with you. If you're lucky the airline may offer to keep that box for your return trip. If you're not lucky, or if you return from another airport, the same hassle starts all over again on the return journey.

Inquire at the airline office at least two weeks before departure date. If you do that in writing, you can also expect a written answer. Use that to back up your claim at the airport if it should be more favorable than what you are told at the check-in counter. Even so, a little polite charm may get your bike on, though it may backfire in some cases, in which case only money will solve your problem—or you may have to go on another carrier, loosing some time.

Actually, I have had good experiences offering my bike without a box and insisting I want to take it that way, and will sign a waiver releasing the airline's responsibility for transit-related damage to the bike: so far, the bike has always arrived unscathed. The advantage, I think, is that everybody can see it's a bike, and not some anonymous box that can be knocked around.

CHAPTER 14

Planning Your Tour

Waiting for the ferry that takes the cyclists to the Gulf Island in Canada. (photo Kimberlee Caledonia)

The first time I proposed writing a bicycle touring book, the reaction of many non-cyclists was that it should contain mainly descriptions of routes to follow. That is not what you will be getting here. You may appreciate how useless that would be, if you consider how slender the chances are of any one rider living close enough to most—or even any—of the rides described that way.

Instead of the cookbook approach, telling you where to start and where to turn off, I will show to do set out your own route with intelligent planning, following your own inclination in the area you have chosen. That, I feel, will be more useful, and will prepare you to use the same skill for any tour in any part of the world.

How to get about once you have selected your route will be covered in some detail in Chapter 16, Finding Your Way. In the present chapter you'll learn how to go about planning your tour in advance. This encompasses all the preparatory work required to successfully pull off a tour of any length, with respect to both the selection of the general route and other planning details. In addition to the remarks in the present chapter, you will find some practical advice in several of the books listed in the Bibliography.

Basic Rules

A few rules should probably be observed to assure the greatest chance of success. Each one of these rules may be individually broken under certain circumstances, without necessarily spoiling the entire trip. However, if you are on a limited time budget, their observation is quite critical. Oddly enough, it is probably less dangerous to start a grand tour improperly prepared than a weekend trip or a two-week vacation. The planning mistakes made in the first case can all be corrected or compensated as time goes by, whereas the short trip just doesn't give you enough time to learn from your present mistakes and correct them until it is too late. Here are the basic criteria for successful tour planning:

☐ Inform yourself adequately about the area ahead of time, to make sure you know what to expect and that it is what you want, both in terms of scenery, terrain, weather, type of accommodation, strenuousness of the trip, and in a more general cultural sense.

☐ When touring with others, agree in advance on what all participants expect. Decide ahead of time what you will be doing and seeing, what to expect of each other, and what each participant wants to do, so you avoid conflicts along the way.

☐ Do not tackle terrain more difficult or remote than what you know from experience you can handle.

☐ Preferably select beginning and end points for the route that can be conveniently reached by public transportation, or make arrangements to leave a car at some place to which you are sure you can return at the conclusion of the trip.

☐ Ascertain that your equipment is suitable for the terrain and that you can carry enough spares and tools wherever help may not be readily available.

☐ Obtain the best mapping material available, consistent with the length of the trip, the remoteness of the region and the nature of the terrain.

☐ For a longer tour, inquire in advance about overnight accommodation facilities, restaurants and stores along the route.

☐ Allow contingencies for emergencies, such as cutting the trip short and returning from someplace along the route by public transportation if that should be necessary.

Learning to Cope

Taking all these points into consideration would be perfect planning, and no doubt you will at times be somewhat in the dark about one or the other aspect. In fact, a little uncertainty is perhaps the spice of life, and it will generally be no disaster if one item or the other is not fully secured. It is important, though, to have considered each of these aspects, even if you check off some of them as being of no serious concern for a particular trip. In fact, I have occasionally found myself insufficiently prepared in one or more areas, but I have made an effort to weigh their relative significance and risk during the planning stage, before starting the trip, which is exactly what I recommend you do.

In general, it is probably smartest to start on a small scale. Go on some relatively short trips, starting with half-day rides close to home. Subsequently, work your way up via day trips to weekend tours over increasing distances. Gradually increase their complexity, from trips without food or overnight problems, via picnics and motel stays, to short camping trips in easy terrain, finally to longer tours that present a combination of many of the problems you can expect to encounter anywhere. Progress from carrying little luggage to touring fully loaded, and from riding in familiar surroundings to well-mapped areas farther away to the relatively unknown. Expand your experiences until you are confident under most conceivable circumstances.

Where and When to Go

The selection of suitable touring terrain is not really as difficult as it may seem. Not so long ago most bike books included the recommendation to investigate a likely area by car first, and then go out the next weekend with the bike. That is not what I propose, since I consider essentially all roads in most parts of the world basically suitable for cycling. Just the same, most people will agree that certain factors make cycling more enjoyable in certain areas. You are probably familiar enough with your own area to be able to guess at suitable terrain, yet you should consider that the world—even your little corner of it—looks different from the bike than it does from behind the wheel of a car. Some of the things that make cycling particularly enjoyable in certain areas and on particular roads should be kept in mind when planning a tour and are listed below:

☐ Terrain or specific roads with minimal differences in elevation.

☐ Areas with little wind and sheltered roads that do not expose you to strong winds.

☐ Scenically pleasant areas with large areas of public lands, especially if these are not quite so popular as to attract excessive motor traffic.

☐ Roads that are well-paved and relatively wide for the volume of motor traffic they carry.

☐ Roads that avoid built-up commercial, industrial and housing areas.

☐ Roads that lead through or past points of interest and small towns, especially if the latter have character of their own and offer facilities you might want to use.

☐ For longer trips, roads that are served at suitable intervals by convenient facilities for overnight stays and shopping for food.

Sometimes you may be riding off-road. But that's not the way to cover significant distances. (photo Dan Gindling)

This list may be a bit of an eye-opener to the less experienced. It has virtually no similarity with the list of points proposed by a class of inexperienced cyclists I taught several years ago. These people all placed as their first preference that there should be separate bike paths on or along the road, closely followed by the desire for narrow roads far away from the nearest town. My list was drawn up in consultation with a number of experienced touring cyclists, and I feel the advice contained here is valid for beginning and advanced cyclists alike.

Time and Area

At the same time as deciding where to go, determine when your trip shall be. You may be restricted either one way or the other. If you have little money or time to travel, you will have to select an area close to home. In that case, select a time when cycling conditions are favorable in your part of the world. If, on the other hand, you are restricted to a certain time, you may have to select a destination that offers good conditions at that particular time of the year.

With respect to the season, remember that good does not necessarily mean hot: milder weather is generally more favorable for cycling, and the most popular vacation time in any one area is rarely the best time to ride your bike there. Any touring cyclist chased off the road along the Pacific coast or in the vicinity of any national park by a stream of incompetently and inconsiderately driven motorhomes can confirm that.

Of course, with suitable equipment, some of the points on my list may be overcome, if not ignored. Thus, unpaved paths and trails may lend themselves wonderfully for mountain bike touring, especially over distances short enough to allow the return to the civilized world, should you need help or supplies. Similarly, you may purposely choose a mountain tour for its scenic character, where there is little point in shying away from differences in elevation.

Once you have decided in which part of the world or of the country to tour, define the area more precisely. The overall pre-tour planning is perhaps best done with the aid of a simple geographical map, such as the state or country map contained in a school atlas. You will be able to get a feel for the terrain, since hills and rivers, towns and major geographical features determine the picture more than the roads, which dominate conventional road maps. This way, you will be able to select one or more likely regions within the larger area selected. Comparing carefully with the scale of the map, you can roughly set out the distance you should be able or willing to cover. In general, it will be best to seek out a more or less circular route, which can be started and discontinued at any point that turns out to be suitable in the next step of preparation.

Detailed Route Planning

For that next step, get down to a more detailed road map. How to select a suitable map, and how to glean a maximum of useful information from it, will be shown in the section entitled *Reading the Map* below. Now define the towns, the points of interest, the roads and the geographical features along your route on the road map. Done with a modicum of imagination, you should be able to judge many aspects of importance by merely interpreting the map intelligently and critically. With the aid of this map, supported by guide books or other literature about the area selected, decide on a suitable route to follow.

To give but one example, a road connecting a suburb with the nearest major town will not be a quiet one. If the tour starts or ends too far from your home to cycle there, take into particular consideration the problem of getting there and back. In America, railway stations and bus depots are often not in very nice parts of town. Airports are generally served only by freeways or similar roads that are generally not legal to ride and which make it very hard to find another way into the nearest town. Long distance buses and trains, and especially ferries in those parts of the world where water is a characteristic feature, on the other hand, are often very suitable for accessing important points on your route by bike.

Reaching Your Starting Point

When traveling to the starting point on public transportation, consider that major towns and cities—I'd say anything with more than 60,000 inhabitants—can be very frustrating to cyclists from elsewhere. Finding your way in or out of such a place can be a veritable nightmare in almost any country. For that reason, I suggest you do not book your trip to such a place but to a minor town nearby that is served by the same line of public transportation, even if that means taking a slower train or bus that stops where the express line does not.

It is of course possible to reach virtually any area by car, carrying the bike. However, there are two hitches. Firstly, you will have to return to the same point for the return journey. Secondly, there is a significant risk to the car. What will happen to it when you leave it overnight or for a couple of weeks? I've once had the experience myself. Having left the car at a gas station for a weekend, I was forced to return after less than an hour. Imagine my surprise to observe how the engine was just being removed, obviously to be exchanged for an older and defective one of the same make and model. Just make sure you leave the car with someone you can trust, or take adequate precautions if you can't.

Direction of Route

Whether this will be a long tour or a short one, consider such factors as the wind direction. There are maps for all parts of the world that show prevailing winds. With the help of these, you should be able to select your route in windy parts to benefit from them as much as possible. Remember that in most regions the winds tend to increase in strength as the day progresses. This means that riding against the prevailing wind in the morning or at night will be a lot easier than it is late afternoon. On the coast, the wind tends to be directed towards the sea in the morning and inland in the evening. Use this kind of knowledge to your benefit when deciding which route to follow.

Reading the Map

There are three different types of maps that are suitable for your purpose at different times, as shown in Fig. 14.1: topographic maps, road maps and street maps. The former show the geographic features most accurately but lack a lot of information

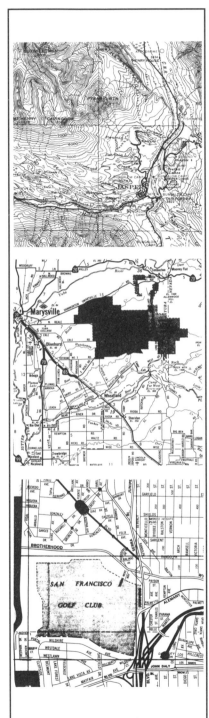

*Fig. 14.1 Comparison of map types.
From top to bottom: topographic map,
road map, street map.*

pertaining to roads and other man-made features. The road maps emphasize just these aspects, while the street maps show even more detail about roads and buildings in built up areas, including specific street names and traffic details such as one-way systems.

For cycling on regular roads in or near populated areas, the road map will generally be the most suitable, whereas topographic maps are more suitable for off-road use or other trips in less frequently traveled terrain. Street maps will help you find your way in cities if they can not be avoided, as should probably be done wherever possible. For shorter trips you may be able to make do with a singe map, while a longer trip in strange surroundings may require a minor library of maps. These may in part be purchased back home, whereas some others can only be obtained locally.

Next to the type of map used, its scale will be the most important feature. That is the ratio between the distance as measured on the map and the corresponding distance in the terrain. For shorter trips in populated areas the most useful one for cycling will be a road map to scale 1 : 100,000, where one cm on the map corresponds to one km on the road (or one inch equals about 1.6 miles). Longer tours will be best covered on road maps to scale 1 : 200,000.

Other scales do have their uses for the cyclist as well. For off-road touring you will need even more detailed topographic maps, say to scale 1 : 50,000 (one cm equals 0.5 km or one inch equals 0.8 miles). Street maps may have a scale like 1 : 25,000, where one cm equals 0.25 km or one inch equals 0.4 mile. The large scale geographical map used for initial planning will have a scale totally unsuitable for cycling, representing large distances in the field by tiny distances on the map, which makes it impossible to show useful details en route.

The most important things on any map are its date of last revision and the legend. Before using any map, first check whether it is reasonably up-to-date, and then get familiar with the particular legend and the symbols used. The legend varies from one series of maps to the other, and any time spent studying it before the trip will save you no end of frustration and errors later on out on the road. For the same reason, I suggest you rely as much as possible on maps from the same series.

For road maps to cover any place in the U.S., those published by the various state or regional automobile associations are often highly suitable, though their scales vary quite a bit, depending on the size of the state or the region they cover. In other countries you will find various series of maps, such as the rightfully famous Michelin maps used in many European countries or those published by Bartholomew for Great Britain and Ireland.

Map Features

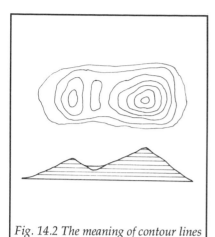

Fig. 14.2 The meaning of contour lines

Some important features for cyclists shown on some maps but not on others include elevations and railway lines. Elevations may be either given in the form of figures or contour lines. Contour lines are most useful to cyclists if they show intervals no greater than 20 meters or 50 feet. This generally means the corresponding maps are to scale 1 : 50,000 or less. The principle is shown in Fig. 14.2: contour lines represent imaginary slices at elevation intervals, each connecting all points at the same height. The more lines are crossed by a road, the greater the elevation difference; the closer they are together, the steeper the climb or descent.

When planning your route, keep the elevation differences in mind and avoid them as much as possible. When unavoidable, you may actually find steeper sections easier to climb than to descend, given the same elevation difference. The short steep section can be taken on the bike, while a very steep descent may actually force you to get off, since it could be too dangerous to stay on the bike if it is heavily loaded and you are not perfectly in control.

To give you an idea of the effect of elevation differences on your cycling performance, refer to Fig. 14.3. It shows the equivalent distances that can be covered at different speeds with the same energy needed to surmount certain differences in elevation. In effect, you may be able to travel a little further in hilly terrain than this graph would suggest, since you will usually benefit from the elevation difference on the downhill sections. However, the benefit on the way down is always less than the hindrance on the way up. There is no doubt that progress is slower in the hills than one would estimate just looking at the map without considering the differences in elevation.

Elevation markings are not the only characteristic features, but they are quite important. If the map contains no other aids, learn to estimate by other features whether a road will be steep

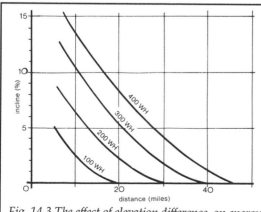

Fig. 14.3 The effect of elevation difference on energy expenditure and distance.

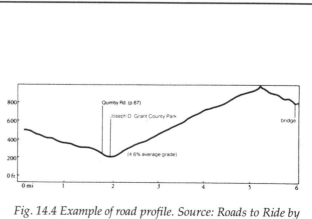

Fig. 14.4 Example of road profile. Source: Roads to Ride by Grant Peterson and John Kluge, Heyday Books, Berkeley.

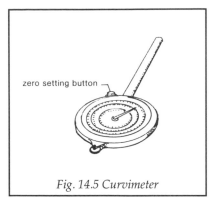

Fig. 14.5 Curvimeter

or not. Snaking roads and suddenly decreasing building and road density are often indicative of mountains. Rivers generally flow relatively gently downhill, while artificial waterways tend to follow the contours of the terrain. Railways often get up and down the hills by the easiest route, as does a road closely parallel.

On the other hand, watch out for the tricks the designers of roads, railways and canals may have played on you: you can't follow the trains through tunnels or over bridges and viaducts. Though any canal has a tow path for maintenance, it may be barred to the public and it may be interrupted or unsuitable for cycling in critical places, such as aqueducts, locks and tunnels. Similarly, beware of nature's tricks: though all rivers flow downhill, there may not be enough room for a road right next to it.

To get a good idea of the distance involved, even at this early planning stage, an additional aid in the form of a curvimeter can be recommended. This device, shown in Fig. 14.5, is used to measure the length of the trip by making its little wheel follow exactly the route on the map, starting after you've set it to zero. The dial is calibrated in a number of different scales, so make sure you read it off at the correct one, as verified by checking with the marked distance in the legend block on the map.

Other Sources of Information

Although the map is no doubt the most useful planning device, it should by no means be the only one. Certainly for areas with which you are not yet fully conversant, I recommend getting some background information from regular tourist guide books. This way, you will get more out of a tour, since you are generally better informed. In addition, there are special bicycle guides. One useful feature often contained in such manuals is a road profile, such as the example shown in Fig. 14.3. This makes it clear very quickly what kind of elevation differences a certain road section has in store for you.

Getting maximum information from maps and guides is not only a matter of studying them ahead of time, it is also a matter of regular use while traveling. Only if you frequently consult the map while traveling, rather than blindly following the road and the signs, will you develop a true appreciation of the benefits offered by various kinds of maps. Consult them frequently and consciously to really benefit from the specific map used, and to appreciate the features that make one map more useful than another. These abilities will greatly help when it comes to finding your way and when planning the next tour.

Part III.

The Practice of Bicycle Touring

CHAPTER 15

Expanding Your Horizons

The chapters of this third part of the book are all concerned more directly with the practical aspects of various forms of bicycle touring. In the present chapter, I shall describe the various ways of bike touring in some more detail, suggesting how you may progress from simple trips to more challenging rides. You will be encouraged to expand your experience to whatever form of touring you choose. Subsequent chapters will deal quite specifically with the various aspects and day-to-day experiences in the many different situations encountered when touring by bike.

As is the case with so many things, even the most demanding type of bike touring can be done without much preparation. On the other hand, it is the consensus of most cyclists with limited time budgets that the instruction gained from talking to others or reading a book like the present is worth every minute, as is a modicum of preparation and the attention to equipment covered in the preceding parts of the book. It will be more enjoyable if you set out adequately prepared.

Getting Ready to Tour

No need to overdo the preparation bit, especially if it is physical fitness you are worried about. I recently read an article in a U.S. cycling magazine, in which a woman cyclist described the agony she went through to work up to her long bike tour. Before going on her journey, this lady desperately tried for months to get fit by spending literally hours each day punishing herself on a home

At Cap des Rosiers, Quebec. (photo Kimberlee Caledonia)

trainer. That's quite ridiculous: except for the utterly feeble, every normal human being is fit enough to go on even quite extensive tours without a special training program. I'm not saying you'll be able to race or keep up with crack athletes, but you should definitely be able to cover distances long enough to give you the sensation of real touring without any special preparatory exercising.

One of my friends set out many years ago on a continental crossing. He astonished all by completing the tour without all the special fitness aids suggested before departure. On the first day he covered a modest distance, and he felt a little sore the next day. But within a week he was daily covering distances that compared favorably with those achieved by much more experienced and trained riders. You don't have to go on a tour from coast to coast, but even a two or three week vacation is long enough to allow you to get into the proper shape as you go along.

Even if you do feel the desire to prepare yourself physically, the obsession with home trainers and wind load simulators, used by some to prepare for their big tour, is totally superfluous. It's simply the wrong way to go about it. A thirty minute exercise bout on one of these machines is a deadly bore, and yet the training benefit for the average person intent on touring is virtually nil. Sure enough, these devices can be used to advantage within an athletic training program. However, the practice it takes to participate in individual or organized bike tours is much more quickly, effectively and enjoyably gained riding a real bike on a real road.

Along the Dempster Highway, Yukon. (photo Dan Gindling)

Whereas on a home trainer you can at best train the few muscles that directly affect the pedaling motion, real life cycling involves the entire process of movement, force, balancing, steering, orientation, fresh air and interest. Who, short of a few insecure crackpots, would feel so insecure as to forego this much wider experience for fear of being physically insufficiently up to the task? Of course, you may be one of those, but I recommend going about it more practically. It is both more effective and more satisfying.

Of all the forms of preparation that are appropriate for bike touring, bicycle commuting is perhaps the most effective. Instead of a twenty-minute car trip or a thirty-minute bus commute, getting to work on the bike will take a little longer. Don't see that as commuting time lost, but rather as cycling time gained. Even if the commute takes ten or twenty minutes longer, at the same time you'll be gaining perhaps 40 minutes or so of true cycling experience. Possibly the beginning cyclist does not feel up to doing this, yet it's a lot more enjoyable and practical than sweating madly on a home trainer will be. You'll be much better prepared for your touring and you'll probably feel fitter and happier all year. It not only strengthens your heart and muscles more effectively than can be done on the home trainer, it also improves your bike handling skills.

From Casual Rides to Day Trips

Even though it is quite possible to start a long tour without extensive cycling experience, it may be smarter to start off with relatively short rides close to your home. This way you will develop an appreciation of the bicycle and the feeling of riding continuously before starting on more demanding tours. It is worth noting in this context that the typical casual ride by people who are not dedicated cyclists is less than two miles in length, while even a one-hour continuous ride will cover about six to ten times as much, depending on the speed of travel. Clearly then, continuous cycling presents a different experience to those who are used to riding a bike only casually.

Don't set out on what will become your first real trip without some defined plan of where to go and how to get there. Choose the distance on the basis of the time available, the points worth cycling to and your ambition. Having a destination is far preferable to just cycling aimlessly. Visiting a beach, a restaurant, a picnic site, a winery, a park, a zoo or a museum—all are likely goals, as are a hundred other places you can probably come up with that are located within reasonable cycling reach even for an out-and-out beginner.

Even on a short trip like this, taking perhaps only an hour there and another hour back, go through the entire planning and preparation process recommended in the various chapters of Part II. Decide when and where to go, which roads to follow, what to take and what to do once you get there. Plan your timing, and consider the contingencies in case one thing or the other does not go according to plan. Pack the food, equipment

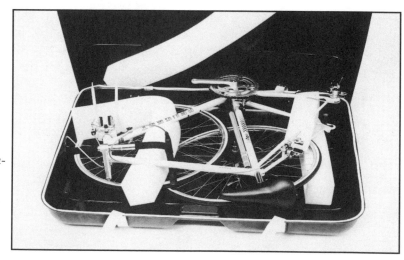

Conveying your bike first class— in a reinforced plastic case. This rectangular case is more convenient than many bike-shaped cases because it can be stacked with other luggage. On the other hand, a cardboard box is even more practical because it can be discarded once you get to your destination.

173

and supplies you want to take along properly, dress right, plan your route and take the appropriate map. If you get into the habit of doing this consistently and systematically right from the start, it will enable you to get ready for longer tours just as systematically and effectively.

You may choose to go on rides of this type alone or in groups. It is my observation that it is probably more enjoyable to first gain some experience alone, and then ride with others who are at least equally experienced. Riding with a whole group of greenhorns may seem like a lot of fun, but often becomes extremely frustrating, since you will probably spend disproportionately many hours waiting for all the other yoyos to get their act together. No need to feel superior, since they'll spend as much time waiting for you. It's just that you'll all delay one another at different times. When starting out alone, you only have to deal with your own inefficiency.

Once you have been on a few excursions like this under the most favorable conditions—selecting nice days, easy terrain and modest distances—start venturing further afield. Go on some rides in more challenging terrain, in less friendly weather, over longer distances or at a higher speed. Then extend the duration of your rides, moving up from trips taking a few hours to half-day and whole day tours. As distances and terrain get tougher, you may have to start carrying more luggage, and invest more thought into planning and preparation. If all is well, you will also start noticing that cycling becomes both more natural and more enjoyable as your level of experience increases.

Overnight Trips

The next stage, for which you may be ready anytime from one to three months after you start bike touring, will be tours that take you over such distances that overnight stays have to be considered. That will also involve more luggage and more preparation. To the insecure it may be a good idea to try a dry run first, taking the kind of luggage needed for an overnight trip, pretending to stay overnight but returning the same day just the same. Some people camp out in their own back yard before they go out on a camping trip, and I see nothing wrong with it.

If your dry run works out, and you establish that you haven't forgotten items that would be essential if it were for real, it will be time to start doing some real two-day tours. The less insecure rider will have little inhibition doing this kind of thing with less practice. It should be easy enough, considering you probably live in a society where real hardship can be avoided with the aid of a credit card or a telephone call.

Decide whether you want to stay in a hotel, motel or hostel, or whether you want to camp out. Consider whether there will be any need to make advance reservations, which may well be the case in some popular areas. In addition to the regular kinds of accommodation just mentioned, you may consider some of the alternatives geared specifically or in part to touring cyclists. In this vein, it may be smart to join a national touring organization, such as Bikecentennial or the LAW in the U.S., or the CTC in Britain. Many of these organizations operate either organized systems of overnight accommodations or a referral service that allows you to find cheap accommodations, or in some cases a free place to roll out your sleeping bag.

Then there is the question of where to go in more general terms. I suggest you do not choose the kind of destination where everybody else also seems to go, since those areas are invariably overrun with motorists and other tourists. Just the same, destinations booked full for people traveling by car may offer accommodations to those who arrive on a bike. That's not unreasonable, since in many cases the facility's capacity is not limited by the number of persons, but rather by the number of cars that can be accommodated. So when making reservations or inquiries, be sure to mention that you will be traveling by bike.

Go on a number of weekend tours like this. Better yet, if you have the opportunity and the time, take two- or three-day tours at mid-week, when fewer people are competing for a place on the road and at the popular destinations. First get to know the areas within the range of sixty miles or so from your home that can be conveniently reached by bike in a half-day ride, while allowing a return trip in comfort the next day. This eliminates a lot of the time-consuming and potentially troublesome decisions regarding transportation to and from the starting point of the tour.

Even if you live in an part of the world that doesn't rate high as a cycling paradise, you are quite likely to find plenty of good touring opportunities on these rides. You will get to know the area well through cyclist's eyes. This experience will also greatly help you think of suitable shorter rides in your home region that do not require overnight stays. By and by, you may start venturing out on longer tours, tackling greater distances and perhaps starting further away, interfacing with public transportation systems or using some kind of carpooling technique if you travel in a group. This latter method can also be used with one car accompanying the cyclists or following them at some distance. This way, you may either take turns driving or perhaps one member of the group may actually prefer driving a car to bike touring.

Longer Tours

Once you have gotten to know the area around your own home base, venture out further afield. First expand your radius to perhaps a hundred miles or more on day and weekend trips of one, two or three days. Next, you may want to travel in more remote

175

areas. Of course, all this is assuming you want to expand your cycling horizons: be my guest if you prefer to stay closer to home. Again, this can be done without all this gradual preparation, but I feel it is advantageous to combine your progress in bicycle touring with the experience of getting to know your own region as a present or potential cycle touring terrain.

In my native Holland, I could not ride more than 100 miles in any one direction without leaving the country, yet I went on literally hundreds of day and weekend rides before I felt obliged to venture abroad. Perhaps your area is less bicycle-oriented than the low countries, where a thousand towns and a hundred thousand miles of various types of roads are contained in a compact area free from really insurmountable natural or man-made bicycle barriers. But even if paradise seems to be far off, suitable bike touring conditions are more prevalent than most people realize.

Your first vacation tours, therefore, must not necessarily take you very much further afield either, although you may prefer to try more distant destinations right away. It will be up to you. But, whether going far or staying near, the type of planning and preparation should be similar. Use the guidelines in the preceding chapters for selecting the route, choosing what to take along and learning how to pack it on the bike. Once you've started, simply expand upon your own experiences to progress from a greenhorn to a confident and competent touring cyclist.

In the remaining chapters of the book, I will present many of the particular aspects that apply most specifically to the longer tours. It will make some difference whether you travel alone or in a group, with adults or children, whether you use a regular bike and travel on well-paved roads or a mountain bike cross-country. There will be different things to consider when touring abroad or at home, when cycling in summer or in the off-season.

In connection with all vacation tours further away from home, you will be confronted with the problem of reaching your destination with your machine. Some more remarks on the subject of transportation—specifically with respect to getting the bike to your destination—are contained in the section entitled *Getting There with Your Bike* in Chapter 19, which deals primarily with foreign travel. The remarks about bike rental there should also be regarded as a suggestion for domestic travel, assuming you can find out in advance whether adequate equipment will be available for rent.

Bike Touring as a Way of Life

All these situations are merely variations on the same theme, and the basic skill of bike touring is not lost on any of these options. Perhaps you will go camping on one tour, whereas you may decide to stay in hotels, motels or hostels at other times. On one

trip you may travel in a familiar society, where it is both easy to
find your way and remains reasonably safe, even if you do get
lost. Another tour may take you to another scene or another
country, where getting lost is the order of the day and the problem of survival may be very real.

Another, though very modest variation on the general bicycle
touring theme is the mid-week evening ride. Certainly in summer and spring, the days are generally long enough to allow
plenty of time for quite extensive bike rides after completion of a
typical working or studying day. Plan your time properly, know
where you want to go and pack your stuff ahead of time. You can
go on a ride of thirty, forty miles or more. It can be combined
with an evening picnic, a trip to the beach or a game of baseball.
Not very ambitious, but one of those additional treats that makes
life so much more enjoyable than merely following the same old
routine.

That is the one extreme, the simple bike trip that can be conducted without much planning or special equipment. On the
other extreme are those really long tours that most people dream
of but never actually carry out. I have experienced both types,
and can't honestly say whether the one is necessarily superior to
the other. Of course, I still have the most vivid memories of some
of my early really long foreign tours. However, the little trips
that are easily conducted and involve nothing more exciting than
many of our other leisure activities perhaps contribute quite significantly to our general feeling of living a meaningful and enjoyable life. Don't neglect those little rides, assuming they don't
compare to real bicycle touring.

On longer tours you may learn to get around in countries
where languages are spoken that you will never even begin to
understand. You may encounter customs and opinions that seem

*Global bike traveler's steed. That's what
it takes to cross the desert. (photo
Dieter Glokowski)*

strange or threatening. But all of these situations can be mastered even by normal mortals, providing you take the trouble to think about what you are doing and how it affects the options available. You can become a really experienced cyclist, whether you travel far or near. You may choose to become a veritable globetrotter, or you may prefer instead to restrict your cycling to more accessible regions and congenial societies. Whatever your choice, you'll enjoy almost any bicycle touring experience if you are well prepared and remain conscious of the problems and advantages offered by the bicycle as a means of getting around.

CHAPTER 16

Finding Your Way

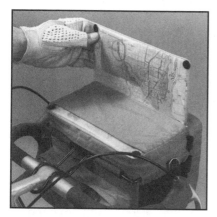

Consult the map frequently right from the start, so you know where you are before you get lost.

In addition to the information imparted in Chapter 14 about planning the route ahead of time, you probably need some practical advice on the subject of orientation. Having mapped out the route is only one aspect of this complex: you will also have to carry out those plans. And, what is perhaps at least equally relevant, you have to find your way once you get out there on the bike. Or you may have to get back when you do get lost despite your gallant efforts to plan ahead and follow the map. These will be the subjects covered in the present chapter.

For most people the problem occurs relatively infrequently in familiar terrain, unless you happen to be punished with the same abominable lack of sense of orientation from which I suffer. In fact, I may be the best guide to the subject, precisely *because* I have so much trouble finding my way myself. As you move further and further away from the straight and narrow, venturing out into remote regions and indeed in foreign lands, you will experience an ever-increasing need for a systematic approach and some additional aids to orientation. In addition to the following remarks, you may find some of the references on the subject that I have included in the Bibliography to be helpful.

Preliminary Orientation

The time to start your orientation work is before you set out on any ride. It will be best if you make an effort of always deciding ahead of time where you intend to go. Before setting out, consult a map and call up in your mind's eye where the various landmarks and points of reference will be relative to your route at different places along your path. Go over the remarks about maps and route planning in Chapter 14 again, so you know how to choose the right map and get the greatest benefit possible from its use.

If you make a habit of doing this work even on relatively simple trips close to home, you will soon develop the systematic approach that allows you to do the same work effectively when you really have to depend on it. Only the person who has frequently gone through the process of consulting a map and planning his route will be able to do it almost unconsciously when it really matters, particularly when traveling in more remote or difficult terrain.

Of course, remote and difficult are not necessarily the same. Very often, it will be much easier to find your way in an area with only few roads than it is in regions that are criss-crossed by

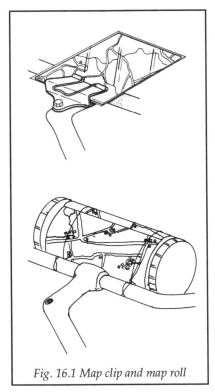

Fig. 16.1 Map clip and map roll

roads leading in all conceivable directions. On the other hand, you should not underestimate the potential difficulty of orientation in areas with only few roads, especially if these few roads wind their way around, up and down and along the slopes of hills, without clear views and devoid of easily recognizable landmarks. You could be traveling down the wrong road for many miles before you find out.

In the pre-tour planning stage, estimate the distances of the various sections of the ride and the nature of the terrain for each section, on the basis of the information gleaned from the map. Also try to see ahead of time whether one landmark or another should be to your left or your right, close by or far away, clearly visible or mostly hidden. Establish whether you should be going uphill or down, traveling through open terrain, woods or built-up areas in particular sections of the ride. Use the position of the sun as a major rough guide if you don't carry a compass, which indeed seems superfluous for touring in most accessible areas.

Especially try to envision the significant points directly along the road: railway crossings, bridges, intersections and outstanding buildings. All this may seem trivial, and indeed it probably is—as long as you are traveling in familiar or well-serviced terrain. After all, in those areas there will probably also be signs telling you which way to go, or there may be people to ask. However, only by consciously taking notice of these features on the basis of your map and pre-tour planning before you leave, will you be able to orient yourself independently once you are traveling. And if that is not significant on your first rides close to home, it certainly will become more important once you venture out further afield.

Orientation Aids

If you have a good memory, you may be able to store all the information pertaining to the pre-planning in your mind. I don't, so I can't. If you should be anything as uncoordinated as I am, you will do well to write a list, summarizing the plan of your route. Keep a systematic list of the directions, landmarks, distances and major reference points in their relative positions on a sheet of paper that can be consulted as you go along. With enough experience—a dozen trips is all it takes—you should be able to write so systematic and comprehensive a list, that you can usually find your way without constant reference to a map. Just the same, don't go out without one.

By way of orientation for longer trips, especially abroad or in other areas further away from home, I suggest you also consult an overall map of the particular region, state or country. Such a map will not be much use when actually cycling—a typical scale for such a map will perhaps be around 1 : 1,000,000, whereas good cycling maps are about 1 : 200,000, i.e. five times more detailed. However, this rough scale map will help you get a feel for the general picture, making you aware of the relationships between towns and mountains, roads and railways, mountains, shores and rivers, forests and plains. Prepare the overall route on this map, and refer to the more detailed one for each daily section.

In addition to one or more maps, you may want to use another simple planning tool at this preliminary stage, namely the curvimeter discussed in Chapter 14. Set it to zero and make the little wheel follow the planned route as accurately as possible, reading out the distances from the appropriate scale on the dial for each section and the overall trip length. It will probably show about 10% less than the distance in the field will register, but it is a convenient guide to the distances to be covered. If you don't use such a tool, you may be able to achieve an adequately accurate estimation with the aid of the map's printed scale and such rough tools as a matchstick. If you add 15–25%, depending on the relative directness of the roads, the result will be accurate enough for a rough preliminary estimate.

Reading the Map

Of course, reading the map starts as early as the preliminary planning stage. However, the practical problems are more relevant once you get out on the road. Certainly if your route plan is less than firm in your mind, or imperfectly summarized on a sheet of paper, you will need to consult the map frequently. Keep it easily accessible, for example in a clip on your handlebars or in the transparent pocket that is provided on the top of many handlebar bags. Or you may make up a reference roll, attached to the handlebars, around which the map is wrapped. If nothing more convenient is available, carry the map in the back pocket of your cycling shirt and don't forget to pull it out frequently for consultation. Keep it folded with the currently relevant section facing out, and protect it against dirt, rain and perspiration by means of a transparent pouch—a plain plastic bag, closed off with adhesive tape, will do the trick.

Recognizing Map Features

Take the characteristics of the map used for planning into consideration. Pay attention to the scale, so you get a feel for the distance or the corresponding traveling time represented by a particular distance on the map. If you have no other guide, measure the scale and the distance in terms of matchstick lengths. Also note that road maps tend to overemphasize the roads, representing them and other road-related information so much that often more significant features are in danger of being overlooked. Thus, the actual configuration of a curve or an intersection, or the relative widths of supposedly minor and major roads, may vary quite a bit from the actual situation in the field. In that respect, topographic maps are much more realistic.

Remember also that each series of maps follows some conventions that are typical for them only. Consequently, it will be smart to try and adhere to maps from the same source as much as possible. If you will be traveling for several days or long one-day rides, and ride on regular roads rather than on minor unpaved cross-country trails, I suggest choosing maps drawn to a scale of about 1 : 200,000. Some people prefer them even more detailed, except that you'd need a trailer full of printed matter to keep up a longer tour.

Also check the date of last revision on the maps you intend to use. If it is too old, you may run into difficulties, especially near built-up areas, where man's industry often outpaces the geographer's pen. Typical examples are the ferry service that has in the meantime been discontinued or the regular road that has been expanded into a freeway, making it off-limits to cyclists.

Although some people like to keep their map looking fresh as the day they bought it, I find it handier to use it for making some of my notes. Certainly the points of interest you definitely want to visit can be marked in on the map at an early stage. This makes it much easier to plan your route so as not to miss them, even if your route is changed on account of other events. I also like to mark the locations of my overnight stays and longer stops, indicating the appropriate date. This will help you gauge your progress as you are traveling. It also helps greatly at a later stage, when it is time to gather the mementos of your tour, as described in Chapter 23.

Map Use in the Field

Practice is the key to effective map use, as it is to so many other aspects of bicycle touring—or any other of life's challenges, for that matter. And though it may seem trivial, you will be best prepared for tricky situations if you start consulting the map well before you need it badly. That means several things. In the first place, you can make frequent use of the map, even in areas where you could also find your way around without it, so you are familiar with the specific map and conversant with orientation when the need arises. Secondly, you should consult the map frequently as you are traveling, so you always know where you should be on the map to avoid getting lost.

The latter point is a quite useful. It will generally be easy enough to find your way, if you can immediately define up to where your position had been verified with the map. But once you realize that you are lost and have no idea how long or how far you have been erring, you may have a very hard time indeed retracking your paces. Conscious cycling is the secret in this respect too. Know during each stage whether you are still where the map suggests you should be. If the next crossing on the map is supposed to be within a mile, you can conclude you went the wrong direction at the last junction if you haven't reached a crossing after two miles.

In the latter case, you only have to go back the two miles to the last junction where you know you must have gone wrong. If you don't know where you took the wrong turn, you may be forced to aimlessly search for many miles before you have even established where you went wrong, let alone how to get back on the correct and proper course. All in all, you will be less likely to get lost and more likely to find your way back if you are thoroughly familiar with the use of your map.

Other Orientation Aids

Maps are not the only tools that may be used to find your way around when bicycle touring. The curvimeter, described in Chapter 14, is of some limited use in orientation, as well as in planning. To keep track of the distances in the field and how they compare to the map, it will be handy to install a speedometer or merely an odometer on the bike, particularly if you can make a habit of keeping track of distances between landmarks and road junctions as you go along. Remember though, that the rougher the map's scale and the hillier the terrain, the greater the discrepancy between the distance measured on the map and the actual distance, which will usually be quite a bit more.

Two other useful devices are binoculars and a compass. The former can help you locate or identify landmarks further afield. Nowadays, small binoculars of very high quality that are light enough to be taken on the bike are readily available. The compass will do a lot more useful things than merely show which way is north. It usually comes complete with an instruction manual, which is worth working your way through before setting out on your first tour, so you get the maximum benefit.

If you don't carry a compass—and I know of very few cyclists who do—there is another simple way to guess the direction. South is where the sun is around twelve noon in the northern hemisphere, and for each hour earlier the sun is 15 degrees further East, for each hour later it is as much further west. Of course, this guideline is most reliable when the sun is relatively low, that is in the spring or fall, or further away from the equator. And in a rainstorm it may be little consolation to know you could find your way—if only the sun would come out.

In addition, you should establish where you are in your particular time zone, relative to its center. That can make a difference of up to 7.5 degrees either way. Finally, in this regard, make an allowance for daylight savings time, called summer time in most parts of the world that use it. It can make an additional difference of 15 degrees. Figure these deviations out before you leave, and summarize the total deviation in a note on your map.

An even simpler aid to orientation is often provided at the state's expense: road signs. In some parts of the world all the preceding advice will seem superfluous, due to society's generosity in putting up adequate directional signs along most roads at virtually all junctions. Even so, you will need a map, since that same thoughtful society may not be aware of your particular short-term destination. As a cyclist, you may not be aiming quite as far as what seems practical to the typical motorist, and your plan may include taking the road in the direction of A only a few miles, followed by a detour in direction B, before finally reaching the road marked for your immediate destination C.

Getting Help

Then there is that other useful orientational institution: asking the way. For the cyclist, there are certain risks involved when following this simple method. One obvious drawback is that most of the potential suppliers of such information are either motorists or pedestrians. The former don't mind making a little detour of twenty miles or so, forget that you can't use the freeway, or don't realize that the shortest way goes over a mountain pass that will take you all day on the bike. The latter, by contrast, often have a very limited perspective on the world. Many pedestrians have no idea how to get to places that are at some distance, and a response like "you can't get there from here…" is indeed not as unlikely as you may think.

Whether questioning motorists or not, there is the risk of being sent to the nearest freeway, which is off-limits to cyclists in most countries. You can't go that way, even if you should be competent enough and willing to put up with the kind of traffic encountered on such a less than rustic road. Another potential problem is that locals often don't know anything about some of the goals that may be of interest to a touring cyclist, which do not necessarily coincide with the places other people want to reach.

Finally there are those areas where most of the passers-by are tourists, who have no idea at all, although most of them at least carry some kind of map. Whatever you do, don't ask anybody the way without consulting the map at the same time, and don't follow any advice without verifying it on the map first. In Chapter 19, you will find a few more remarks that are particularly relevant when trying to find your way abroad.

CHAPTER 17

Food for the Road

Preparing an elaborate roadside picnic. (photo Kimberlee Caledonia)

Compared to the demands of a sedentary lifestyle, bicycle touring is a strenuous affair, and a lot of food is needed to keep you going. Consequently, the questions of what to eat and how to go about it are often raised in cycling circles. Considering that most bike tours are not really all that monstrous in their energy demands, and that most people have acquired an impressive store of body fat, the chance of literally running out of energy supplies is quite remote for the average touring cyclist. What does need to be said will be covered here.

Before getting hung up about the subject, realize that there is hardly a topic about which more nonsense has been written and about which more people hold preconceived notions than that of food and diet. So, at the risk of being accused of adding more of the same, here's my limited view as a touring cyclist. In cycling circles you will encounter staunch vegetarians and veritable carnivores, carrot munchers and pill poppers, all claiming the key to their fitness, endurance or peace of mind lies in the way they fill their bellies. Though the subject is not without interest, I would suggest considering it more soberly: forget about fad diets and concentrate on selecting your food consciously instead.

Although this chapter is pretty concise compared to what is found in any other general cycling book, there is a lot more to the subject. In this context I can recommend Richard Rafoth's book *Bicycling Fuel* (see Bibliography for details).

Diet for Endurance

Especially in America, cyclists typically seem to stem from the same ranks as health food freaks and other diet-conscious people. Nothing wrong with that, but many of the theories propounded in those circles are only relevant for people with a sedentary lifestyle. However, it makes a great difference whether you spend the day lounging about in office, car and home, or spend a good part of each day burning up calories on a loaded bicycle. What the touring cyclist needs is not a diet but a clear understanding of the function of food as it applies to his performance and overall health. Most of all, active cyclists should consider the following facts:

☐ Endurance activity requires much more in the way of calories and allows the kinds of food that would be fattening or otherwise undesirable to the inactive person.

☐ A two or three-week tour does not determine a permanent life style, so your diet should vary, reflecting the energy level required during active and inactive periods, respectively.

☐ As for the supposedly superior nutrients, such as proteins, vitamins and minerals, an active person does not necessarily require more of these than an inactive person of the same weight.

☐ More is not necessarily better: if X grams of protein or Y milligrams of some vitamin or mineral are required, then it does not follow that twice these quantities will improve your health, strength or endurance even one bit.

The Tasks of Food

Your body needs food to function properly. The tasks that must be fulfilled by the things you eat and drink boil down to providing the following:

☐ Energy to keep the body's temperature at the necessary level for the various systems to operate.

☐ Energy needed to perform mechanical work by means of muscle action.

☐ Liquids to conduct heat, to control body temperature and to allow various physiological processes to function.

☐ Building materials needed to grow and replace cell structures.

☐ Enzymes that allow the other processes to operate efficiently.

Types of Food

The most important substances to ingest so these functions can be carried out are listed as follows:

- Water
- Carbohydrates
- Fats
- Proteins
- Vitamins
- Minerals
- Fiber and bran

In the following sections, each of these major substances will be briefly described, followed by an analysis of the tasks for which the body needs the various types of food and drink. I'll show how the different food substances fit into the complex of functions that must be fulfilled for the human body to operate effectively, especially under such physically demanding conditions as presented by long-distance bicycle touring. Finally, I will give some practical suggestions for solving the food problem en route.

Water About 70% of your body weight is water. It is the major carrier for other substances in the body and is essential for the process of temperature control. Water must be replenished as it evaporates or is excreted. It need not always be taken in the form

186

Food for the road—conveniently packed in the top compartment of a rack-top puck, where it won't get squashed.

of plain water, since it is contained in most foods, especially in fruits, vegetables and meat. And of course almost any beverage provides it quickly.

Many substances needed within the body, such as sugars and minerals, are dissolved in water and pass into the cells by means of osmosis. That is the process of filtering an aqueous solution through a thin membrane. In osmosis, the transfer is always from the side with the higher concentration to the side where it is lower. Consequently, the concentrations of essential substances (such as sugar and in some cases table salt) in the water you drink should be at least as high in the liquid as it is in your body's cells. Thus, the way to introduce sugars is to bind them in what is referred to as an isotonic solution, meaning it has at least the same concentration of dissolved materials as the liquid in the body cells.

Water is particularly important for regulating the body's temperature. During vigorous cycling in hot weather, the cyclist may lose water faster than the rate at which his system can possibly absorb it. Half a liter, or about one pint, per hour is all the body will absorb, while it may evaporate at twice that rate. To keep the body at the optimal temperature for muscular and mental work, water is required. Whenever the temperature threatens to get too high, the pores and sweat glands are opened and perspiration is excreted, the natural evaporation of which cools the body.

Especially in hot weather and on long exhausting rides, you may need more water than you can carry in bottles on the bike. Start drinking well before the start, and drink frequently in moderate quantities during the ride. Allow perspiration to evaporate, rather than wiping it off. Since water is also an excellent medium to tie up sugars and electrolytes isotonically, it is frequently suggested to carry two bottles on a hot and exhausting ride: one with plain water for cooling, the other with a water-based mixture containing 2–2.5% sugar and up to a teaspoonful of table salt per pint. Personally, I prefer natural fruit juice over this man-made mixture. It serves the same purpose but tastes a lot better.

Carbohydrates This predominant energy source, comprising both sugars and starch, is present in virtually all foods. The difference between sugar and starch is that the latter takes about two hours longer to provide energy, as it must be turned into usable sugar first, while most sugars can be taken up in the bloodstream very shortly after they are consumed. However nice it may seem to get something that works quickly, starch-rich foods are preferable over sugars, since they also provide other nutrients and keep the

187

body's digestive system in better trim. They should be the staple of the active cyclist's diet.

Particularly rich sources of starch are all grain products and potatoes. Yet starches are also contained in virtually all other vegetables and in meat. Natural sugars are contained in most fruits and honey, while refined sugars are provided only too generously by just about all ready-made foods and drinks. Whether natural or refined, they provide energy equally efficiently—ordinary refined sugar at the lowest cost. Though you may want to take a sugared drink for quick energy on the road, try to avoid sugars in your everyday diet, except in the form of fruits and natural juices, which also contain other valuable nutrients and digestive aids.

Fats as Food   Although justly derided as a no-good in the inactive person's diet, fat is the most energy-efficient nutrient, which makes it a legitimate food for the endurance cyclist. However, fat as consumed is very slowly digested and converted to energy only indirectly. In the body, fat is used as a store of energy and an insulator. The body converts excess nutrients of any kind into body fat. Nutritive fat is present in meats and dairy products, but also in many nuts, seeds and various other vegetable sources. The distinction between polysaturated and unsaturated fats is probably not as significant to the active cyclist as it is to the sedentary person.

Fat can be used as an energy source in the form of free fatty acids (FFA), dissolved from the stored body fat. These are carried in the blood stream and are used for energy much like sugar. After it is consumed, the fat first builds up as padding in various places, to be released in the form of FFA as needed to supply energy when work must be done at a certain level. This will be covered in more detail under *Food for Energy* below.

It is probably true that the majority of people in the western world have accumulated too much body fat. But it is very hard to avoid eating it altogether, since it is tied up with proteins in so many products that we have grown fond of. The tender American steak contains twice as much fat as the tougher stuff consumed in the rest of the world, and it is hard to convince most people they don't need to eat as much meat as they do, or that tougher meat would be better for them.

Protein   Protein comprises various combinations of a group of amino acids. These are contained in meats and dairy products, as well as—though in lesser concentrations—in legumes and grains. For the body to use proteins for cell building, the amino acids must be present simultaneously in a particular ratio, which is most closely approximated by egg white, fish and meat. Other forms of protein foods are only adequately efficient if eaten in some combination of various types, for instance lentils or peas with potatoes, bread with milk, or beans with rice.

Contrary to popular belief, cyclists don't need more protein than other people of the same age and body weight. Only about 1 g of protein is required per day for each kg of body weight. Slightly more may be needed by growing youngsters, pregnant women and during the initial building-up phase when a previously inactive person first takes up cycling, developing new muscle tissue. Most American adults get enough protein to allow for these instances. On the other hand, protein deficiency may become a problem on a long tour, especially in other countries, when you rely too much on food that is either simple to prepare or easy to find ready-made.

Excess proteins—those that are not used for cell building—are simply burned up to provide energy or stored in the form of body fat, much like carbohydrates. A crying shame, since proteins are on average five times as expensive and considerably harder to digest. For the latter reason, protein-rich meals should not be eaten during or shortly before really hard trips. Breakfast and lunch should be heavy on starches, minerals, vitamins and bran, whereas they should be low on fats and protein. The best time to eat meals containing more protein is perhaps about 6–7 PM: late enough not to interfere with demanding physical activity, yet early enough to be digested before the night.

Vitamins Vitamins are primarily a group of acids, required in small quantities to provide the enzymes necessary for operation of various functions. They are divided into water soluble and fat soluble types. The water soluble vitamins (B and C) leave the body quickly in the urine, so they must be replenished daily, while the fat soluble ones (A, D, E and K) can be stored in the body over longer periods. Various vitamins are contained mainly in fresh fruits and vegetables, organ meats and whole grain products. A well-balanced and varied diet provides all the essential vitamins you ever need.

Consequently, there is probably no need for vitamin supplements if you have an adequate variety of vitamin-containing foods in your diet, and there is no need to take vitamin tablets even during the toughest rides. Especially the fat soluble vitamins should be taken in moderation to avoid large build-ups with questionable effects on your health. The water soluble vitamins B and C, being necessary for energy production in the body, may have to be supplemented if performance falls off and no other cause is evident. Since any excess of these is excreted, there's no risk of getting too much. In some cases you may benefit by taking modest doses of multi-vitamin tablets on a regular basis, certainly if you are for some reason not able to adhere to a properly balanced food intake during a prolonged tour.

Minerals Also referred to as electrolytes, some minerals are required in small quantities for enzyme functions. Those that are only required in the minutest quantities are referred to as trace elements. Most are present mainly in vegetables, fruits and grains. The most familiar of these elements is the sodium that becomes free when ordinary table salt dissolves in water. Others, such as potassium, calcium, and iron (the latter needed as a carrier of oxygen in blood and certain muscle fiber cells) are equally needed. Since these electrolytes are water soluble, their excess is excreted with urine and perspiration. Consequently, after a very long and hard ride in hot weather, a case may be made for their replacement if heavy perspiration depletes their levels below their required minimum concentration in the body.

Back in the early 70s a medical layman analyzed perspiration, assuming all substances lost in it should be replaced. No medical evidence has ever been presented to support this assumption, but that has not stopped dozens of manufacturers from introducing similar potions. They are all expensive and taste awful, containing too much sugar and useless electrolytes. Totally unnecessary of course: the water and sugar can be provided in a more appetizing form and better balanced proportions, while the only electrolytes that matter (sodium and potassium) can be replenished by adding some table salt in hot weather and by eating a banana, respectively. Beyond that, eating a reasonably balanced diet will take care of all your electrolyte needs.

Fiber and Bran Fibrous materials, which are contained largely in unprocessed vegetable and grain products, are necessary to stimulate the digestive cycle. With the exercise of your cycling, you will not need it as much as most inactive people, but you may not get enough to feel well. Cycling with clogged intestines is not very enjoyable. Again, the famous balanced diet, with whole grain bread instead of the white pulp usually dished up in most households, cooked and raw vegetables and various fruits, will keep you well supplied. If not, use bran cereals or add bran flakes to other foods. Going for a walk after the main meal also works wonders.

Food for Energy

The overwhelming majority of the food you eat will be used to provide energy—both the heat energy to keep your body warm and the mechanical energy that allows you to do muscle work. Carbohydrates, fat and proteins all lend themselves to that purpose. They can all be converted to the glucose that is transported in the blood or the glycogen that may be stored in the liver and muscle tissue. Thus, they can ultimately all be burned to form the ATP (adenosine triphosphate) that constitutes the raw material for muscle work. However, these three foods are not all equally efficient, and they require different proportions of oxygen to perform their tasks. Furthermore, different kinds of foods—even with similar constituents—require longer or shorter digestion periods before they can be used effectively. Table 17-I summarizes the major differences between the three basic energy sources.

Your Energy Needs

The amount of work expended and the food energy consumed can best be measured in kJ (kiloJoules). To relate this to more familiar units, 4.2 kJ = 1 kcal (kilocalories), which is what's really meant when calories are referred to in older works about nutrition. An average person leading a quiet life needs about 7,000 kJ of energy per day. A hard day's cycling requires up to 4,500 kJ in mechanical energy in addition.

Considering the human engine's efficiency of approximately 25%, that means an additional 18,000 kJ must be provided, adding up to a total daily energy requirement of about 24,000 kJ. That is also just about the maximum your body can take in per day. Any energy expended in excess of this (which may happen in a tough mountain tour or a double century, which is cycling jargon for a 200-mile ride) will go at the expense of your body weight. On the other hand, eating more than enough to supply that will not make you fatter: it goes straight through your system.

As you can tell from Table 17-I, fat is easily the most energy-efficient nutrient, offering twice as much energy per gram as either carbohydrates or protein. The fat you burn passes into the system as free fatty acids (FFA). That's not the fat you have just eaten. Rather, it derives from the stuff that has accumulated in

Food type	Energy content kJ/g	(kCal/g)	RQ	Time to digest hours
carbohydrate	17.2	(4.1)	1.0	
sugars				0.1–2
starch				2–3
fat	38.9	(9.3)	0 .7	6–8
protein	17.2	4.1		6–8

Table 17-I Characteristics of various foods for energy

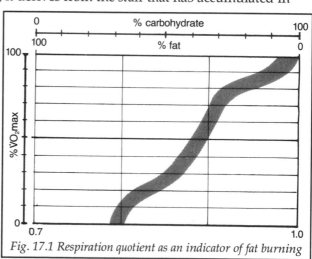

Fig. 17.1 Respiration quotient as an indicator of fat burning

various places in your body. These fat stores are formed by all excess foods not needed for immediate energy supply, which is always converted into fat, except if it exceeds the maximum digestive limit mentioned above. At most levels of output the body uses a combination of free fatty acids and glycogen for aerobic energy production: mainly fat at low levels, mainly glycogen at higher levels, as represented in Fig. 17.1.

RQ: Fat or Carbohydrate

It is possible to determine what proportions of the energy come from fat and carbohydrate metabolisms, respectively, at any time. This is done by comparing the volumes of exhaled carbon dioxide and inhaled oxygen, called RQ (respiratory quotient). If RQ is 1.0, all energy comes from carbohydrates; if it is 0.7, all comes from fat. Any intermediate ratio allows the physiologist to determine how much fat and how much carbohydrates are being burned. On really long exhausting rides, such as mountain tours, the supply of carbohydrates is in danger two ways. At high output levels it is used up first and fastest, and its supply is limited to what can be taken in by the body in a day. You may run out before your destination is reached.

No such problems occur at low output levels, such as relaxed touring rides, where free fatty acids are preferably burned. The supply of fat on even the leanest body will probably suffice to cycle half way around the world at a modest speed. But to the mountain touring cyclist, who has to keep up a high output all day, the supply problem may become evident. Anywhere beyond 75% of his maximum output level, he'll be burning virtually only carbohydrates, as evidenced by an RQ close to 1.0. The glycogen in liver and muscles, the glucose in the blood and the food in the belly are the only energy supplies available. Once these are gone, it's all over.

The obvious way to prolong your energy supply is by reducing your pace to a level below 75% of the maximum, whenever possible. That's one good reason to take it easier by riding sheltered, which may be achieved by taking turns in the front with your companions. This reduces the wind resistance enough to make all the difference on a long fast ride. This tends to shift the balance more towards the fat metabolism.

Caffeine

Finally, there is some evidence that the fat metabolism can be stimulated by taking caffeine. Everything in moderation though: probably not more than 4 mg per kg of body weight (2 mg per lb.). That is the equivalent of about two small cups of strong coffee at the beginning of a hard ride for the average person.

Even when used as suggested, there is a problem with caffeine, since it also works as a diuretic. That means it encourages liquids to leave the body in the form of urine. Consequently, in hot weather, particularly for tours involving a lot of climbing, the excessive use of caffeine may be dangerous: you will need all the water you can drink to act as a cooling medium.

Carbohydrate Loading

Carbohydrate loading is a technique used by some cyclists who want to perform well in a duration activity only once in a blue moon. It's of no use for short or really long rides, nor for vacation tours, and dubious at best even for its intended purpose. The idea, is to exercise to exhaustion several days well before the big events, after which you start eating carbohydrates in generous supplies, without doing very much in the way of hard work. The assumption is that the muscles will absorb lots of carbohydrates in the form of energy-carrying glycogen. For bicycle touring it is a highly questionable technique. Don't fool around with it.

Weight Loss

The quickest, easiest, healthiest and cheapest way to cycle more effectively may be by reducing your body weight. That's assuming you are like most people in the industrialized world, who carry unnecessary ballast in the form of excess fat. The body fat percentage can be accurately determined by means of several techniques, most simply by measuring certain skin folds, which any sports physician or paramedic can do. For a touring cyclist, looking in the mirror will probably suffice. To limit your weight, use a combination of various techniques: eat less and differently, taking more fibrous matter and less fat and sugar; do more physical work in addition to your cycling—walk or use your bike instead of the car, the stairs instead of the elevator.

Only on a very long tour is there any risk of running out of body-stored supplies. Typically, the touring cyclist, however big his appetite, eats a little less than the energy he consumes each day during a longer tour. You can easily verify that by comparing your weight before and after any tour of a week or more. On really long tours—say four weeks or longer—it is conceivable that you eventually use up essentially all stored body fat. This may lead to symptoms similar to those described in Chapter 11 for the overtraining syndrome. If you should develop these symptoms, take it easier for a couple of days and make sure you get a varied and adequate diet.

A Meal Planner

It is possible to eat adequately without any other advice than that contained in the preceding sections. If you follow those suggestions, you'll be adequately prepared for even the toughest bicycle tours. However, for those who prefer some additional guidance, here are some specific hints on how one might divide the required food intake over a touring day.

Breakfast Aim for a high starch intake, combined with vitamins, fibers and minerals, and modest amounts of proteins, avoiding sugars and fat.—fruit or fruit juice, whole grain cereal with a banana or dried fruit, low fat milk or natural plain yogurt, whole grain bread. Try to eat breakfast at least an hour before the start of your tour and at least two hours before really hard mountain climbing sections.

Lunch On the road, aim for a relatively light lunch after a big breakfast, again containing more starch than proteins, avoiding fats and sugars. Eat salad with bread or other starchy foods, combined with small quantities of meat, fish, egg or cheese. A sandwich should not be lots of meat or cheese with a little bread, but rather lots of bread with little meat or cheese and very little in the way of butter, margarine or mayonnaise. Drink plain water, tea or low fat milk, and have a dessert of plain yogurt and fresh fruit.

Supper When bicycle touring, this should be the heaviest meal of the day and the one time to include more protein foods, though it will still be preferable to go easy on tender (read: high-fat) meats. In addition to meat or other protein foods, eat generous quantities of starch foods and fresh or cooked vegetables and fruit. Drink water, tea, natural fruit juice or low fat milk. Hold off on salad dressings, gravies and sauces. Try to have dinner relatively early in the evening. Exercise after dinner, even if it is only a 20 minute walk to help digestion.

Snacks

If the urge strikes during the day, the active cyclist can indulge in snacks between meals. In fact, it will be even wiser to eat six small meals than three big ones during a cycling day. When eating between meals, avoid junk food, though. Instead of sugared and fatty stuff, choose any of the relatively light foods that give you something to munch on and which contain starch, fibers, minerals and vitamins. You can eat fruit, crackers, raw or cooked vegetables and plain yogurt; drink water, tea, low fat milk or unsweetened natural fruit juice.

On the road, it will be smart to have some snacks for nibbling readily accessible. For long rides in relatively deserted terrain, you may also have to carry supplies for at least one meal, sometimes more. Try to adjust your eating pattern to the above recommendations, so the items for lunch are easy to carry, and the meal quickly prepared on the road during a picnic break. The larger meal at night and the preparations for some of the next day's meals can be taken care of at the location of your overnight stay. In the Bibliography, you will find references to some books with recipes for dishes that can be easily prepared on a little camp stove with a minimum of simple ingredients.

CHAPTER 18

Bicycle Camping

Although there are many other suitable forms of accommodation, most touring cyclists end up camping at least some of the time. To be frank about it, I am beginning to have my fill of camping and I enjoy every chance I get to stay in a hotel—with a hot shower, good food and a comfortable bed. But done properly, camping can still be a very enjoyable experience. Without the right equipment, inadequate preparation or with the wrong attitude and expectations, on the other hand, bike camping can be quite frustrating. In the present chapter you will find the advice needed to make your bicycle camping experience a pleasant one.

In most cases, you probably want the emphasis of your trip to be on the cycling. That is perfectly legitimate, providing you pay just enough attention to the camping aspect so it does not result in excessive work or frustration. That would spoil the fun of cycling as well. In short, taking the various considerations necessary to make you as competent a camper as you are a cyclist will be handsomely rewarded. You'll have a more enjoyable touring experience.

Choosing and Packing Your Gear

The correct selection of your camping equipment is of course of utmost importance. In order to handle the selection process most competently, I suggest you read through Chapter 7 once more. In addition, it may be a good idea to get several catalogs from camp-

Bike campers in the Colorado Rockies (Photo David Epperson/Bicycle Sport)

ing and backpacking equipment suppliers. You may also consider the possibility of making some of your own gear. If you are not already an experienced lightweight camper and an accomplished seamster, you should only venture into that particular field with the aid of very thoroughly tested patterns. You may be as impressed as I was with the sew-it-yourself kits developed by the Frostline company.

After solving the equipment selection problem, that of packing it all in the various bags and attaching these to the bike will be the most important. Refer to the relevant advice in Chapter 5 for the selection of bicycle bags and Chapter 13 for the choice of items to take and the way to pack them. If you spend the night in a tent and a sleeping bag, you will have so much more to carry on the bike that all these recommendations become even more critical than they are for other bicycle tours.

Campsites

Assuming you have managed to work out all the equipment and packing questions satisfactorily, you will now be faced with the practice of camping. Even if you have often spent the night outside before, it will not be quite the same as when you are backpacking or traveling by car. Unlike the backpacker, you will probably travel quite significant distances between overnight stops, and your campsites generally have to be those along the road. Many of those, you'll soon learn to your considerable disappointment, are less idyllic than you may have imagined.

In the first place, these sites may be quite far apart, since motorists—for whom these sites are primarily intended—don't mind traveling a hundred miles out of their way. As a cyclist, you probably object to "wasting" even ten miles. In addition, most of these campsites are overrun by people in cars. There'll be lots of trailers (caravans to the English) and mobile homes, not to mention the televisions, refrigerators and other achievements of modern civilization that go wherever motorists penetrate. But there are other drawbacks. In the U.S., I have more than once found campsites paved wall to wall with asphalt, where pitching a tent was plainly impossible.

Even so, all in all, there are enough suitable campsites, though it will be smart to plan your trip carefully to make sure the ones you intend to use are equipped for your kind of use. The positive side of the motorist domination is that there will almost always be a little corner for a cyclist and his tent somewhere, even on a site that is otherwise full. And, as a cyclist, you can more easily pitch your tent outside the official camp sites, much like the backpacker. Certainly in the U.S., where private property is a fetish, I must recommend not doing that on land that appears to be privately owned without specific permission from the owner. In areas where people live near the land they work, it should often be possible to round up the owner, who will rarely object when asked for permission.

Many roadside campsites have the advantage of very sophisticated facilities, though they are often rather expensive. The opportunity to take a shower, do your laundry or buy many of your essential supplies will be particularly welcome to the cyclist. To make maximum use of these advantages, get an up-to-date guide that shows the facilities available at all the campsites in the relevant area.

The biggest problem is that you may have an awfully long way to go if the anticipated facilities are for some reason not available, for instance to obtain the food you thought could be bought locally. However, you can probably find a motorist at the site who will either give you a ride to the nearest store or bring you something back. In countries like the U.S. and Canada, this nearest store may be beyond cycling reach, certainly after you've already spent a long day in the saddle. If you can't get a ride or if even the remote shop is closed, motor campers often have so much in the way of supplies (and compassion) that you can scrounge enough for one or two meals without difficulty or embarrassment.

Free Camping

I have had some of my most memorable experiences camping with permission on private land. Many land owners were delighted to have a visitor, and quite a few were extremely helpful and hospitable. This does seem to work out best in foreign countries, since most people feel a particular obligation to show themselves from their most favorable side when they are given an opportunity to help strangers. I have been invited in for meals and baths, spent long nights in animated discussion and made good friends in such cases. Certainly if there are only one or two in your group, this can be a wonderful way to camp.

In many countries this is of course the only practical way—there may not be any official campsites. In other countries, such as Sweden, it is considered so natural, that it is not even necessary to ask for permission (as long as you don't pitch your tent in front of someone's house). The law there protects everybody's right to access. In fact, you can feel free to pick berries on some private land as well—a very pleasant change from the property-crazed society most of us are used to.

Pitching Your Tent

The ultimate way of camping, to my mind, is under the stars with nothing more than a sleeping bag between you and the heavens. Unfortunately, a tent can rarely be considered dispensable. Although it may at times be quite possible to camp without putting up a tent, I suggest you carry one on all camping

197

trips, especially if rain, insects or the need for a modicum of privacy may become a problem. When bike touring, one or the other of these criteria seems to apply most of the time. In this section I will discuss the considerations needed to put up the tent wisely.

The tent should properly be considered a shelter that can be used to protect you from rain, wind, cold, insects and improper curiosity. Clearly, it must be pitched with the relevant objectives in mind. In addition, you will want to be assured of a reasonable night's sleep, so it will be necessary to put up the tent in such a way that it is on a level surface. Here are the considerations necessary when surveying the overall site to choose where you choose to pitch your tent:

☐ The spot for the tent must be level, free from protruding rocks, and large enough to accommodate the tent, allowing all guy lines to be extended.

☐ If there is any chance of rain, find an area that is elevated slightly above the rest of the terrain; at a minimum avoid a location that is just below a likely downward path for water.

☐ If strong winds are likely, make sure the tent opening faces either a dense and high windbreak or the downwind side.

☐ Keep an adequate distance from your present or future neighbors, public facilities, car parking areas, roads and pathways.

☐ Find a place so generally sheltered that you have at least a modicum of privacy.

☐ Before pitching the tent, remove all sticks, stones and other protrusions that might damage the ground sheet and fill up any holes that would make it uncomfortable to sit or sleep.

☐ Make sure you can keep your bike locked up close to the tent and within your view.

Inside and Around the Tent

The way you arrange your household in and around the tent can be of great significance for your comfort and convenience. Having everything needed regularly within easy reach, while keeping things you don't need where they are out of your way, must be learned. Experience eventually solves that problem, but a little thought and practice beforehand may be very helpful. Don't hesitate to try it all out in your own back yard or in any public place, before you actually go out on your first serious camping trip. Even then, I would suggest you start off with a weekend trip to get additional practical experience. Either way, thinking it all out beforehand, as well as during the time you are

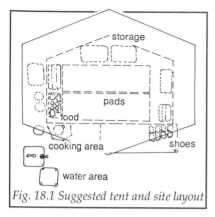

Fig. 18.1 Suggested tent and site layout

out there, will make the whole experience more enjoyable and efficient.

Fig. 18.1 shows a suggested layout for the tent and your equipment. As you can see, the tent's central area should be its entrance. When sitting in the entrance, and protected within the tent, though maintaining access to the things arranged to either side of you, everything may be taken care of conveniently. The things that must be kept dry at all cost, such as clothing and sleeping bag, are kept inside the tent, near the back. Cooking equipment, including camp stove, pots, utensils, food and water container, are arranged to one side, just outside the entrance, sheltered by the front part of the tent's fly sheet.

Items to which you need quick access, such as matches and utensils, are near the side of the tent. The stuff you don't need to get at very often can be kept just outside the tent under the extended sides and in the back under the fly sheet. Near the entrance of the tent, the ground is covered with a small extra ground sheet. Shoes and rain gear, if appropriate, are also near the entrance. Items of value are kept in a bag in a fixed place, that should not be too obvious to others. This allows you to take them with you whenever you leave the tent, certainly when you do not have a companion with you who can guard tent and gear while you are gone.

Most inexperienced campers either sit inside their tent with the opening closed, or stand outside. The experienced camper, on the other hand, has found the method explained above much more effective. This way you are at the interface between your tent and the outside world. Getting up to fetch water, or to take care of any other chore, is no problem. Even if it is windy or rainy, this arrangement, together with the smart selection of the location and orientation of the tent, sees to it that you are adequately sheltered.

Meal Preparation

You can cook or do other household chores from your station at the front, without getting smoke, flames or fumes inside.

If it does get too cold, you can still close the tent opening and move the entire operation in by about two feet. That way you'll bring the dangerous cooking operation into the tent as well, so you must take a little more care to avoid fires, breathing in fumes or spilling the contents of your pot. The entire cooking procedure is a tricky thing, but I'm afraid doing it really effectively with limited facilities takes more than anybody can adequately describe in a book.

You'll learn as you go along, especially if you give the whole operation some thought and if you plan ahead. Working in the right sequence, it is possible to cook an entire meal on just one flame, using only two or three saucepans and a frying pan. You can keep items just cooked warm on top of the pot with the next dish you prepare. Alternately, you can wrap certain items up in a towel and a sleeping bag to keep them warm (that's the ultimate way to cook rice, to give just one example).

Excellent freeze-dried dishes are available in great variety in most parts of the world these days. Although specialized backpacking stores may have the most complete (and the most expensive) selection, you may find enough variety in ordinary supermarkets at home or along the way. But you need not limit your cooking to the reconstitution of freeze-dried mixtures. Preparing meals from scratch is not impossible on a camp stove. This makes even more sense if you are with a larger group. If you are traveling in a group of three or more, you can carry two separate cookers and enough pots to prepare a full meal using fresh foodstuffs. Just select the ingredients with the required preparation time in mind, and shy away from dishes that need too many different ingredients or spices. Those few spices you do need should be selected before you leave, and they can be carried in small waterproof containers, such as empty film canisters.

Sleeping in the Tent

At night, also arrange everything with some thought. To make sure your pad will be comfortable, you can try out the ground before you even pitch the tent. Sometimes pitching the tent a few inches one way or the other can make all the difference in comfort. Keep the sleeping bag packed away until you are ready to go to bed, though the mattress pad may be used during the day to sit in the tent more comfortably, especially if it is cold.

Arrange all the items you will not be needing during the night, or when getting up in the morning, along the back and the sides of the tent. Articles you may need during the night or when first getting up, such as matches, candle or flashlight, shoes, jacket or rain wear and the next day's clothing, should be easily accessible near the entrance, as appropriate to their function. In addition to your sleeping bag and pad, you probably want to have something that can serve as a pillow—if nothing else, fold some clothing together and wrap it in a towel.

In very cold weather, you may find even your sleeping bag is not enough to keep you warm. You can easily extend your bag's comfort range by wearing socks, a sweater and a woolen cap, in addition to your usual night wear. I like to use a sheet sleeping bag liner inside my down bag, to keep the latter clean under normal circumstances. Putting this sheet bag around the outside of the down bag will keep you quite a bit warmer in the cold, thin though it is. In particularly hot weather, you may want to make do with sleeping on top of the opened sleeping bag, sleeping uncovered or with only the sheet bag. Sleeping directly under the stars without a tent, keeping the tent open, or closing only a mosquito netting flap, will also keep you a lot cooler during a hot night.

Breaking Up Camp

Next day, if you intend to continue on the bike right away, you may either pack up before breakfast, or you can first treat yourself to a comfortable breakfast in camp. It all depends on the time you get up and the number of hours you want to spend on the bike. If you have a long trip ahead of you, it will make a lot of sense to hold off with breakfast, breaking up camp right away instead. If you stay in camp until after breakfast, first hang your sleeping bag out to air or dry, assuming it is not raining. Keep the tent pitched until all is taken care of, packing the tent last of all, especially if the weather is cold or wet. Make sure you forget nothing and that everything is properly packed on the bike.

Ride and Meal Timing

If you are in a hurry to get back on the bike, you may have to pack up in a bit of a rush, so you may not have time to air your sleeping bag or to eat breakfast. Take the time for a proper breakfast after one or two hours, especially if you anticipate some hard cycling that day. While stopped for breakfast by the roadside, air the sleeping bag, the tent and any laundry or other clothing, if it was not completely dried when you packed up.

This late breakfast after one or two hours of cycling can be taken in the form of a roadside picnic. Buy your supplies fresh along the way, and stop in a scenic location. It is perhaps one of the most delightful experiences to be having breakfast under the sky at a time long before most others are traveling. You will feel even better when you realize that you have already covered twenty, thirty or even more miles of cycling, bringing you that much closer to the day's destination. On a really long trip, you

View from the tent. This tent has a large extended porch, which is ideal for rainy climates. (photo Catharina Halter)

can even have supper on the way, continuing the bike trip afterwards, to put up camp quite late. This is particularly suitable in northern regions in the northern hemisphere—or far south in the southern hemisphere. In spring and summer, days are very long in those regions.

If, on the other hand, you want to make the most of your camping experience, and want to keep the day's cycling distance down to something manageable without interruptions, you may decide to cycle only half days, either mornings or afternoons. In the former case, have an early breakfast at the campsite and get going early. Travel up to a late lunch, which you have at the next campsite. This way you will have the entire afternoon to spend in camp, which will be very desirable if you are camped in a location where some activity—whether sightseeing, a museum visit or an afternoon at a swimming pool—is possible conveniently close to the campsite. Conversely, you can stay put until after lunch; in that case, cycle only afternoon and evening, getting to the next campsite in time for supper.

CHAPTER 19

Bicycle Touring Abroad

Bicycle touring is a fine way to travel in foreign countries. The formalities and the material risks associated with traveling abroad by car are eliminated. At the same time, you retain the freedom to travel at will at your own pace and on your own schedule, where you want and when you want. It is usually both more convenient and cheaper than conventional ways of traveling. The latter applies especially if bike touring is combined with camping or staying in youth hostels. This chapter is devoted entirely to the specific problems associated with traveling abroad by bike. For a more thorough treatment of foreign bike touring, you may want to consult Kameel Nasr's book *Bicycle Touring International*, also published by Bicycle Books.

Clearly, riding a bike in a foreign country is not very much more difficult than it is in your own. Though the roads may be better paved here than they are there, the traffic less murderous in one society than it is in the next, the weather more congenial to cycling here than it is there, the differences are gradual, rather than absolute. In fact, you are likely to encounter at least as many positive and negative extremes in your own country as you will abroad.

Overlooking one of the Swiss lakes. (photo Nadine Slavinski / Cycling Europe)

As an additional bonus, you may consider combining your tour abroad with some bicycle-related activities. Perhaps you'll have an opportunity to watch a major stage race, such as the Tour de France, while touring on the European continent. A visit to a major manufacturer's plant may well be an eye-opener to the interested cyclist. On a more practical level, you may be able to purchase some of the more exotic bicycles, bike components or cycling clothes that are not readily available at home. Or how about a visit to the Science Museum in London or another one of several European museums with extensive bicycle collections?

Preparation

Of course, it will pay off to prepare well for your tour, because purposeful preparation and planning is critical to the success of your bike tour abroad. But so are they when you're traveling abroad with any other means of transportation. Adjusting to foreign motoring habits or parking restrictions, getting used to railway time tables or staying sane aboard a guided touring coach are at least as tricky, and they require the same kind of thorough preparation if you want to do them successfully.

Much of the work that goes into preparing your tour abroad can be done the same way it should be done for any other kind of travel, providing you keep your particular mode of transportation in the back of your mind.

Only *you* know what you want out of a bike tour. You can only arrive at a satisfactory program if you are given a chance to base your decisions—to take one route or another, visit one place or the other, go at one season or another—on comprehensive and unbiased information.

Most of the items that matter to other tourists abroad are just as important to the cyclist. You will need some kind of identification, and perhaps other traveling documents. Depending on your destination, that may include anything from a simple ID or Driver's License to a passport, a visa or special exemptions. For the countries immediately bordering the U.S., a Driver's License is usually all you need, unless you are a resident alien, as I am. In that case you will need more—if only to get back into the country. Passports and visas (a visa is nothing but a rubber stamp in your passport) are required for some countries, and in some cases you will need vaccinations. If you are in doubt about these matters, inquire about such things at the host country's consulate or travel bureau before you leave.

Of course, you will also need foreign money, although it will usually be much easier to exchange dollars into local currency once you are abroad than it is to get money changed anywhere in the U.S. This is something to keep in mind if you are living in another country and visiting the States.

Sources of Information

Almost all the information about preparing for your tour, ranging from these formalities and money matters to specific suggestions about the things to do at your destination, can be learned from the kind of general guide book other tourists would use. There are specific bicycle touring manuals for many countries, and there is at least one book that provides basic bicycle-relevant information for almost any country in the world (Kameel Nasr's *Bicycle Touring International*).

Excellent general tourist guides are available for most countries and for many general or specific regions. Of these, the Michelin guides, which are available in English for many countries, are perhaps the ultimate, while the Lonely Planet guides are excellent for budget travel. In a very systematic way and with astonishing economy of space and language, these guides present the essential information about a region and each of the individual points of interest.

Even if no Michelin or Lonely Planet guide is available for the country or the area you plan to visit, I suggest you take a close look at one of these for another country or region. Compare the guides that exist for your destination with the way the Michelin guide is arranged. If the other one appears to be similarly encyclopedic, it may well suit your purpose admirably. If, on the other hand, it is less systematic, wordier or with too much emphasis on pretty pictures, it may perhaps be useful only to get background information before setting out.

In that case, you'll probably have to choose another book to help you with more practical matters along the way. A second series of useful books are those based on the scheme of the original *Europe on $5 a Day* (yes, really: that was possible in the late 60s) by Arthur Frommer. These guides are especially suitable if you are on a budget, don't want to go camping, and are more interested in the towns than the countryside. A few less well-known, though excellent, guides for the major continents are included in the Bibliography.

Tourist Boards

An additional, a good, if subjective, source of information will be the host country's national tourist board in your home country. Many countries maintain tourist offices in major cities abroad, others have at least one office in the U.S. and other major countries, with whom you can deal by mail or telephone. They will send you free maps, schedules of events and hotel or campsite directories. Of course, these tourist boards are set up primarily to deal with conventional tourists who travel by car or plane—people who like to visit beaches or overrun tourist traps and stay in expensive hotels. Just the same, upon request, most of these offices will provide the specific type of information that interests you. That is under the proviso that you give them enough time: start your preparation at least three months before leaving.

Let me give you an example of the type of bicycle-specific information that may be obtained from a tourist board. In many countries you may at some time or another wish to travel some distances by public transportation. For that purpose, it will be a good idea to ask in writing for the schedules of major carriers and an English-language copy of their policy on transporting passenger-accompanied bicycles. In most cases, you will receive adequate information to plan your tour, so you'll know where you can take the bike and how to go about it. Even if some local station officials, drivers or conductors balk or don't know the policy, assuming they just can't accept a bike, a polite and respectful confrontation with a copy of the letter you received from their national tourist office usually has the desired effect.

Another example of such very important kind of general information pertains to cultural or commercial customs and opening hours. Anybody who has ever tried to get a drink or food at an English pub, or who has attempted to do grocery shopping evenings, weekends or certain weekday afternoons in countries like England, Holland or Germany, or to go to a museum on Mondays anywhere, can confirm the usefulness of exact information about these matters. Don't think foreign visitors to America have fewer difficulties: just try changing foreign currency, or even getting an out-of-state check cashed, if you are used to European banking efficiency.

In addition to the conventional guide books and tourist board information, which both almost invariably show the sunny side of a country, you would do well to charge yourself up with some socially, culturally and environmentally relevant information. Read, cut out and collect all the articles that appear about your destination in the newspapers and other periodicals, so you are up to date on relevant current issues. Inform yourself regarding the geographic details of the country in a school atlas, almanac or encyclopedia. This will make you an informed visitor—one who understands and appreciates what he sees and experiences.

Foreign Maps

Maps are another essential ingredient of the preparation process. Enquire locally what maps are available, and anticipate having to buy the more detailed ones at your destination. In most big cities there are bookstores that specialize in maps and other travel literature, so try to find such a store in or near your home town. The minimum you will need is an overall map, showing the entire country or region you intend to visit in relief, to use as a preliminary planning tool. In addition, get a road map, showing the area in one piece and, if possible, some more detailed maps, on which you can plan out the actual route and itinerary more accurately with the help of your tourist guide book and other literature.

Finally, another source of pre-trip information should not be overlooked: talk to those who have visited the country of your destination, preferably people who have traveled by bike themselves. If you are not talking to a cyclist, make sure you don't get carried away with reports of ventures that will be much harder or impossible on the bike. On the other hand, you are not married to your bike, so you could well consider the possibility of leaving it in safe keeping, while you go off on a shorter trip by bus, train, ship, plane or on foot. Good places to leave bikes reasonably safely in most countries are the railway stations.

Getting There with Your Bike

Unless you live close to the border and want to visit the neighboring country, you will have to consider the transportation problem. Getting yourself to your destination is easy enough: the same way any other tourist would go about it. But you'll want to get your bike there too. From the U.S., different airlines have different policies. Many either leave it to their airport personnel or the latter take it upon themselves to make or bend the rules. This practice may work in your favor or against you, as I have experienced myself at different times. By and large, you'll actually find most airlines to be much more cooperative to cyclists on international routes than on domestic ones.

You may be charged a hefty sum if the total weight of bike and luggage exceeds the personal weight limit. To avoid or minimize that, make sure you pack for absolute minimum weight,

You've come a long way. Touring cyclists with young admirers in Nepal. (photo Dieter Glokowski)

207

keeping the weight of the items you check in at the counter to no more than 20 kg (44 lbs.). Put all heavy items in a bag that can be carried on. Usually you can get away with carrying a small backpack and a hand-carried bag on board as cabin luggage.

If it all sounds like too much of a challenge, you may consider renting a bicycle at the other end. Whether you can rent an acceptable machine will depend on the country of your destination and on your taste in bicycles. In France and England reasonable bikes are readily available for rent, while you may as well forget it in most other countries, unless you have been able to secure the use of a suitable machine by mail in advance. On the other hand, don't insist too much on the kind of equipment you are used to: the bikes available for rent at your destination may be quite suitable for the terrain encountered, even if you think they are heavy clunkers—it's probably what the locals use, and they get by somehow.

Choosing Maps

Maps for trips in foreign countries present essentially the same problems as maps for your own country. Consequently, you are referred once more to my comments in Chapter 14 about route planning and those in Chapter 18 about orientation. Once you have learned to handle a domestic map effectively, you will have no problems gleaning the essential information from a foreign map. The legend of many foreign maps is actually printed in English, as well as in the native tongue. If not, the country's tourist board or your domestic touring or automobile association may be able to provide a list of translations of such terms. Similarly, you can generally obtain a guide to the meanings of road signs—both directional and regulatory ones.

The criteria for a good cycling road map are the same abroad as they are at home: a detailed scale of about 1 : 200,000, not too much distortion in the road widths and other topographic details, and the need for reliable information pertaining to elevations. Finally, it should be as up to date as possible, to avoid frequent surprises with freeways and other man-made barriers that are not shown on the maps. In almost all Western countries, you will be able to find several adequate series of maps once you get there. In Eastern Europe and some other former communist societies, suitable maps are hard to get locally.

You may want to do some off-road cycling when you are in the country of your destination. To find your way off-road, you will need maps to scale 1 : 50,000. Generally, it will be impossible to obtain such detailed maps, except locally. Don't cover all the terrain with maps of that scale: a friend of mine carried three pounds of mapping material just to follow the Rhine from its source downstream for about 300 miles. Instead, decide ahead of

Looks more exotic than it is. Taoist temple in Vancouver, Canada. (photo Kimberlee Caledonia)

time where will be a good area to cycle off-road, and buy topographic maps to cover only that specific region.

In most cases, you will have to wait until you are in the country of your destination before buying the detailed maps. Once you get there, that should be your first priority of things to take care of. Even there it may take a search for a special bookstore to get hold of the right maps. At the first shop you find, don't just ask for the particular maps: if they don't have them, buy something else and ask for the address of a shop that would have the kind of maps you are looking for.

Done even slightly diplomatically, you will find out the source for good maps quite soon. Once you have discovered such a store, buy all the maps you think you may need, erring rather on the high side than risking the chance of your trip taking you to uncharted regions. Perhaps that does not sound very adventurous, but most experienced travelers agree that a trip without reference to a good map brings a much less intensive experience than a well-prepared and properly documented journey.

Understanding One Another

When you have to ask the way during your trip, always consult the map at the same time. You will find that, though the locals perhaps do not understand your pronunciation of a place name, they will recognize it when you are pointing to it on the map. Similarly, it will be much easier to follow their instructions while making reference to the map. Even if you soon forget the verbal instructions, you will find it quite easy to reconstruct the route with the aid of the map.

In most foreign countries you will have to overcome the language barrier. Even between English speaking countries there are problems, since different words may be used for the same things, while the same word may mean different things on either side of the Atlantic. That the Englishman calls an intersection a junction, and means the sidewalk when he says pavement, are just a few examples.

Much more unexpected sources of confusion sometimes completely obliterate sensible communication. Thus, the American asking for a *rest room* or a *bath room* in England or Australia should have a strong bladder, while the Englishman asking for a *toilet* is probably unaware how much embarrassment he causes some American. That may seems trivial, and it is, except that people have got hopelessly lost on account of such differences.

Whether you are traveling in another English-speaking country or in a place where a truly foreign tongue is spoken, it is not impossible to prepare for sensible communication and understanding. Before you leave on your tour, take the trouble to get familiar with the differences you can expect to encounter.

Of course, there are also weights and measures to consider, where the difference between metric, American and imperial systems can be quite bewildering. But converting pounds to kilograms and kilometers into miles or vice versa is just as easy as converting meters into feet when it comes to expressing elevations. Table 4 in the Appendix will prove quite helpful in this respect.

Not only different variants of English, but even foreign languages can easily be learned well enough to allow the very basic level of communication required to avoid getting lost. Simple expressions like left, right, straight ahead and back will be quickly learned in any language. Similarly, you can learn to pronounce the names of most towns and major landmarks with some semblance of the authentic. It's a matter of preparation, and it adds to the interest of the tour when you at least manage to come across as somebody who tries, rather than as the proverbial ugly American. Be receptive to your hosts and their language, and you and your country will be treated with equal respect.

Timing Your Tour

One of the charms of foreign or otherwise remote regions is the fact that the weather can be quite different at certain times of the year. Thus, you will find that when it is high season and too hot to do anything enjoyable in your part of the world, it may be quite delightful and not half as overrun with people somewhere else. Conversely, you may be able to benefit from the relative unpopularity of early or late season travel to get to an area where the weather is just perfect for cycling at that particular time, a subject that was covered in Chapter 12.

This is again the kind of information to be found out when doing your preliminary planning. In general, I suggest you shy away from the summer months in flat and lower lying regions, as well as from popular summer seaside destinations. The weather prevalent there at such times may be acceptable to those who prefer to stay in a hotel swimming pool most of the day, but it won't make for enjoyable cycling.

On the other hand, really high mountainous areas can be incredibly cold, especially in the late and early season, and high summer may be the only even remotely comfortable period there. Of course, these considerations also apply when traveling in your own country, certainly if it is a land as big as Canada or the U.S. However, the views of foreign countries in our minds are colored by their generalized representation. Consequently, it may be as hard to imagine a heat wave in Canada or Iceland as it is to believe that there is perennial snow on Indian and central African mountains, or for that matter that the French Alps can get quite chilly, while sun-tanned beauties bathe topless at the beaches only two hundred miles away.

It will also be smart to try and avoid major public holidays, such as Easter, in most Catholic countries, especially in religious or cult centers. Of course, that advice does not apply if your particular interest is precisely in witnessing such a celebration. The problem is usually that accommodations and travel are greatly hindered during such events. If you're not coming for the show, especially if you are not prepared, it can be quite frustrating to be stranded somewhere on account of a head hunting heyday among the cannibals or an Easter procession in Spain.

Where to Travel

Whether at home or abroad, major roads are generally the most convenient routes to follow. Of course, it will be wise to steer clear of heavily traveled arterials and real freeways (certainly where it is illegal to use them with a bike) and to avoid roads that form direct connections between neighboring major centers or a metropolis with its satellites and suburbs.

Some people like to avoid all major roads, fearing motor traffic more than getting lost or stuck in the dirt. In some countries, it is quite possible to avoid really major roads, and still travel on well-paved roads with good facilities. France is a good example. In that country most major roads are quite closely paralleled by nearly equally direct minor roads. These may be just as well-paved but carry much less motor traffic. Besides, they lead through many more interesting places and are generally more scenically attractive.

In some other European countries you will find specific bicycle paths. In countries such as Holland and Denmark, these

A rough road. But unlike most rough places in the U.S., you're not alone in most of Asia. (photo Dieter Glokowski)

paths are generally of adequate quality, certainly if you don't use very delicate equipment. In other countries, like Germany and Belgium, they seem to be created solely to keep cyclists off the much safer and better surfaced roads. In general, even the best bicycle paths are more dangerous and less convenient to cyclists than just about any road. For that reason, I suggest you try to steer clear of them as much as you can. Wherever a parallel connection exists without a separate bike path, use it in preference if you want to enjoy your trip, while maximizing your chances of living to tell others about it.

Off-road cycling came along with the mountain bike in the U.S., although it has long been practiced in many other countries by folks who never knew they were doing it—and hadn't waited for the mountain bike. In many countries, there is an entire network of paths and trails that are off-limits to motorists. Some of them may be on private land but with public access.

Certainly with a mountain bike, you'll be in a good position to combine transportation rides on regular roads with sections that go cross-country to explore the more remote terrain. In general, you will do better not to try and ride off-road for an entire tour. Instead, combine regular travel on the road with excursions and short sections cross-country. See Chapter 22 and the remarks on maps above, to make sure you are adequately prepared.

Where to Stay

In numerous foreign countries the accommodations available are generally quite a bit more primitive or harder to find than they are at home. When doing your general preparation for the tour, also establish what type of accommodations to expect where. Their availability, their accessibility and the services provided may well influence your choice of accommodations. Thus, in a country where hotels are few and far between and where cyclists are frowned upon, you may decide to camp out, since in many cases campsites are actually more numerous and adequately equipped.

If you want to go camping, also use the host country's tourist offices. Most of these have specific materials available for campers. Certainly the list of official campsites and the country's police policy regarding camping on private or public land will be of great importance to you, if that is the way you intend to spend the nights. If not available from the tourist office, your own country's automobile association or certain bookstores that cater to travelers may be able to supply you with a campsite guide, or you may have to wait until you arrive at your destination.

Don't expect foreign campsites to be similar to those in your own country. Read up on the facilities offered and any regulations that may apply. To give just a few examples, French and

Danish campsites are each in their own way superb for cyclists, while Dutch campsites generally have so little available space and so many restrictions that I prefer to steer clear of them. In other countries, for example in Eastern Europe, there are only very few and extremely large campsites, set up for people who spend three or four weeks in the same spot.

Hostels and Private Rooms

In most European countries, Australia and New Zealand, but more and more also on the North American continent, there is a type of accommodation known as hostels. Formerly they offered only separate dormitory sleeping facilities for men and women. Though differing quite a bit from one country to the next as regards the services and supplies available, many now have private and semiprivate rooms, sometimes with their own bathroom. Enquire at your local or national hostel association about the facilities in the country of your destination, if you are interested. I have my own prejudices as to which of these I like and which not. Try them out and decide for yourself whether you prefer the regimented type with clean trim and noisy school kids or the slightly run-down variety with interesting people to meet. In the U.S. their existence seems to be a guarded secret, hardly known to those for whom they are intended.

Each country has its own peculiarities with respect to overnight accommodations. Thus, the British and Irish bed & breakfast houses and the German, Swiss and Austrian private pensions are excellent choices—they are found everywhere, except in the big towns. In addition, many of the national cycling organizations have listings of cheap or free overnight facilities for members. Some of these are as good as staying in a commercial facility, while all will help you keep within a more modest budget, even if you don't want to spend every night in such simple quarters.

Staying Healthy Abroad

The chances of getting sick or hurt while traveling abroad are—if anything—higher than they are at home. Yet most people are both hopelessly unprepared for this, and do little to prevent it. By way of preparation, make sure you know what kinds of medical services are available in the host country and check into the best form of insurance. The better conventional tourist guides or your own country's automobile association can give you information about what is available and how to go about getting treatment. See any independent insurance broker to obtain travel insurance coverage that includes accident and health risks, as well as liability and theft. Take the appropriate health insurance ID and any other documents that tell you what to do when you go on your trip.

Entering the Ukon along the Dempster Highway, Canada. (photo Kimberlee Calddonia)

If you do get sick, you will perhaps be better off if you can locate a physician who is used to dealing with English-speaking patients. In the address list in the Appendix you will find the address of the International Association for Medical Assistance to Travelers, who can supply you with a directory of English-speaking doctors in the country you will be visiting. All member physicians agree on a modest standard fee per consultation and accept certain forms of insurance.

To prevent health problems from developing or getting serious, follow all the precautions commonly suggested. Make sure you have an adequate supply of any prescription medicines you regularly need, kept in a waterproof container. Take care to feed yourself well, especially making sure that your diet is at least as varied as it would be at home. Protect yourself and your companions by avoiding excessively strenuous trips without adequate rest. Make yourself familiar with the basics of first aid, checking Chapter 11 for particularly relevant issues for cyclists. Finally, minimize accident risks by studying the traffic peculiarities in the host country and being particularly careful while cycling or walking in city traffic.

CHAPTER 20

Touring with Children

Bicycle touring with children is not impossible, even though it presents some additional problems that are not encountered when cycling with adults alone. If you are willing to take the special needs and wishes of your offspring into consideration, all of you will find it to be an enjoyable and educational experience, whatever the children's ages. My parents took me touring and camping from the time I was a toddler, and I only regret not having been able to share real bike touring with my own children quite as much as they did. Even so, my family and I have gathered enough of the direct experience needed to help you in this chapter. You will learn how to make the most of your touring with children.

I feel a full awareness of the children's cycling needs and abilities on the part of the parents is a basic criterion for successful family touring. However, if you are not an experienced cyclist yourself yet, there is no need to shy away from sharing your own learning experience with the entire family. In that case, just avoid the really ambitious tours. It will be smarter to first get used to competent cycling together and individually, before setting out on a major tour. Together, go through the basic advice contained in the first two parts of this book, and practice what you learn, going on modest family trips first.

Family cycling using a child trailer

Age and Ability

The most important thing to consider when planning a family bicycle tour is the child's interest and ability. Though younger children are not always very demanding, your first task as a parent is your responsibility to the child. The touring schedule should primarily be determined by what corresponds to the child's needs, not by what you would do if you were traveling alone. On the other hand, there is no need to subordinate your own wants completely. There will be instances when the child has to wait his turn, just as there are many times when you have to accommodate the child's special needs or wishes.

Of course, each child is an individual—although they all go through similar development stages. At a very early age they are quite satisfied sleeping and idling. After some time they want to be occupied, meanwhile learning to keep themselves busy, which occurs in the next stage. Then comes the stage of interaction, when they need the presence and response of others. Finally, they have developed into youngsters, who distinguish themselves mainly from adults in the particular nature of their interest: whereas the parents may want to converse about one thing, their offspring may be more interested in another; while the parents want to visit a museum, they'd rather spend their time at play.

The age at which a child is in any particular stage is not quite as fixed as to allow categorizing. It is more important for the parents to be aware of the particular stage the child is in and what interests him most at this time. Your children will not be replicas of mine, just as my daughter was no carbon copy of her elder brother, and neither of them are similar to me or my sister at corresponding ages. If you occupy yourself with your children enough at other times as well, you should be able to evaluate their development and interests. This in itself should make it relatively easy to consider these factors when planning you family bicycle tours.

Well-designed child carrier from Troxel

Unless your child happens to be one of those rare creatures who themselves want to ride a bike for its own sake, make sure the tour also serves other purposes. If your children are interested in horseback riding, try to combine the tour with one or more visits to rental stables. If the children are fascinated by the sea and bathing, plan your tour to include some opportunities to go to the beach. If your children don't feel happy without other companions, suggest taking one or more of their friends along. In the latter case, start off with some practice rides together, to get the friends used to responsible cycling practices.

Allow the child to participate in the preparations for the tour right from the start. Consult him when doing initial planning and when selecting particular destinations within the tour's itinerary. Convince the child you take him seriously, by actually including as many of his suggestions as possible and heeding his

Your child can take care of his own bike. At least teach him to clean it regularly. (photo Bob Allen)

warnings. Even during the tour, the child can be given the feeling of being a full-fledged participant. Invite and respect feedback and suggestions. Don't be too rigid in your planning, since it is only too easy to overestimate the abilities of a child, which would not only spoil this one tour, but may also nip a developing cycling career in the bud.

Teach the child the basic skills of effective cycling, as well as some appreciation for the various aspects of touring. Children can develop an understanding for where they are and how much work it will be to get to the next place. A child old enough to learn reading and writing is also adequately developed to understand the principles of mapping, including the distances to be covered and the symbols used to represent various landmarks on the map.

Especially when the child rides a bike himself, you may be astonished at the insatiable appetite he or she develops. I found my nine-year old daughter eating like a grown man, devouring food she would have declined back home. That makes the family experience all the more pleasant, and increases the children's willingness to participate in the jobs of shopping and cooking. When camping, delegate certain responsibilities to the child—providing they are not only the kind of chores the child detests. Try to include jobs that can be seen as a kind of reward for his performance during the day. By involving the child in this manner, you will find the tour can be a delightful communal experience.

After completion of the tour, or shortly before the goal is reached, is a good time to reward your children with a durable memento of the tour in the form of a desirable or practical present. Things like a bicycle speedometer, a Swiss army knife, a pair of binoculars or a simple camera make excellent presents. You may look for things that increase the child's interest in bike touring, as well as providing something enjoyable in and by itself. It all depends on the child's interest—one child may be more interested in a doll, another in a book.

Ways to Carry the Child

Depending on the age and development, there are a number of different potential methods of taking your child along when cycling. Not all of these methods are equally recommended or suitable for serious bike touring, but here they are summarized:

☐ in a papoose type backpack (also referred to as a Gerry Pack) on the back of one of the parents;

☐ on a child's seat mounted in the front of the bike;

☐ on a child's seat mounted in the back of the bike;

☐ in a trailer or a side car, pulled by one of the parents;

☐ on the back seat of a tandem;

☐ on a bike of his own.

During the first six months or so, when the child cannot keep his back upright, the only even remotely satisfactory solution would be to carry the child in a sidecar or trailer, equipped more like a baby carriage or perambulator. Hardly the thing for long tours, but it has been done successfully.

Gerry-Pack

Carrying the child papoose-style on the back of one of the parents only lends itself to very limited use, for transporting small children up to the age of perhaps 18 months. It is potentially unsafe, uncomfortable for the parent and not much better for the child over a longer distance. Though possible for short trips—we often carried one of our children this way if we had to take two on one bike—I'd consider it totally unacceptable for touring over longer distances.

Children's Seats

A front-mounted seat can be suitable for younger children. Whether it is safe to do so depends on a number of factors. The child's seat must be installed firmly to a fixed part of the bicycle, not to the steering system. His feet must be well protected from accidentally getting caught between the spokes of the front wheel. The frame must be so long and the handlebars so high that the parent's sight of the road and control over the bike are not imperiled. Provided that all these criteria are met, this position allows good interaction between child and rider. It also gives the child a chance to see more than in the back. Children over the age of about four are generally too big for this method of carrying.

Children's seats installed in the back of the bike are by far the most common. The same criteria regarding sizing, foot protection and mutual interference apply as in the front, except that the steering is of course not effected. Since some of these seats are intended, or will be used, for quite sizable kids up to the age of perhaps six, you will have to make doubly sure the construction is really adequately sturdy to take the weight and to offer sufficient support and protection to the child.

When choosing a child's seat, and before you buy it, try it out. Install it on the bike, and put the child in it. Now take the bike by the handlebars and sway it in a lateral motion. If the whole affair starts oscillating precipitously, the seat's carrying frame and attachment are not adequately rigid. When a child is carried in the back, assuming you have found a suitable seat, you will have to transfer some of the luggage otherwise carried there to the front with the aid of a sturdy low-rider front luggage rack and sizable front panniers.

Trailers

Trailers and side cars are now available in quite a number of different versions, although not many are really adequately equipped to carry children. The trailer should be equipped with smoothly running wheels, incorporating high pressure tires and ball bearings. It must be big and sturdy enough, so the child's movements will not upset its balance or negatively effect the bike's handling and steering characteristics. Finally, it must be equipped with an adequately safe seat, complete with harness and weather protection. Give the younger child some toys that are tied on to the trailer, so they can't be lost on the way.

Children's Bikes

Children over the age of seven or eight are usually strong and coordinated enough to participate in bike tours on their own bikes. That only applies under close parental supervision, since children up to age ten are neither sufficiently coordinated, nor mentally advanced enough to understand some of the basic phenomena necessary to ride safely in traffic. At this stage, they cannot decide by themselves what is the right action in a critical situation on the road. Before going on a tour, take the child out cycling on several trips, and get him used to the skill and routine of predictable cycling. Make him understand and execute your advice and commands while riding. Develop a communal riding style and, conversely, learn to observe the child to estimate what his needs are.

A child's bike should be selected just as carefully as an adult's machine and ought to be of comparable quality. That will make it about as expensive too, since the price of most components is not a function of their size, but rather of the care that went into

Waiting for the ferry on a family tour.
(photo Dan Gindling)

making them. Do not purchase a bike that is clearly too big for the child, assuming he will eventually grow into it. He probably will eventually, but before he reaches that stage, he may have learned to hate cycling on an unsafe and uncomfortable machine that is too big.

Unfortunately, there are only few stores—and even fewer manufacturers—offer an adequate selection of high-quality children's bikes, while suitable components and accessories may be even harder to locate. You will probably find the few stores that do stock such items by simply asking other cycling parents who appear to have found good equipment for their offspring. If you should ever get abroad, you will find France and Italy to be wonderful places to purchase high quality components for children's bikes. So you may want to take the opportunity to investigate purchasing certain parts or even complete bikes while you are there. Similarly, tandem parts, including conversion kits to make the tandem suitable for a child stoker (that's cycling jargon for the rear rider), are more readily available in England and France than they are anywhere on the North American continent.

Riding with Children

This chapter is not the appropriate forum to show how you teach a child bicycle-riding skills. However, it will be imperative that the child be adequately prepared and develop all the basic skills necessary. Once he has learned these basics, the only proper way to prepare him for serious touring is to take him along on as many supervised rides as possible. Instruct junior in the kind of lessons contained in the chapters of Part II of this book. Even on the tour, remain aware of the child's probable need for instruction—just avoid bombarding him with unwanted warnings and superfluous advice.

Depending on the child's development, you can load his bike up with some luggage. Making even the smallest member of the party carry at least something will boost his confidence as a full-fledged participant. Younger children's bikes should of course be loaded lightly: give them items that are relatively bulky for their weight. I've always made my children carry their own sleeping bag and clothing, right from the first trip. Later we added some of the other items that have to be carried. By the time my son was 14, he was indeed carrying as heavy a load as that of an adult.

Tandems

Perhaps the best way to introduce a child to cycle touring is on a tandem as the stoker. If the child is still quite small, you will need either a specially built tandem with a very small rear frame, or an adaptor kit to raise the rear cranks to a level that suits the child's leg length. Although the latter gadget, illustrated in Fig. 20.1, seems more like a do-it-yourself solution, it is in some ways the preferable way: the child sits so high that he sees more than the parent's back, and it is easier to adapt when junior grows bigger. If money is no object, you can get an experienced tandem frame builder to construct a special tandem that is designed right from the start for a short but growing stoker. At a later age, a standard tandem with a suitably small rear frame may be used.

Even tandem riding has to be learned and practiced before-hand—both for the person in front and the one in the rear. How-ever, it can be mastered quickly if you put your mind to it. The tandem has less luggage carrying capacity than two individual bicycles. That needn't be a serious drawback, since you would probably not load the child's bike up with very much luggage anyway. For additional advice, you are referred to Chapter 21, which is devoted specifically to tandem touring. There you will find general comments regarding this type of bicycle and the spe-cial problems associated with its use.

Overnight Stays with Children

The first few trips with children should probably be short ones. Very soon, it will be possible to make tours that include over-night stops. I have found that children prefer to stay at camp-sites and youth hostels. Neither camping in isolation in the wilds, nor staying in the boring solitude of a motel, nor the or-ganized splendor of most hotels, seems to satisfy their need for relaxation and playful activity. The only drawback of camping is the fact that quite a bit of luggage has to be carried.

At campsites, they usually find other children with whom to spend their time and whom they can impress with their bicycle touring achievements. Generally, they seem to enjoy getting in-volved in the improvised household chores associated with camp-ing. Youth hostels are appreciated for similar reasons, especially in those countries where it is customary for the visitors to prepare their own meals. Many hostels offer family rooms, in addition to the characteristic sex-segregated dormitory accommodations. The advantage of youth hostels over camping is the reduction in the volume of luggage that must be carried: neither tent, nor cooking equipment, nor down sleeping bag will be required.

Certainly when camping, it will be a good idea to stay two nights at the same site occasionally. This should be made depend-ent on the degree to which the children feel at home at one campsite or another. When you have reached a site where the children find plenty of playmates or absorbing occupations, the suggestion to stay on an additional night will probably be wel-comed enthusiastically. An occasional rest day like this is probably just as enjoyable and relaxing for the parents as it is for the children. You may take the opportunity to visit some local places of interest on unloaded bikes, either with or without the

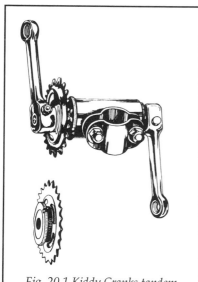

Fig. 20.1 Kiddy Cranks tandem
drivetrain adaptor

221

Another trailer. This model is covered and has large wheels for greater comfort and better handling.

children, or you may just loaf about if that's your preference at the time.

Hotel and motel stays require even less in the way of essential equipment. On the other hand, perhaps the main reason for kids to object to that kind of accommodations is the fact that they feel out of place in their cycling garb. In fact, children are generally even more concerned about their parents' appearance than they are about their own clothing. So you would do well to make sure you carry enough normal clothing for children and adults alike to come across to the other guests and personnel as quite respectable visitors, just as if you'd arrived in a car like everybody else.

Contrary to popular fears, cyclists are not treated like paupers or poor relatives at most hotels. That applies to most places, both abroad and at home, including really fancy hotels. You may find that many people have an innate sympathy for those who do something different and more interesting than what they encounter every day. In fact, staff or owners often go out of their way to make sure their young cycling guests lack nothing. In most cases they will also help you find a safe place to put your bikes.

CHAPTER 21

Tandem Touring

Tandems have become increasingly popular in recent years. Although most are used for recreational riding, the tandem is also quite suitable for bike touring. It has several important advantages that make it ideally suitable for touring purposes. You can cycle together without losing one another. You will always be close enough for communication. It allows riders of unequal abilities to go at the same pace. Besides, since the wind resistance of a tandem is much less than the total for two single bikes, driven by the same two human motors, tandem riders usually move faster and smoother.

In the preceding chapter I emphasized the value of the tandem for family cycling. You are referred to the information contained there for specific comments about the adaptation of a tandem to carry children. In the present chapter many of the general issues relevant to tandem touring and the technical peculiarities of the machine will be covered in some depth.

Tandem Skills

Excellent European touring tandem by Hans Mittendorf of Germany.

Delightful though it is, tandem touring has disadvantages too. In the first place, you can carry less luggage on one tandem than you can on two single bikes. That makes the tandem somewhat less suitable for camping, although the smart selection of light-

weight equipment, together with good luggage racks and bags, or the use of a luggage trailer, can overcome most of the tandem's inherent weaknesses in this respect.

Tandem riding is a very unique experience, and the problems associated with it are equally singular. Other and more experienced tandem riders are your best source of relevant information and advice. In Great Britain there is an active organization of tandem riders, the Tandem Club, whose address can be found in the Appendix. This association has what is probably the world's greatest storehouse of technical and practical expertise in the field, and their handbook is far and away the most comprehensive printed source of tandem facts. A membership in the Tandem Club is highly recommended to present and prospective tandem riders alike, wherever they live.

Transporting a Tandem

Like any other bike, the tandem is most practical when you ride it: transporting it any other way can be a bit of a headache. These things are mighty big. Whereas a normal bicycle is about 1.70 m (5 ft. 8 in.) long, the typical tandem measures a full 2.40 m (8 ft.). And when you remove the wheels, the difference seems even more striking, since the tandem frame turns out to be nearly twice as long as that of a normal bike. That's not a problem in everyday use, but it becomes apparent when the thing has to be put in storage or transported.

You may have to be particularly inventive and imaginative to solve some of the transportation problems you'll encounter with a tandem. In the case of public transportation, inquire well ahead of time how it can be done. And if all else fails, decide not to transport the bike, except the way it was meant to travel in the first place: on its wheels, with you and your companion in the saddles. That limits your range of operation a bit, but it may save you a lot of headaches.

Except in a full-size station wagon, you will usually find no room for the tandem in a car, and it will be equally hard to transport one on a trunk-mounted rack. When carrying it by car, only a specially adapted roof rack will do the trick. In America, the Amtrak railway system does not accept tandems on account of their length. An unreasonable ruling, because Amtrak's luggage cars are big and empty enough to handle a whole flock of tandems. Bus drivers probably don't welcome tandem patrons either. Most airlines balk when you arrive at the check-in counter with a tandem. If they accept it at all, they may charge a hefty excess luggage surcharge, even if the overall weight of your luggage— including the bike—stays within the total allowance for the number in your group.

A tandem couple of my acquaintance had travelled much of the Middle East. Finally, they discovered that getting the bike back to Greece from the African continent would be nearly impossible, at least within their budget in terms of time and money. So they did something original: with a hacksaw, they severed the rear triangle, shortening the frame just enough to allow transportation as regular airline luggage. Upon their arrival in Greece, they went in search of a competent bicycle mechanic who joined the two parts up again with the aid of accurately fitted reinforcing inserts and brass brazing technique. I'm not suggesting you do that each time the tandem has to be shipped, merely that you often have to be imaginative when it comes to overcoming tandem difficulties.

Renting a Tandem

It is not impossible to rent a tandem, and could certainly be recommended—if only tandem riders weren't so fussy. And with good reason, because a tandem is a lot more than a bike with two saddles. It has to really stand up to its task, and there are only a few bicycle shops that are familiar with the problems associated with tandem set-up, riding and maintenance. Consequently, most of the tandems offered for rental are not adequate for serious touring over longer distances. In France and England you will probably be able to find respectable tandems, as you may in those places in the U.S. where a local bike shop has attained some standing as a tandem specialist. But, by and large, however inconvenient it is to transport a tandem, it will be the lesser of two evils.

Mechanical Problems

At least equally serious as the transportation problem is another one: the frequency of mechanical breakdowns with a tandem, and the associated difficulties in getting repairs executed satisfactorily. In subsequent sections of this chapter you will be introduced to some of the equipment selection considerations relevant to the purchase or modification of the machine, to minimize the likelihood of such mishaps. Before you take up tandem riding, though, it will be fair to warn you of the kind of hardships you may be saddled with.

The touring tandem is always a heavily loaded machine. Carrying twice the weight, accelerating twice the mass, with twice the propulsive output, often at a significantly higher speed, it is subjected to hard punishment. In addition, all these higher demands are placed on a structure that is considerably longer between supports (the wheel axes). To the mechanically or structurally enlightened, that translates into potential trouble. Consequently, tandem design is a serious matter. Only the products of specialized tandem frame builders and manufacturers should be considered.

Not only the frame, but also the various other components get a lot of abuse. Wheels, brakes and drivetrains are heavily

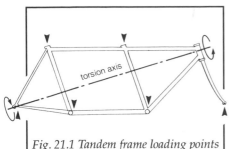

Fig. 21.1 Tandem frame loading points

loaded and often fail. That is the time the unprepared tandem rider gets the next shock, because most of these tandem components are non-standard. Consequently, the repair or replacement of even a relatively minor component may be quite expensive and time consuming.

To prevent such difficulties, which of course are most likely to happen when you are touring far away from home with limited time available, always choose the sturdiest, rather than the lightest or most fashionable equipment, for use on a touring tandem. As an additional safeguard, ride and treat your machine carefully. When in doubt about the quality of the road, go slow or even get off the bike. Get up from the saddle when riding over bumps, if they are unavoidable. Walk up the very steepest hills and slow down enough to eliminate the need for excessive braking when going downhill.

Tandem Frames

The frame of a tandem bicycle is a very heavily loaded structure. Fig. 21.1 illustrates the major points where forces are applied to it. The various forces working on the frame result in the tendency to twist around an axis that runs from the rear wheel axle to the head tube, also represented in the illustration. To satisfy the structural and mechanical criteria for adequate strength and reliable tracking, steering and braking, the torque-induced movements around this axis must be kept to a minimum.

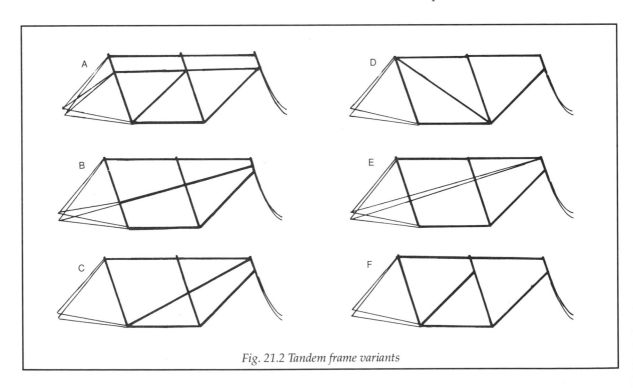

Fig. 21.2 Tandem frame variants

The structural design of the tandem frame determines whether or not adequate rigidity around the torque axis is achieved. Frame builders and tandem manufacturers have come up with several designs to try and achieve the desired effect without making the bike quite so heavy and stiff as to be uncomfortable. Structurally ideal would be a very large diameter tube that runs the length of the chain-dotted line in Fig. 21.1, split only in the rear portion to accommodate the rear wheel.

This design is indeed used by some manufacturers. Unfortunately, it involves a number of practical problems, brought about by such factors as material and part availability, poor shock absorption due to excessive vertical rigidity, and the visual impact on the observer. Consequently, various other, more or less adequate designs have been used. Several designs for touring tandems are illustrated in Fig. 21.2. The ones on the left all have sufficient rigidity, whereas the RH details include examples of common, though inadequate, designs.

As you can tell from the positive and negative examples of these two illustrations, the most critical thing to avoid is an open frame design, even if only in the rear. Both parts of the frame should have a continuous horizontal top tube. "Women's" designs, on which the rear top tube is either lacking or lowered to run parallel to the down tube, are no-no's for touring tandems. Furthermore, diagonal bracing in the form of twin lateral tubes, if anything, to the desired rigidity, which is so critically important for the stability and integrity of a touring tandem.

As for the size of the frame, these machines are usually available in a stepped design, on which the forward seat tube is about five cm (two inches) longer than the one in the rear. That suggests a convention which is indeed very hard to break: the big man as captain in the front, with his small companion, usually female, as the stoker in the back. I don't agree that it must necessarily be this way, and feel that many women would feel better about tandem riding if they could take the reins in their own hands. Conversely, I'm not macho enough to consider the place in the back with disdain for a male rider.

If you agree, you may have to order a custom-built tandem, with equally long seat tubes front and rear. In fact, even a reverse design, one that's bigger in the rear than it is in the front, should be possible. If you choose the front of a conventional design small enough to accommodate the smaller partner, you may still be able to swap places by using a special (strong and long) seat post in the rear. In recent years such items have become readily available for mountain bike use.

The Tandem Drivetrain

The most popular set-up for touring tandems includes fifteen-speed gearing. The problem with this configuration is that it locks you into special tandem components for most of the drive-train parts. I feel that for most applications a ten-speed design may be quite satisfactory. This allows the use of a standard triple chainwheel crankset in the rear and a single chainring model in the front.

Actually, in less undulating terrain 6- and 12-speed systems would usually be quite adequate. These are less complicated to operate and maintain. In that case, choose big steps between the individual sprockets, to obtain reasonably wide range gearing. For any given type of terrain, tandem riders generally need some-what more widely spaced gears than those listed for solo riders in Table 9.I in Chapter 9. Invariably, wide range derailleurs should be selected for touring tandems.

Fig. 21.3 illustrates a number of different drivetrain configura-tions. Those that keep the two chains on the same side allow the use of conventional components, as long as you are satisfied with a 12- or 14-speed system. Special tandem drivetrain com-ponents are expensive and hard to find, especially if you get into trouble on your tour far from home. If one accepts the need for special tandem components, then most experienced touring riders seem to agree that the rather odd looking arrangement with the very long chain, driving the rear wheel from the front crankset, is the most convenient to use.

The connecting chain between the front and rear cranksets must be kept reasonably tense. This may be either achieved with a spring-loaded chain tensioning device, or by adjustment of the position of one of the crank spindles. For the latter purpose, most

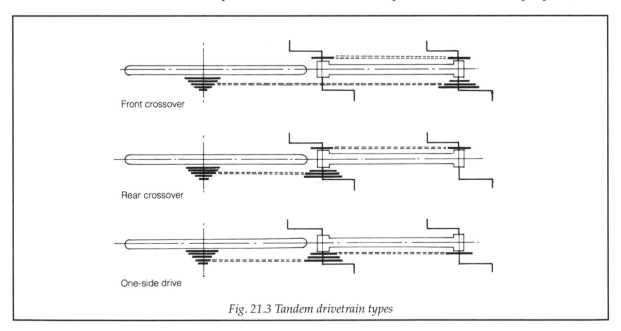

Front crossover

Rear crossover

One-side drive

Fig. 21.3 Tandem drivetrain types

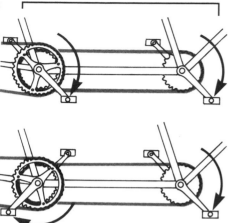

Fig. 21.4 In-line and off-set tandem cranks.

quality tandems are equipped with an oversize forward bottom bracket shell and an eccentrically located set of bearings. By selecting a different eccentric orientation of the bearings, the spindle can be moved further to the front or the back, thus loosening or tensioning the connecting chain. Ideally, the system with a long driving chain should have this adjustable bottom bracket in the rear, while tensioning and loosening are achieved by adjusting it in the opposite directions, respectively.

Many touring tandem riders like to modify the synchronization between the two sets of cranks so that the cranks are not parallel, as shown in Fig. 21.4. This way, the propulsive power output is more constant, since the one rider's minimum and maximum power points in the dead center and forward crank positions, respectively, never coincide with the corresponding orientations for the other rider's cranks.

This off-set can be achieved by undoing the connecting chain and putting it back when the cranks are held in the desired relative orientation. Alternately, a 90-degree difference may be achieved by undoing the cranks on one crankset, and re-installing them in the off-set position. It's a matter of preference, but it is certainly worth trying to see whether you and your tandem partner benefit from this configuration.

Tandem Wheels

The most trouble-prone parts of a tandem seem to be the wheels. Reasonable enough, if you realize that they have to carry twice the weight as compared to what similar wheels used on single bikes have to stand up to. It should be obvious that tandem wheels must be selected on the sturdy side, rather than on the light side. If you've ever heard the tales of broken spokes and bent rims told by most tandem riders, you'll feel no desire to take any chances yourself.

Most tandem tourists agree that touring tandems should have strong 26 inch (650 mm) wheels. The advent of the mountain bike, with its sturdy 26-inch wheels, is perhaps the best thing that has happened to tandem wheel design in recent years. Now once more regularly available are sturdy hubs, some models even with solid axles, held by means of axle nuts with integral washers instead of quick-releases. Such hubs should be suitable for relatively thick spokes, preferably at least 13 gauge or 2.2 mm diameter. Also available are strong aluminum rims (36 spokes are quite adequate for 26-inch tandem wheels) and strong fat tires, that nevertheless take a high air pressure. All these are essential factors in the construction of a satisfactory tandem wheel.

Of course, the tandem frame geometry must be designed generously enough to accept these rather hefty mountain bike wheels, with their slightly smaller diameter and much greater

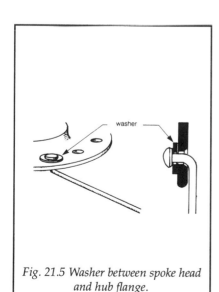

Fig. 21.5 Washer between spoke head and hub flange.

229

tire cross section. However, the narrowest mountain bike tires of size 26 x 1.5 in., also known by their ETRTO designation 559 x 38 mm should be about the right size to fit many properly designed touring tandem frames. As long as the brake pivots for cantilever or cam-operated brakes are mounted in the appropriate relative position, as explained in the final section of this chapter, such wheels are eminently suitable for tandem touring use.

Tandem Brakes

The much bigger mass put on the road by a loaded tandem can become correspondingly much harder to slow down than that of even a heavily loaded single bike. Add to that the higher speed at which tandems roll downhill, and you should be able to appreciate how difficult it can be to provide adequate tandem brakes. For touring machines, the industry standard has become cantilever brakes on both wheels and an additional drum brake, which is usually mounted on the rear wheel.

Due to the tandem's great length on the one hand, and the strength of a properly constructed tandem fork on the other, it does not much matter whether this additional brake is installed on the front or the rear wheel. Either brake solution, however, frequently seems to be associated with the incidence of spoke breakage. Make sure the thickness of the hub flanges matches the bend at the spoke heads, or install thin washers in between flange and spoke head, to make up any difference that may be present. Keep those spokes tight by frequently adjusting the nipples, and you'll avoid the most common problems of this kind.

The use of cantilever brakes (or some of the modern frame-mounted cam-operated models) brings with it the question of the location for the pivot bosses. These are usually set for a specific rim size. Although the difference between the formerly most common sizes 630 mm (for 27-inch wheels) and 622 mm (for 700 mm wheels) is so small that adjustment of the brake shoe location generally provides adequate compensation. Mountain bike wheels, with their much smaller and at the same time wider rims, require different boss locations. Make up your mind about the wheel size and brake model to be used before ordering the frame, so these bosses can be located appropriately. If you are buying a standard factory-made tandem or frame, you may have to get the bike shop to arrange for their relocation by a competent frame builder.

Eccentric front bottom bracket adaptor. Allows tensioning the chain by rotating it, bringing the bearing unit forward.

CHAPTER 22

Mountain Bike Touring

The greatest cycling revolution of the 80s has doubtlessly been the sudden emergence of mountain bikes and the increase in the popularity of off-road cycling. Of course, this modern fat-tired bicycle lends itself to much more than cross-country cycling alone. It has indeed become the favored machine of many experienced and novice cyclists alike. Despite its slightly lower efficiency when it comes to cycling on the open road, its advantages are not lost on many touring cyclists. It is an excellent choice for heavily loaded bicycle touring, especially when less than perfectly paved roads are encountered, as will often be the case abroad.

The mountain bike and its application have so many fascinating aspects that distinguish it from regular bicycles and their use, that I should recommend the interested reader purchase a copy of a special book devoted to the subject. In this vein, you may find my *Mountain Bike Book* and *Mountain Bike Magic*, also published by Bicycle Books, of considerable benefit. However, to go touring, there is no need to know quite that much about the mountain bike. The present chapter will probably suffice to get the most out of your mountain bike for touring purposes.

Off-road touring at its best. (photo Dan Gindling)

Rough Trail Cycling

When people talk about *off-road, cross-country* or *all terrain* cycling, they don't usually really mean what they say. In fact, the majority of cycling done with most mountain bikes is probably on the same kind of roads as you would use with a regular bike. And even if you leave the regular smoothly paved road, that doesn't necessarily mean you're in the jungle, the mountains or the desert. In practice, off-road cycling generally means nothing more than riding on any non-asphalted surfaces, be they fire roads, forest trails, or abandoned regular roads.

Without knowing it, I have been doing this kind of cycling since I was a kid. In Holland and England, as well as many other countries, cyclists are less obsessed with asphalt than Americans used to be before the advent of the mountain bike. We rode our ordinary bikes, which admittedly were equipped with relatively fat tires, on dusty paths and gravel trails, cobblestone streets and muddy tracks quite frequently, without thinking anything of it.

We didn't make quite the spectacularly fast progress that can be attained on smoothly paved main roads, but this kind of cycling always had a charm all its own. What a difference it makes, not to hear the constant rumble of motor traffic. How delightful to meet nothing but walkers, cattle and a few other cyclists for miles on end. No anxious looking back, ready to dive into the ditch, should an overtaking motorist threaten your right to the road. No inhibitions about suddenly turning off without concern about following traffic. Everybody probably needs to experience this from time to time, if only to realize what he has to endure the rest of his cycling life.

Even when I settled in California, back in the late 60s, I sometimes left the beaten track and found short cuts and paths that few other cyclists seemed to have discovered, or didn't care to use if they had. Some local cyclists shared my appreciation of the unpaved outback, but not until the mountain bike boom of the mid 80s, did it even begin to get crowded on any trail. Even today, only a very few of the many paths seem to have been discovered by the mountain bike masses. And that is in Marin County, the nation's number one off-road cycling area. There must be lots of trails left for uncrowded off-road cycling all over the country.

Much of the United States, as well as millions of square miles elsewhere, is criss-crossed with trails that are virtually undiscovered by cyclists, though they offer the potential for great off-road cycling. It can be done with any good touring bike, providing it is not equipped with the skinniest tires. It's even more accessible with a real mountain bike. In the section that follows we shall have a closer look at this fat-tired machine. Before we do, let me once more give you the advice not to skimp on the price when buying one of these: the more expensive models definitely pay off the price difference in greater riding pleasure and reduced trouble.

Off-Road Cycling Skills

To really appreciate the difference between a mountain bike and a regular touring bicycle in a positive sense, you have to use it off-road, even though these machines do quite well on surfaced roads as well. Before you take your mountain bike on an extensive bicycle tour, get familiar with the art of off-road cycling closer to home and without luggage. For this kind of work you need not find a spot of real wilderness, since suitable terrain to practice the kind of maneuvers required can be found almost everywhere.

Practice riding on soft ground and rough terrain. Get a feel for the gearing ratios and the pedaling rates best suited for certain conditions. Learn to climb in the saddle and out of the saddle, to mount and dismount quickly, without stopping or falling. Get used to the feel of braking under off-road conditions, going steeply downhill or riding on ground that is either soft or so uneven that the bike bounces wildly about.

All these things can be learned with a little conscious practice, since they don't really differ completely from the techniques described in the various chapters of Part II. It's not an absolute difference, but one of degree. If you practice enough, you can teach yourself these skills, as indeed most of today's successful off-road racers have done. Once you can ride confidently off-road, try doing the same with a loaded bicycle, especially if that is what you will be doing on tour. If you want to delve further into these matters, you are referred to my *Mountain Bike Book* for more detailed instructions and advice.

Cross-Country Touring

There are three perfectly respectable ways to use your mountain bike for touring:

☐ instead of a regular touring bike on normal roads;

☐ on normal roads with occasional off-road excursions;

☐ for real continuous off-road touring.

No doubt the latter is the ultimate off-road experience, but I suggest you start off by selecting one of the two less stringent alternatives. This way you learn to appreciate the advantages and disadvantages of this kind of equipment under different circumstances. That will help you select the riding style and equipment optimally to match terrain conditions encountered during subsequent tours.

Mountain Biking on the Road

If your choice is to tour on regular roads and to see your mountain bike rather as a more rugged type of regular touring machine, you are in a position to travel on rougher roads and to take steeper terrain than you would otherwise have been able to handle. There are parts of the world where this is obviously beneficial. My first trip to Baja California was in a car, but it immediately became clear that bicycle touring in that environment would require something like a mountain bike—which unfortunately did not yet exist at the time. The same can be said for much of Latin America and in fact for all countries outside the industrialized Western world.

To find your way on this kind of tour, you will need the same type of maps as you would choose when riding a regular bike. After all, the roads are not of a different category but of a different quality within the given category. Even so, you should probably count on making less rapid progress, and you may need more orientation and map-reading stops in this kind of terrain. For that reason, I still suggest you use topographical maps in addition to regular road maps, whenever you can get hold of the former in the less well-mapped parts of the world.

Mixed Touring

If you want to use your mountain bike to combine a longer tour on regular roads with excursions into the outback, I suggest you concentrate these trips to only one or two areas within your overall tour. National or state park lands, wilderness areas and the like all lend themselves to this kind of use. One way is to plan your tour to include one or more stops, perhaps at a campsite in or near such an area. Make your excursions from there, returning

Cycling in the Douglass County wine country in Oregon. (photo Dan Gindling)

to the base camp after the day's ride. In many popular mountain biking areas, this kind of thing is also possible using a mountain bike that is rented on the spot for the day or for a longer period.

A more demanding, but also more flexible, method is the one I would recommend you use. Plan your tour through such an area with good paths for off-road cycling and several campsites or other facilities. Travel to that destination on regular roads, covering considerable distances each day, until you get to a base camp. Next day, load the bike up with your camping gear again, to venture out on the trails to another campsite at a day's distance in off-road cycling terms. That distance is probably less than half what you may be used to doing on the road, though still quite a bit more than backpackers can cover. You'll be camping out in the wilds, meeting at best some backpackers and at worst a bear. Take all the precautionary and other measures with respect to food and safety you would take as a backpacker.

For this kind of touring, you can get by using perhaps only one or two detailed topographical maps for the off-road area you cover, in addition to road maps to cover the entire tour. Except for having to dismount each time you consult the map, orientation is no more problematic on the bike than it is when hiking, and it is no more difficult doing it this way than when making day trips. The added advantage is that, should you get lost, at least you have the equipment and the time to stay out another day before you have to get concerned about finding your way back to the civilized world.

Staying Off-Road

Once you have tried this technique, you may be ready to move up to the ultimate in off-road bike touring. That would be an entire vacation, traveling essentially only off-road. To reach the start of a mountain bike tour, you can travel by car or bike to a base camp. From there, take the bike and your camping equipment for a tour through woods and mountains, deserts and plains—a tour that may be purposely designed so as to avoid the roads as much as possible. In some areas, you need not even bring your own mountain bike for a trip like this, since you may be able to rent a perfectly good mountain bike and have it equipped with the appropriate luggage racks before you leave for the back country.

You will have to take a lot of food, and you should plan quite accurately how, when and where you can get to a town or a store to replenish your supplies. I have never ventured into the wilds this much myself, but those who have done so agree that it is a most impressive experience. You may be most surprised to note what distances you can cover on a tour like this. Returning on the main road, you may be following your earlier cycling route for hundreds of miles from some distance away.

This will probably do much for your appreciation of what a wonderful means of individual transportation the bicycle is—a machine that allows you to go where no other vehicle can, and to cover unbelievable distances in a limited time. With a mountain bike, this can be done miles away from the rush of everyday traffic that otherwise seems so pervasive and omnipresent in our society.

CHAPTER 23

Keeping a Record of Your Tour

It is quite possible to ride a bike for years, without ever feeling the need to preserve any of your experiences—whether for posterity or for your personal pleasure. If so, don't feel obliged to bother. However, if you are like most people I know, you will consider many of your bicycle tours so enjoyable or eventful that they warrant keeping some kind of mementos. From a more pragmatic standpoint, whether the whole trip was that enjoyable or not, each of your touring experiences can be used to advantage as a learning factor for the future. For all of these reasons, it is a good idea to keep a reasonably accurate and systematic record of your bicycle tours.

The simplest and most useful form of record keeping is the pocket diary. If you don't keep writing the most important facts down from day to day, you won't have traveled very far before you have forgotten how many days you've been gone, how far you've traveled, what day it is and what point you had intended to reach tomorrow. Though the modern digital wristwatch with display of weekday and date can help you keep on track as far as the date is concerned, keeping a minimal daily record in your diary seems essential for a successful trip. There are, however, more comprehensive, systematic and rewarding ways of recording your touring experiences, which will be covered below.

The Photo Log

One obvious way of tying your records together is by means of a photo log, systematically collecting the photographs you take while touring. In its simplest form, the photo log is no more than a conventional photo album. Most people take photographs here and there along the route. These can be organized in the photo album in such a way as to remain in their context as records of a specific trip to a defined goal at a known point in time. If you take slides, you can of course do the same with your slide collection, keeping the pictures from one trip together with the notes that pertain to them. You can also have both, since good prints can be made from properly exposed slides with the Cibachrome process.

For the photo album, arrange your photographs in the sequence of the tour on one or more two-page spreads. Add references to the locations, the dates and the names of the participants. Perhaps you can include a piece cut out or photocopied from a map in which the route is drawn in, referencing the places where you took the individual pictures, as well as start and finish and the locations of your overnight stops. Any additional pictorial mementos, ranging from postcards to hand-drawn sketches, from ferry tickets to dried plant or flower leaves, can also be added.

To do this really effectively, it will prove very helpful to maintain a systematic record during the tour. Keep a little note pad and pen with your camera, so you can record when and where each photo was taken, what the subject was and whether it contains any additional details that you might overlook or forget when you put the photos in the album, once you get home. Doing this conscientiously helps you get the most out of your photo records, and it avoids a lot of frustration later on. You may refer to Chapter 13 for some remarks about the selection of a camera and the best way to carry photo equipment on the bike.

The Touring Log

The concept of the notebook, mentioned above for recording information about the photographs you take, can be expanded to provide an even more useful set of records. Take a 4½ x 6 inch notebook (or the international size A-6), and keep all your records pertaining to your touring experiences in there. I already suggested such a notebook in Chapters 13 and 14, where I proposed using it to write down your various remarks about the items to take and the route to follow. Combine it with the kind of information used to back up your photographs, and you'll have a pretty compact and complete record of your tour.

Use a new notebook for each season or for each longer tour. Start off by collecting the preliminary systematic and random notes taken while preparing for the trip. As you go along, add the day-to-day remarks, specifically remembering to record the date, day of week, starting and termination points and a few details about the route as it was planned. During the day, add the details about the places where you stopped, as well as the subjects and locations you photographed. At the end of each day, update your entries with remarks about the actual trip.

All this may seem trivial, and it is to those who operate systematically by nature. But for us basically disorganized and impulsive folks—I guess we are about 99 percent of the populace—this must be organized consciously to be done right at all. What we also have to learn is to write legibly enough that it can be deciphered upon our return. It is also useful to keep the book in such a place and in such a state that the information can be located and the book can be found when it is needed. Take the trouble to go through all these notes almost immediately upon your return, when the experiences are still fresh in your mind, to get the maximum benefit from them.

The Mapping Log

In addition to the notebook, maps are your most valuable and concise recording tool. Some people cringe at the thought, but I think maps are more useful if you add your own remarks to them. Recording the locations of your stops makes it easier to find your way on the map as you are traveling. It helps even more in reconstructing your overall tour at the record keeping stage. Certainly the beginning and end points of each day's ride with the relevant date are worth recording on the map, using an indelible pen.

Then there are those who take a big marking pen and draw in the proposed route long before they set out. I've ruined perfectly good maps myself that way. However, I have never managed to adhere to those routes as I went along, nor has anyone else I know. In practice, you will soon find out, as I did, that the route actually travelled only rarely coincides with the one you had initially planned to take. The actual route you follow evolves as you go along, and the very purpose of a map is to find your way in the field, much more than planning it out at home.

The time to draw in the route you followed is *after* the day's ride. Only then can you be sure which way you actully went, while it is still fresh enough in your memory to remember the exact routing. In addition, this is the time to make some comments about the trip, perhaps drawing in some remarks of your own. The sites from which you took photographs are just as useful to indicate as the precise locations of worthwhile places to stop, scenic sections and really bad parts of the road, to give some examples.

These remarks will not only help you reconstruct the tour when collecting records afterwards, they also serve several other important purposes. You can learn from earlier experiences in bike touring, as in other pursuits, by referring to your records, whether consciously or not. Having recorded on the map where it was good or bad may help you seek out or avoid either the same sites or those that are characterized by the same features in other locations. Finally, you will be able to use these records to help others who are planning to travel in an area where you have been. If you can show on a map where you went and how it was, your friends will be much better prepared when they leave on their trip.

All this record keeping, whether documenting photos, routes or anything else, is of course strictly up to you. Many cyclists don't want to be bothered, since they enjoy the experience of riding more than that of digesting their experiences. Others have such organized minds that they can do without, although these are more typically exactly the ones who keep meticulous paper records as well. And finally, my way is not the only right way to do it. This description may help if you don't know at all how to go about it, but it is entirely up to you to find a method of recording your touring experiences, using the tools and the form you enjoy most.

Feel free not to keep any records at all, except in your mind. However, I know lots of people who were sorry they did not take systematic notes afterwards, while I have never met anybody who regretted keeping such a record of his touring experiences.

Getting Published

Some of your photographs and writings may well be suitable for publication in one of the increasing number of bicycle, camping or adventure magazines. If it doesn't provide much extra income, at least it may serve to boost your ego. Especially for magazine articles, the pictures are at least as important as the text. So your photographs had better be good: only perfectly exposed and brilliantly sharp color slides will be accepted to maintain today's standards in magazine publishing.

If you are thinking of getting your work published in book form, you'll have to count on it being done in black and white. So in that case, instead of color slides, use black and white film and make sure you can offer perfectly sharp large glossy black and white enlargements (at least 5 x 7 inches). Actually, with today's technology, it is possible to get decent halftones (the technical term for black and white photos as reproduced in print) from color prints. But they have to be at least 5 x 7 and must be brilliantly sharp glossy prints. As with magazine material, if your publisher can print in color, color prints will not do; you must supply color slides.

If you are more artistic and skilled than most of us, really good drawings or water colors may also be suitable, and are gladly accepted by some editors. Whatever the chosen form of illustrations for this purpose, they are of no use unless they bear directly on the text of the article. The latter should be relatively short and to the point (where exactly, what, who, when, and why), avoiding any unnecessary detail and background information—at all cost avoid showing pictures of yourself, except for one single photo of the author with or without bike. Include a clear description of the location and distance of your tour, as well as a map showing the route in relation to nearby major cities or other landmarks. Before you get down to writing, take a critical look at some of the other material published, to give you an idea what editors and publishers are looking for.

Back Matter

Appendix:
Tables
Packing List
List of Addresses

Bibliography

Index

Table 1. Frame sizing

inseam size inch (cm)	road bike cm	road bike inch	mountain bike cm	mountain bike inch	touring bike cm	touring bike inch
28 (69—70)	45	17	42	16	46	18
29 (71—72)	46	17.5	44	16.5	48	19
(73—74)	48	19	46	17	50	20
30 (75—76)	50	19	48	19	52	21
31 (77—78)	52	21	54	22	50	20
32 (79—80)	54	21.5	56	22	51	20.5
(81—82)	56	22	58	23	53	21
33 (83—84)	58	23	60	24	55	22
34 (85—86)	60	24	62	25	57	22.5
35 (87—89)	62	25	63	25.5	58	23
36 (90—92)	64	26	65	26	60	24

Remarks:
1. This table applies to bicycles with 26 in, 27 in, 650 mm and 700 mm wheels.
2. Inside leg measurement is taken per Fig. A.
3. Maximum recommended seat height as defined in Fig. B, dimension X. If measured per dimension Y, a nominal frame size must be selected that is 1.5 cm or 0.5 inch smaller.
4. See Chapters 2, 8 and 22 for additional explanations.

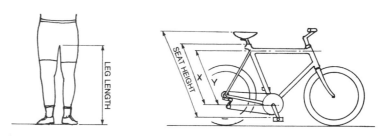

Fig. A. Inseam leg length determination   Fig. B. Frame size determination

Table 2. Gear table in inches

number of teeth on chainring	12	13	14	15	16	17	18	19	20	21	22	23	24	25	26	27	28	29	30
28	63	58	54	50	47	44	42	40	38	36	34	33	31	30	29	28	27	26	25
29	65	60	56	52	49	46	43	42	39	38	35	34	33	31	30	29	28	27	26
30	67	62	58	54	51	48	45	43	41	39	37	35	34	32	31	30	29	28	27
31	70	65	60	56	52	50	47	44	42	40	38	37	36	34	32	31	30	29	28
32	72	67	62	58	54	51	48	45	43	41	39	38	36	35	33	32	31	30	29
33	74	69	64	60	56	53	50	47	45	43	41	39	37	36	34	33	32	31	30
34	76	71	66	61	57	54	51	48	46	44	42	40	38	37	35	34	33	32	31
35	78	73	68	63	59	56	53	50	48	45	43	41	39	38	36	35	34	33	33
36	81	75	69	65	61	57	54	51	49	46	44	42	40	39	37	36	35	34	32
37	84	77	71	67	63	59	56	53	50	48	46	44	41	40	39	37	36	35	33
38	86	79	73	68	64	60	57	54	51	49	47	45	42	41	40	38	37	35	34
39	87	81	75	70	65	62	58	55	53	50	47	46	43	42	41	39	38	36	35
40	90	83	77	72	68	64	60	57	54	51	49	47	45	43	42	40	39	37	36
41	93	85	79	74	70	65	62	59	56	53	51	48	46	44	43	41	40	38	37
42	95	87	81	76	71	67	63	60	57	54	52	49	47	45	44	42	41	39	38
43	97	89	83	77	73	68	65	61	58	55	53	50	48	46	45	43	41	40	39
44	99	91	85	79	74	70	66	63	59	57	54	52	50	48	46	44	42	44	48
45	101	93	87	81	76	72	68	64	61	58	55	53	51	49	47	45	43	42	41
46	104	96	88	83	78	73	69	65	62	59	57	54	52	50	48	46	44	43	41
47	106	98	91	85	79	75	71	67	63	60	58	55	53	51	49	47	45	44	42
48	108	100	93	86	81	76	72	68	65	62	59	56	54	52	50	48	46	45	43
49	110	102	95	88	83	78	74	70	66	63	60	58	55	53	51	49	47	46	44
50	113	104	96	90	84	79	75	71	68	64	61	59	56	54	52	50	48	47	45
51	115	106	98	92	86	81	77	72	69	66	63	60	58	55	53	51	49	48	46
52	117	108	100	94	88	83	78	74	70	67	64	61	59	56	54	52	50	48	47
53	119	110	102	95	89	84	80	75	72	68	65	62	60	57	55	53	51	49	48
54	122	112	104	97	91	86	81	77	73	69	66	63	61	58	56	54	52	50	49
55	124	114	106	99	93	87	83	78	75	71	68	65	62	59	57	55	53	51	50
56	126	116	108	100	95	89	84	80	76	72	69	66	63	60	58	56	54	52	50

Number of teeth on sprocket (column header)

Table 3. Conversion from inch gear to development in meters

Gear number (inches)

```
     30    40    50    60    70    80    90   100   110   120    in
     |     |     |     |     |     |     |     |     |     |
   2,0   3,0   4,0   5,0   6,0   7,0   8,0  10,0  11,0   m
```

Development (meters)

Remarks:
1. See Chapter 9 for derivation and explanations.
2. See Table 2 for gear numbers in inches.

LOW GEAR
SHORT DEVELOPMENT

HIGH GEAR – LONG DEVELOPMENT

Suggested packing list

Note:

This compilation is only intended as a starting point to help you make up your own packing list. Select only the appropriate items from the various groups applicable to your situation; delete or add items and avoid duplication.

Removable bike accessories:

pump	lights	bike cover
lock	warning device	straps, belts, bungees
water bottle	rear view mirror	
map holder	saddle cover	

Tools, etc.:

tool pouch	adjustable wrench	spray lubricant
screw driver	pliers	hand cleaning paste
patch kit	spoke wrench	cleaning rags
3 tire irons	crank tool	repair instructions
Allen keys	chain tool	
wrenches (spanners)	freewheel tool	

Spare parts:

brake cable	light bulbs	brake blocks
gear cable	batteries	special spares
insulated electric wire	inner tube	
spokes	chain links	

Bike clothing:

shorts	underwear	helmet
jersey, shirt	shoes	visor
socks	gloves	

Cold weather wear:

long pants	helmet liner	helmet cover, Sou'wester
sweater	long underwear	spats, leggings
thick socks	pedal covers	shoe covers, pedal covers
lined gloves, mittens		overshoes, plastic liners
jacket	Rain gear:	
scarf	jacket, cape	

Off-bike clothing:

shoes	slacks, skirt, dress	track suit
socks	jacket	pajamas
shirt	swim wear	

First aid items:

first aid pouch	scissors	disinfectant
band aids	prescription medicines	water purification tablets
aspirin	insect repellent	
tweezers	insect bite ointment	

Toilet gear:

small and large towels
toilet bag, pouch
soap
wash cloth
tooth brush
dental floss

tooth picks
tooth paste
cotton swabs
shaving equipment
mirror
nail scissors

nail file
comb, hair brush
shampoo
sun screen, lotion
tissues, toilet paper

Documents etc.:

document pouch, wallet
cash
ID, driver's license

credit cards
address, phone no. list
transportation tickets

insurance documents
address book

Orientation aids:

maps
spare map pouch
map cover

curvimeter
compass
binoculars

note book
pen, pencil

Various:

pocket knife
can opener
scissors
sewing kit
cold water detergent
chamois cream
laundry line
clothes pegs
clip board, plain board

protector for stationery etc.
stationery
envelopes
stamps
note book
pen, pencil
flash light (torch)
camera, accessories
films

spare glasses, sun glasses
literature
pocket radio
wrist watch
tissues
toilet paper
ziplock bags
carrier bags
small backpack

For roadside eating:

pouch for utensils
knife, fork, spoon
flat tray, bread board

cup
bowl, plate
can opener

dish towel
plastic sheet

For foreign touring:

passport
visa
vaccination record
foreign currency

traveller's checks
special insurance
guide book
phrase book

dictionary
special address list
special medicines

For camping:

groundsheet
sleeping bag
sleeping pad, air mattress
cushion
sleeping bag liner
tent with accessories
spade
electric light, candle
wind shields

stove
fuel
cooking pots
can opener
matches, lighter
salt, spices
staples (sugar, flour, etc.)
dehydrated or canned food
storage bags or containers

screw-top bottles
water container
wash basin
dishwashing liquid
dish brush
scouring pad
dish towel
(also see *Roadside eating*)

List of Addresses

Alliance Internationale du
Tourisme (AIT)
Department de Cyclisme
Quai Gustave Ador 2
1207 Geneva
Switzerland

American Youth Hostels, Inc.
1332 - I Street
Suite 800
Washington, DC 20005
USA

Association of Cycle and
Lightweight Campers
11 Grosvenor Place
London SW1W OEY
Great Britain

Australian Cycling Council
153 The Kingsway
Cronulla
Sydney 2230
Australia

Bicycle Federation
1055 Thomas Jefferson Street
Washington, DC 20007
USA

Bicycle Federation of Australia
399 Pitt Street
Sydney 2000
Australia

League of American
Wheelmen, LAW
PO Box 988
Baltimore, MD 21203
USA

Bikecentennial
Box 8308
Missoula, MT 59807

USA
British Cycling Federation
70 Brompton Road
London SW3 1 EN
Great Britain

Camping Club of Great Britain
and Ireland, Ltd.
11 Lower Grosvenor Place
London, SW1
Great Britain

Canadian Cycling Association
Touring Department
333 River Road
Vanier, Ontario K1L 8B9
Canada

Canadian Youth Hostel
Association
268 First Avenue
Ottawa, Ontario
Canada

Countryside Commission
John Dower House
Crescent Place
Cheltenham GL50 3RA
Great Britain

Cyclists' Touring Club
69 Meadrow
Godalming, Surrey GU7 3HS
Great Britain

Effective Cycling League
726 Madrone
Sunnyvale, CA 94086
USA

International Association for
Medical Aid to Travellers
736 Center Street
Lewiston, NY 14092

USA

National Parks Foundation
PO Box 57473
Washington, DC 20037
USA

Sierra Club
540 Bush Street
San Francisco, CA 94108
USA

Rough Stuff Fellowship
c/o F.E. Groatcher
65 Stoneleigh Avenue
Worcester Park, Surrey KT4
8XY
Great Britain

Tandem Club
c/o Peter Hallowell
25 Hendred Way
Abingdon, Oxfordshire OX14
2AN
Great Britain

Touring Bureau
3 Moor Lane
Lancaster
Great Britain

Travel and Services
Department
29 John Adam Street
London, WC2
Great Britain

The Youth Hostel Association
Trevelyan House
8 St. Stephen's Hill
St. Albans, Herts AL1 2DY
Great Britain

Bibliography

Advanced First Aid. New York: Doubleday / The American National Red Cross, 1973.

American Youth Hostels Handbook. Delaplane, VT: American Youth Hostel Association, (annual).

Ayres, M., *Cycles and Cycling*. London: Butterworth, 1981.

Ballantine, R. and R. Grant, *Richard's Ultimate Bicycle Book*. London: Dorling Kindersley, 1992.

Bicycle Touring Atlas. New York: American Youth Hostel Association, 1969.

Biestman, M., *Travel for Two*. Sausalito, CA: Pergot Press, 1986.

Bridge, R., *Freewheeling: The Bicycle Camping Book*. Harrisonburg, PA: Stackpole Books, 1979.

——,*Bike Touring*. San Francisco: Sierra Club Books, 1979.

Brooks, J. and Candy, J. (ed.), *The South America Handbook*. Bath (GB): Mendip Press, Chicago: Rand McNally, 1980.

Bunelle, H. and Sarvis, S., *Cooking for Camp and Trail*. San Francisco: Sierra Club Books, 1984.

Campground and Trailer Park Guide. Chicago: Rand McNally, (annual).

Carlson, R. (ed.), *National Directory of Budget Motels*. New York: Pilot Books, (annual).

Clark, J., *Cycling the U.S. Parks*. San Francisco: Bicycle Books, 1993.

Climates of the States. Port Washington, NY: United States National Oceanic and Atmospheric Administration, 1974.

Coles, C.W., and Glenn, H.T., *Glenn's Complete Bicycle Manual*. New York: Crown Publishers, 1973.

The Complete Guide to America's National Parks. Washington, DC: The National Park Foundation, 1984.

Crane, N. (ed.), *International Cycling Guide*. London: The Tantivy Press, New York: Zootrope, (bi-annual).

The CTC Handbook. Godalming, Surrey (GB): Cyclist's Touring Club, (annual).

Cuthberson, T., Anybody's Bike Book. Berkeley, CA: Ten-Speed Press, 1984.

——,*Bike Tripping*. Berkeley, CA: Ten-Speed Press, 1984. Cyclists Reference Dictionary. London: F.C. Avis.

Davis, A. (ed.), *The On Your Own Guide to Asia*. Rutland, VT: Charles E. Tuttle, 1979.

DeLong, F., *DeLong's Guide to Bicycles and Bicycling*. Radnor, PA: Chilton Books, 1978.

Eastman, P.F., *Advanced First Aid for All Outdoors*. Centerville, MD: Cornell Maritime Press, 1976.

Editors of Bicycling Magazine, *Best Bicycle Tours*. Emmaus, PA: Rodale Press, 1981.

Faria, I.E., Cycling Physiology for the Serious Cyclist. Springfield, MA: Thomas, 1978.

Fletcher, C., *The New Complete Walker*, New York, Knopf, 1974.

Food and Nutrition Board, *Recommended Dietary Allowances*. Washington, DC: National Academy of Sciences, 1974.

Forester, J., *Effective Cycling*. Cambridge, MA: MIT-Press, 1984.

Gatty, H., *Finding Your Way on Land and Sea*. Brattleboro, VT: Stephen Green Press, 1983.

Gausden, C. and Crane, N., *The CTC Route Guide to Cycling in Britain and Ireland*. Oxford: Oxford Illustrated Press, Harmondsworth: Penguin Books, 1980.

Greenhood, D., *Mapping*. Chicago: University of Chicago Press, 1964.

Hawkins, K. and G., *Bicycle Touring in Europe*. New York: Pantheon Books, 1980.

Hefferson, L., *Cycle Food*. Berkeley, CA: Ten-Speed Press, 1976.

Howard, J., *The Cyclist's Companion*. Brattleboro, VT: Stephen Green Press, 1984.

Inside the Cyclist. Brattleboro, VT: Vitesse Press, 1984.

International Bicycle Touring. Mountain View, CA: World Publications, 1976.

Kals, W.S., *Land Navigation Handbook*. San Francisco: Sierra Club Books, 1971.

Kellstrom, G., *Map and Compass*. New York: Charles Scribner's Sons, 1973.

Knotty, P., *Cycle Touring in Europe*. London: Constable, 1976.

Murphey, D., Full Tilt: *Ireland to India with a Bicycle*. London: J. Murray, 1978.

Nasr, K., *Bicycle Touring International*. San Francisco: Bicycle Books, 1993

Palister, N. (ed.), *NOLS Cookery*. Emporia, KS: Emporia State Press, 1974.

Rafoth, R., *Bicycling Fuel*. San Francisco: Bicycle Books, 1993.

Slavinski, N., *Cycling Europe*. San Francisco: Bicycle Books, 1992.

Sloane, E., *Eugene A. Sloane's Complete Guide to All-Terrain Bicycles*. New York: Simon & Schuster, 1985.

——, *The New Complete Book of Bicycling*. New York: Simon & Schuster, 1981.

Thomas, D., *Roughing it Easy*. Provo, UT: Brigham Young University Press, 1974.

Van der Plas, R., *The Bicycle Repair Book*. San Francisco: Bicycle Books, 1993.

——, *Bicycle Technology*. San Francisco: Bicycle Books, 1992.

——, *The Mountain Bike Book*. San Francisco: Bicycle Books, 1993.

——, *The Penguin Bicycle Handbook*. Harmondsworth (GB): Penguin Books, 1983.

——, *Roadside Bicycle Repairs*. San Francisco: Bicycle Books, 1990.

Watts, A., *Instant Weather Forecasting*, New York: Dodd Mead & Co, 1968.

Westell, F. and S. Martin, *The Cyclist's Body Book*. Huddersfield (GB): Srpingfield Books, 1991.

Whiter, R., *The Bicycle Manual on Maintenance and Repairs*. Chicago, IL: Contemporary Books, 1972.

Whitt, F.R. and Wilson, D.G., *Bicycling Science*. Cambridge, MA: MIT-Press, 1982.

Wilhelm, T. and G., *The Bicycle Touring Book*. Emmaus, PA: Rodale Press, 1980.

Youth Hosteller's Guide to Europe. London: Youth Hostel Association, Riverside, NJ: Collier Books, 1977.

A

accessories
  attaching to bike, 55–57
  fenders, 57–59
  lights, 59–62
  locks, 64
  maintenance for, 56–57
  for mountain bike, 40
  for poor weather, 147
  pump/tire gauge, 62–63
  selecting, 16
  spares, 65–66
  tools, 65–66
  for touring bike, 26–27, 55–66
  warning devices, 64–65
  water bottle, 63–64
accidents, 129, 133–136
  avoidance procedures for, 130–133
  diverting type, 134–135
  falls/collisions, 133–134
  fork damage from, 35
  high-risk periods for, 131
  loss-of-control type, 135–136
  skidding type, 135
  stopping type, 134
  See also handling; safety
air mattress, 92
  See also camping gear
airplanes
  bike transport on, 159–160, 207
  tandem bike transport on, 224
  for travel to tour site, 165
  See also foreign touring; transportation
alloys, for frame, 31
aluminum
  fenders, 59
  frame, 30, 32, 33, 35
  handlebars, 36
  luggage racks, 70
  rims, 48, 146
  water bottles, 63
ANSI Z-90.4 helmet standard, 80, 137
arms
  correct positioning for, 104
  injuries to, 135, 136, 137
  length of affecting fit, 102, 103
  See also hands; safety

B

backache, 140
  See also injuries
backpacks
  for food supplies, 156–157
  pannier bag as, 74
  pros/cons, 71–72
  See also bike bags; luggage racks
batteries
  for lights, 61–62
  See also lights
bearings
  cartridge (sealed), 42, 146
  in crankset, 42
  cup-and-cone, 42
  in headset, 35
belt pack, 72

See also luggage
bicycle bags, 23
  See also luggage
bicycle parts, 29
  See also components
bicycle paths
  disadvantages of, 213
  See also off-road riding
Bicycle Touring International, 204, 205
bicycles
  for children, 219–220
  renting, 208, 225, 235
  transporting, 72, 159–160
  See also mountain bike; racing bike; tandem bike; touring bike
Bicycling Fuel, 185
bike bags, 23, 67, 71
  personal bags, 71–72
  See also luggage racks
bike stores
  selecting parts at, 29
  for supplies, 19, 20
  See also mail order
Bikecentennial, 17, 130, 175
  accident frequency rates, 130, 131
binoculars, 183
Blackburn, Jim, 57, 69
Bluemels, 58
bottom bracket, 30
  bearing systems for, 42
bottom tube, 29–30
brakes
  adjusting, 52–53
  block style factors, 53, 146–147
  braking techniques, 121–123
  cable replacement, 53–54
  cam-operated, 52
  Campagnolo C-Record, 29
  cantilever, 41, 52
  cantilever, for mountain bike, 38, 146–147
  cantilever, pivot bosses for, 35, 38
  hub brakes, 51
  lever types, 53
  Modolo D-0015 brake blocks, 147
  for parking, 64
  rim brake types, 51–52
  Sachs drum, 41
  safety testing, 53
  selecting, 29
  sidepull, 51–52
  in stopping procedure, 105–106
  for tandem bike, 230
  of touring bike, 26–27
braze-ons, for accessory attachment, 55–56
brazing, 70
Breeze, Joe, 39
bungee cords, disadvantages of, 74, 156
  Burden, Dan, 17
buses, 165
  transporting tandem bike on, 224

C

cables
  brake, 52
  brake, adjusting, 52–53
  brake, replacing, 53–54
  Campagnolo, 52
  derailleur, 113
  guides for, 56
  shifter, 45
caffeine, 192
  See also food
cameras
  handlebar bag for, 73
  for photo log, 237–238
  selecting for tour, 154
Campagnolo
  cables, 52
  C-Record brakes, 29
camping, 195–202
  breaking camp, 201
  campsite selection, 196–197
  with children, 221–222
  in foreign countries, 212–213
  meal preparation, 199–200
  on private land, 196–197
  in poor weather, 149–150
  See also motels
camping gear
  air mattress, 92
  campsite clothing, 84
  cooking gear, 92–93
  other equipment, 94
  packing procedures for, 156
  selecting, 85–94, 195–196
  sleeping bags, 86–89
  tents, 89–91
carbohydrates, 187–188, 190–191
  carbohydrate loading, 192–193
  metabolism of, 191–192
  See also food
cars
  for touring support, 175
  transporting tandem bike in, 224
chain
  construction details, 44
  maintenance of, 44
  on tandem bike, 228
chain hanger, 30, 56
chain rivet extractor, use of, 44
chain stays, 30, 33
chainring
  attachment detail, 43
  attachment to spider, 43
  selecting, 114–116
chainset. *See* crankset
children
  bicycles for, 219–220
  bike adjustments for, 104
  carrying on bike, 217–218
  Gerry-Pack for, 218
  overnight tour with, 221–222
  special bike seats for, 218
  tandem biking with, 220–221
  touring capability of, 215–216
  trailers for, 218, 219
chrome, in frame alloy, 31

cities, route considerations for, 165, 211
clamps, for accessory attachment, 56–57
clipless pedals, 44
　　See also pedals
clips, for accessory attachment, 56–57
clothing, 77–84, 78, 144–145
　　for accident prevention, 133
　　arranging in tent, 200
　　campsite wear, 84
　　for children, 222
　　cold weather, 82–83, 140–141
　　essential items, 152–153
　　gloves, 80
　　helmets, 80–81
　　for injury prevention, 134
　　limited, for touring, 153–154
　　plastic bags, 82, 83
　　for preventing saddle sores, 139
　　rain gear, 81–82
　　shirts/tops, 79–80
　　shoes/socks, 77–78
　　shorts/slacks, 78–79
　　street clothes, 83–84
cold weather
　　clothing for, 80, 82–83
　　cycling practice for, 146
　　health concerns for, 140–141
　　related injuries from, 139, 140
　　riding style in, 147–149
　　sleeping bag for, 87
　　See also clothing; rain gear
Coleman Peak 10 stove, 93
collisions. *See* accidents; safety
comfort
　　frame weight affecting, 30–31
　　handlebar sleeves for, 80
　　riding posture affecting, 97–98
　　sleeping pad enhancing, 92
　　tube/tire weight affecting, 49
　　See also clothing; safety
commuting by bike, 172–173
compass, 180, 183
　　See also maps
components
　　bike parts, 29
　　specialized, 29
　　specialized vs. general, 27
　　See also accessories; quality
Consumer Product Safety Commission
　　(CPSC), 58, 220
containers, for supplies, 157–158
cooking gear, 92–93
　　packing tips for, 158–159
　　See also camping gear; packing
CPSC. *See* Consumer Product Safety
　　Commission
cranks
　　cotterless, tightening, 42
　　cotterless, attaching, 42
　　offset, on tandem bike, 229
　　straightening, 42
crankset, 42
　　cottered vs. cotterless, 42
　　See also drivetrain
CTC. *See* Cyclists' Touring Club
curvimeter, 181
　　See also maps
Custom Cycling Fitments, 82

cycling clubs, 17–19
　　in Great Britain, 18, 19
Cyclists' Touring Club (CTC), 18, 175

D
derailleur
　　function and position, 45–46, 108–109
　　indexed, 46
　　See also gearing system
diet. *See* food
down tube, 31, 32, 33
drafting, 125
　　See also group riding; wind resistance
drivetrain, 41–42
　　crankset, 42
　　derailleur system, 41
　　drum brake system, 41
　　for tandem bike, 227–229
　　of touring bike, 26–27
　　See also gearing system
drop-outs, 30
　　for accessory attachment, 56
　　derailleur placement on, 45

E
Effective Cycling, 117
electrolytes. *See* minerals
elevation
　　evaluating for tour, 163, 167
　　See also hilly terrain; maps
endurance
　　carbohydrate loading for, 192–193
　　considerations for, 171–173
　　diet for, 185–186
　　gear selection enhancing, 107
　　gradual build-up of, 162–163
　　pedaling rate enhancing, 110, 113
　　safety concerns for, 130–131
　　vitamins enhancing, 189
　　See also food; speed; training
equipment
　　renting, 20
　　selecting, 16
　　specialized vs. general, 27
ESGE, 59
ETRTO designation, 49
Europe
　　buying supplies in, 154
　　children's bike availability in, 220
　　See also foreign touring
Europe on $5 a Day, 205
eyelets, for accessory attachment, 55–56

F
fat, in weight loss, 193
fatigue failure, 59
　　in luggage racks, 69–70
fats, 188
　　metabolism of, 191–192
　　See also food
feet
　　affect on saddle height, 101
　　See also shoes
fenders
　　benefits of, 57–58, 82
　　clearance required for, 35

fiber-reinforced, 59
　　installing, 58
　　metal, 59
　　for mountain bike, 40
　　mud flap for, 59, 82
　　plastic, 58–59
fiber/bran, 190
　　See also food
fit
　　for child's bike, 220
　　for handlebar/saddle, 98–103, 99
　　for mountain bike, 38
　　selecting frame for, 33–34
flat tire. *See* tires, puncture repair
Flick Stand, 64
food
　　caffeine, 192
　　camping meals, 199–200
　　carbohydrate loading, 192–193
　　carbohydrates, 187–188, 190–191
　　endurance diet, 185–186
　　for energy, 190–192
　　fat, in weight loss, 193
　　fats, 188, 190–191
　　fiber/bran, 190
　　functions/types of, 186
　　isotonic solutions, 187
　　liquids requirements, 186–187
　　meal planning, 189, 193–194
　　meal timing, 201–202
　　minerals, 190
　　for off-road touring, 235
　　packing tips for, 158–159
　　proteins, 188–189, 190–191
　　respiratory quotient concerns, 191–192
　　scrounging for, 197
　　snacks, 194
　　sugars, 187, 188
　　for touring, 155, 185–194
　　for touring children, 217
　　transporting on bike, 156–157
　　vitamins, 189–190
foreign touring, 203–214
　　accommodations for, 212–213
　　language difficulties, 209–210
　　maps for, 206–207, 208–209
　　preparing for, 204–207
　　route selection for, 211–212
　　safety concerns for, 129–130
　　timing for, 210–211
　　See also planning; touring
Forester, John, 117
fork, 34
　　components of, 34–35
　　front fork, 34–35, 35
　　threaded bosses for, 56
fork crown, 34
fork-ends, 30
frame
　　braze-ons, 55–56
　　components of, 29–30
　　custom-built, 28–29, 33, 103
　　English vs. French threading, 35
　　frame dimensioning, 32, 33–34
　　frame joints, 30–31, 31
　　geometry of, 32
　　materials for, 30, 33
　　men's vs. women's, 28
　　of mountain bike, 33, 38

pump attachment to, 63
rigidity requirements, 31–32
of tandem bike, 226–227
of touring bike, 26–27
touring vs. racing, 32, 33, 34
tubing materials, 33
frame bag, 73
frame dimensioning, 32, 33–34
France, typical touring bike, 28
freewheel
cassette hub, 44–45
Maillard Helico-matic, 44
separate, 44–45
freewheel block, 44
French valves. See Presta valves
Frommer, Arthur, 205
front fork, 34–35, 35
full tuck position, adjustments for, 102
functionality, checking components for, 29

G
gearing set-up, for mountain bike, 39
gearing system, 45–46, 107, 111–113
chainring/sprocket selection, 114–116
derailleur, 46, 108–109
derailleur adjustment, 113–114
derailleur, front, 45, 108–109
derailleur, rear, 45, 108–109
gear selection procedure, 113
hub gears, 41, 45
indexed, 46, 111
practice procedures for, 110–111
shifters, 45
start-up procedures, 105
for tandem bike, 227–229
theory for, 109–110
of touring bike, 26–27
generators, 60
See also lights
geometry, 32
fork angles, 35
steering geometry, 35
See also frame
Gerry-Pack, 218
See also children; luggage
Girvin Flexstem, 40
gloves, 80
for injury prevention, 134
for numbness prevention, 140
See also clothing
Gordon, Bruce, 25
Goretex clothing, 81
See also clothing; rain gear
Grab-On, 104
Great Britain
cycling clubs in, 17
Cyclists' Touring Club, 18
touring in, 18
typical touring bike, 28
See also Europe
grips, for handlebars, 39
ground sheet, 90, 91
See also camping gear; tents
group riding
drafting, 125
riding style for, 148
tandem bike for, 223

tour planning for, 162, 174

H
handlebar bags, 73
for instant-access items, 155
See also luggage
handlebar stem, 34
replacing, 103
sprung, 40
handlebars, 34
adjusting, 36–37
bar-end shifters for, 46
drop style, 52
foam sleeves for, 80, 104, 140
height/position adjustment, 102–104
for mountain bike, 39
handling
acceleration procedure, 124–125
basic procedures, 104–106
bike balance affecting, 118–119
braking techniques, 121–123
forced turn, 120–121, 126–127
jumping the bike, 127–128
natural turns, 119–120
obstacle avoidance, 126–127
safety concerns for, 131
speed consistency, 124
start-up procedures, 105
steering principle, 118
stopping procedures, 105–106
See also safety; turns
hands
cushioning for, 80
hand signals, 133
handlebar position affecting, 103–104
injuries to, 130
numbness in, 140
See also arms; safety
head lugs, 30
head protection. See helmets
head tube, 29–30
headset, 34
components of, 35–36
English vs. French threading, 35
headset bearings, 34
health
in foreign tour, 213–214
See also safety
helmets, 80–81, 134
for injury prevention, 134
safety functions of, 137
See also safety
hilly terrain
accident risks with, 130
avoiding, 162
brake use in, 123
caffeine use in, 192
climbing skills for, 125–126
clothing for, 82–83
elevation considerations, 163, 167
food requirements for, 191, 192
gearing system for, 46
health concerns for, 140–141
identifying on maps, 167, 183
meal planning for, 193–194
orientation in, 180
preparation for, 210–211
Hite-Rite, 39

Hodges, Mark, 100
home trainers, 171–172
See also training
honking, 126
hotel. See motels
hub brakes, 51
Sachs drum brakes, 41
hubs
high/low flange, 46
quick-release, 46
See also spokes; tire; wheel

I
identification, for foreign tour, 204, 214
injuries
abrasions, 136
backache, 140
to brain, 137–138
from collisions, 134, 135, 136–138
evaluating, 130–131
fractures, 137
to knee, 139
numbness, 140
from overtraining, 141–142
sinus/bronchial complaints, 140–141
sprains, 136–137
sunburn, 141, 146
tendonitis, 139–140
See also handling; safety
instruction, bike clubs providing, 17–18, 19
insurance, 129
for foreign tour, 213–214
Ishiwata, 33
isotonic solutions, 187
See also food

J
jumping the bike, 127–128
See also handling

K
Kaplan, Jerrold, 130
knee injuries, 139
See also injuries; safety

L
language difficulties, in foreign tour, 209–210
laundry, 78–79
See also clothing
League of American Wheelmen, 18, 175
leather belts, for securing luggage, 156
lights
attachment of, 56
battery powered, 61–62
fender mounting of, 59
generator lighting, 60
for mountain bike, 40
for poor weather, 147
reflectors, 62, 132, 147
required for safety, 131–132
See also safety
locks, 64

Lonely Planet guides, 205
lubrication
    for pedals, 43
    for poor weather, 147
    for threaded parts, 56
    See also maintenance
luggage
    accident risks with, 130
    affecting handling, 105, 120
    bicycle bags, 23
    children's seats, 218–219
    for child's bike, 220
    for foreign travel, 207–208
    gearing system for carrying, 46
    Gerry-Pack, 218
    loading procedures, 67–69, 105,
      156–157
    securing to bike, 156
    for tandem bike, 223–224
    for transporting bike, 72, 159–160,
      207–208
    weather protection for, 148–150
    See also packing
luggage carrying equipment, 67–76
    backpacks, 71–72, 74
    bag details, 74–76
    bike bags, 23, 67, 71, 72–76
    bike bags, personal, 71–72
    frame bags, 73
    handlebar bags, 73
    pannier bags, 73–74
    rack-top bags, 74
    requirements for, 67, 70–71
    saddle bags, 72–73
    trailer, 67, 76
    See also packing
luggage racks, 25
    fork attachments for, 34–35
    installation points for, 55–56
    loading, 67–69
    for mountain bike, 40
    mounting to bike, 70
    types of, 57
lugs, for accessory attachment, 55–56

M
mail order
    for bike supplies, 19–20, 67
    for camping supplies, 85, 195–196
    for clothing, 81
    See also bike stores
maintenance
    for accessories, 56–57
    for chain, 44
    for derailleurs, 113–114
    for tandem, 225–226
    weather affecting, 147
    See also lubrication; repairs; spares;
      tools
manganese, 31
Mannesmann, 33
maps, 162, 166–167
    accessibility for, 155
    additional orientation aids, 183–184
    cases for, 40, 157–158, 181, 182
    curvimeter for, 168, 181
    features of, 167–168
    for foreign touring, 206–207, 208–209

mapping log, 239–240
    for off-road riding, 234, 235
    for preliminary orientation, 179–180
    proficiency with for children, 217
    reading tips, 181–182
    relative scale readings, 180–181
    types of, 166
    See also planning; touring
meals
    planning, 189, 193–194, 201–202
    See also food
Michelin guides, 205
Michelin maps, 167
minerals, 190
    See also food
molybdenum, 31
money, exchanging, 206
motels, 150, 154, 174, 176, 195, 222
    in foreign countries, 212–213
mountain bike
    accessories for, 40
    adjusting for fit, 104
    brake levers, 52
    brakes, 38, 146–147
    frame, 33, 38
    gearing set-up, 39, 126
    handlebars, 39
    luggage racks for, 40
    shifters for, 108
    tires for, 49
    touring accessories for, 55
    touring with, 25, 37 39, 231–236
mountains. *See* hilly terrain
mud flaps, 59
    See also fenders

N
Nasr, Kameel, 204, 205
nature, appreciating on bike, 15, 16
Nordlicht generator, 60

O
obstacles
    avoiding, 126–127
    collisions with, 133–136
    See also accidents; safety
off-road riding
    avoiding on tour, 162–163
    bicycle paths, 213
    bike adjustments for, 104
    combined with touring, 234–235
    in foreign country, 208–209
    jumping techniques, 127–128
    mountain bike for, 232–236
    skills for, 233
    tire pressure for, 62–63
    tires for, 38–39, 49
    warning device for, 64–65
    See also mountain bike
109% rule, for saddle height, 99
overnight trips, 174–175
    See also planning; touring
overtraining
    injuries from, 141–142
    See also injuries

P
pacing, 125
    See also handling; wind resistance
packing
    determining priorities for, 152–153
    luggage attachment techniques,
      156–157
    procedures for, 155–156
    weight concerns for, 155, 156, 158
    See also luggage
paintwork, protecting from damage, 56
    pannier bags, 73–74
pedaling rate
    for acceleration, 124–125
    affecting endurance, 110, 113
    affecting knees, 139
    affecting respiratory quotient, 192
    for honking, 126
    for injury repair, 139, 140
    See also endurance; handling
pedals
    adjusting, 43
    clipless, 44
    position for start-up procedure, 105
    removal/installation, 43
    removing, 43
    toeclips for, 43–44
Penguin Bicycle Handbook, 21
pivot bosses
    for brakes, 35, 38, 56
    for mountain bike, 38
    for tandem bike, 230
planning
    basic rules for, 161–162
    for foreign tour, 204–207
    including children in, 216–217
    road evaluation for, 163
    for short trips, 162–163, 173–174
    timing concerns for, 164
    for tour route, 164–165, 179–180
    for touring, 161–168
    See also maps; safety
plastic
    avoiding in luggage racks, 70
    for fenders, 58–59
    plastic bags, 82, 83
posture. *See* riding posture; riding style
    potassium, 190
    See also food
Proofide, 156
protein, 188–189
    See also food
pumps, 62–63
puncture repair, 49–51, 50–51
    See also tires

Q
quality
    for bike tools, 66
    determining for bike selection, 28, 146
    for luggage selection, 74–75
    for maps, 162
    for sleeping bag, 86–87
quick-release, for wheel removal, 46

R

racing bike
    brakes, 52
    clothing for, 77
    clubs for, 18
    components, 29
    fork offset, 35
    frame geometry, 32
    frame size selection, 34
    handlebars, 36
    riding posture for, 97–98
    shifters, 108
rack-top bags, 74
Rafoth, Richard, 185
rain
    accidents in, 135
    affecting brakes, 121–122, 147
    affecting lighting system, 60, 61–62
    affecting sleeping bag, 86
    cycling practice for, 146
    fenders for, 57–59
    packing procedures for, 156
    riding style in, 147–148
    tent design for, 90–91
    tent siting in, 198
    touring techniques in, 148–149
    weatherproof luggage for, 74
    See also weather
rain gear, 81–82, 145
    packing tips for, 155–156
    plastic bags, 82, 83, 158
    See also clothing
Randonneur handlebars, 36
rear triangle, 29, 30
reflectors, 62
    danger of, 132
    for poor weather, 147
    See also lights
repairs
    lighting system, 60–61
    puncture repair, 49–51, 50–51
    spoke replacement, 47–48
    tire pump, 63
    wheel truing, 48
    See also maintenance; spares; tools
respiratory quotient (RQ), 191–192
responsiveness, frame weight affecting, 30–31
Reynolds, 33
riding posture, 37, 97–98
    brake use affecting, 122
    See also comfort; fit
riding style
    affecting wind resistance, 148
    with children, 219–220
    for cold weather, 147–149
    for cornering, 148
    for group riding, 148
    in rain, 147–148
    See also turns
rigidity, 31–32
    for brakes, 52
    for fatigue prevention, 69
    for luggage loads, 68
    for luggage racks, 70–71
    in tandem bike, 227
rims
    aluminum, 48, 146, 229
    generator operation by, 60

matching to tires, 49
    mountain bike, 38
    for tandem bike, 229
    See also tires; wheels
roads
    analyzing before tour, 179–180
    bicycle paths, 213
    evaluating for tour, 163, 179–180
    freeways, 184
    identifying landmarks on, 180
    maps for, 166
    mountain bike touring on, 233–234
    road sign analysis, 184
    selecting for foreign tour, 211–212
    See also planning

S

Sachs drum brakes, 41
saddle
    Brooks 66 Champion, 39
    fitting concerns, 37
    heels-on-pedal adjustment, 99–100
    height adjustment, 99–101
    injury from, 130, 138–139
    Mark Hodges adjustment, 100
    mountain bike, 39
    109% rule adjustment, 99
    position/angle adjustment, 101–102
    saddle bags for, 72–73
    and seatpost, 37
    of touring bike, 26–27
    width determination, 37
saddle sores, 130, 138
safety
    accident risk reduction, 130–131
    for bike at campsite, 198
    brake testing, 53
    with bungee cords, 74
    foreign health concerns, 213–214
    installation of accessories, 55–56
    lights enhancing, 59–61
    locking procedures, 64
    locknuts for, 57
    luggage loading procedures, 68
    luggage mounting system, 76
    for stored auto, 165
    tire pressure concerns, 62
    traffic hazards, 131
    for transported bike, 159–160
    See also handling; packing
seat covers, 66
seat lug, 30
seat pin. See seatpost
Seat Post Thing, 73
seat stays, 30
    threaded bosses for, 56
seat tube, 29–30
seatpost
    and saddle, 37
    saddle attachment to, 37
shifters, 45
    bar-end, 46
    indexed, 46, 111
    racing, 108
    See also gearing system
Shimano components, 29
    cantilever brakes, 41
shock absorption

foam grips enhancing, 39
    fork thickness affecting, 35
shoes, 43–44, 77–78
    for preventing numbness, 140
    safety concerns for, 105
    See also clothing
shorts/slacks, features for, 78–79
Sigg bottles, 63
sightseeing, 144
sinus/bronchial complaints, 140–141
    See also injuries
SKS, 58–59
sleeping bags, 86–89, 200
    caring for, 88–89
    covers for, 89
    designs for, 87–88
    liners for, 89, 200
    packing, 156
    See also camping gear
snacks, 194
    See also food
socks
    for preventing numbness, 140
    requirements for, 77–78
    See also clothing; shoes
sodium, 190
    See also food
Softride Frankenstem, 40
spares
    for lighting system, 61–62
    recommended, 65–66
    See also repairs
specialized shops, for bike supplies, 19
speed
    affecting handling, 118–119
    brakes regulating, 121
    gear selection enhancing, 107
    maintaining consistency of, 124
    nominal, for touring, 130
    on tandem bike, 223
    reducing for safety, 134, 135–136
    See also handling; safety
spiders, chainring attachment to, 43
spokes, 46–47
    ferrules reinforcing, 48
    replacing, 47–48
    retensioning, 48
    rim tape, 48, 51
    spoking patterns, 47
    See also rims; wheels
sprockets
    selecting, 114–116
    See also gearing system
stainless steel, for spokes, 47
start-up procedures, 105
    See also handling; safety
steel frame, 30–32
steerer tube, relationship to frame size, 35
steering principle, 118
    See also handling
steering system
    adjusting, 35
    attaching bags to, 69
    components of, 34
    of touring bike, 26–27
sunburn, 141, 146
    See also injuries

supplies
  bike shops providing, 20
  buying on tour, 154
  renting, 20
  shape of affecting packing, 157
  See also mail order
suspension
  Flexstem, 40
  mountain bike, 39, 40, 40

T
tandem bike
  bike adjustments for, 104
  brakes, 230
  drivetrain, 227–229
  frame, 226–227
  frames for, 32
  touring on, 223–230
  transporting, 224
  use with children, 220–221
  wheels, 229–230
Tange, 33
tendonitis, 139–140
  See also injuries; safety
tents, 89–91
  efficient use of, 198–199
  materials for, 91
  packing, 156
  site selection for, 197–198
  sleeping arrangements in, 200–201
  See also camping; camping gear
tetanus immunization, 136
theft, 64
Therm-A-Rest pad, 92
  See also camping gear
tire patch, for protecting paintwork, 56
tire pressure
  nominal values for, 49
  safety concerns for, 62
  tire size affecting, 39
  touring values for, 62–63
tires
  matching to rim, 49
  mountain bike, 38
  mounting on wheel, 46
  nominal sizes for, 48–49
  pump for, 62
  puncture repair, 49–51, 50–51
  selecting, 49
  sidewall affecting, 49
  sizing details, 49
  tire gauge, 62
  tools for, 65
  valves, 49, 63
  for wet/cold weather, 147
  See also rims; wheels
toeclips, 43–44, 105
tool pouch, 66
tools
  carrying on tour, 155
  for crank tightening, 42
  recommended, 65–66
  See also maintenance; repairs
top tube, 29–30
Tour de France, 204
touring, 15–17, 162–163, 173–174,
  176–178
  accident risks from, 130

automobile support for, 175
by Bikecentennial, 17
with children, 215–222
with commercial tours, 18
components for, 27
cottered crankset for, 42
day trips, 173–174
endurance diet for, 185–186
in foreign countries, 203–214
high-risk periods for, 131
in inclement weather, 148–150
insurance for, 129
log book for, 237–240
longer trips, 175–176
on mountain bike, 37–39, 231–236
on tandem bike, 223–230
overnight trips, 174–175
planning for, 161–168
preparations for, 171–173
research for, 161–162, 164–165, 168,
  179–180
timing concerns for, 164
tire pressure for, 62–63
tire width for, 49
weekend tours, 174–176
  See also foreign touring; packing;
  planning
touring bike
  accessories, 26–27, 55–66
  brakes, 26–27
  fork offset, 35
  gearing system, 107
  insurance for, 130
  selecting size for, 33–34
  women's, 28, 33
tourist boards
  for tour information, 205–206
  See also foreign touring; planning
traffic hazards
  avoiding, 131–133
  See also handling; safety
trailers, 67, 76
  for young children, 218, 219
  See also luggage racks
training
  considerations for, 171–173
  home trainers, 171–172
  overtraining injuries, 141–142
  See also endurance
trains, 165
  transporting tandem bike on, 224
transportation
  to foreign-country tour, 206–207
  for tandem bike, 224
  to tour site, 162–163, 165, 176
trouble-shooting. *See* repairs
tubes
  bottom, 29–30
  butted, 31
  down, 31, 32
  head, 29–30
  materials for, 33
  for mountain bike, 38
  nominal diameters for, 33
  protecting from damage, 56
  seat, 29–30
  top, 29–30
tubes (tire), selecting, 49
turns

forced, 120–121, 126–127
natural, 119–120
riding style for, 148
safety for in traffic, 132–133
traction concerns for, 147
  See also handling; safety

V
valves
  Presta valves, 49, 63
  types of, 49
  See also tires; tubes
vitamins, 189–190
  See also food

W
walking, for digestion, 190, 194
warning devices, 64–65
water bottle
  attaching, 56, 63
  types of, 63–64
weather
  affecting touring, 143–144
  choosing clothing for, 144–145
  tour timing concerns for, 164
  See also cold weather; rain
weight
  affecting braking, 122
  affecting comfort and performance, 31
  affecting handling, 31, 156
  affecting rigidity, 31
  awareness for in packing, 155, 156, 158
  of frame, 30
  reducing for wheels, 48
welding, 70
wheels
  for children's trailer, 219
  on tandem bike, 229–230
  parts of, 46
  quick-release, 46
  rear wheel centering, 47
  relative wheel symmetry, 47
  sizing details, 49
  of touring bike, 26–27
  truing procedure, 48
wind
  evaluating for tour route, 163, 165
  tent siting in, 198
wind resistance
  drafting technique reducing, 125
  on tandem bike, 223
  posture affecting, 97–99, 98
  riding style affecting, 148
women
  clothing concerns, 79
  fitting problems, 32–33
  saddle fitting concerns, 37
  special bike for, 32–33
women's bike, 28
  hazards of, 32
  tandem bike concerns, 227

Y
youth hostels, 213
Youth Hostels Associations, 247

Other Titles Available from Bicycle Books

Title	Author	US Price
All Terrain Biking	Jim Zarka	$7.95
The Backroads of Holland	Helen Colijn	$12.95
The Bicycle Commuting Book	Rob van der Plas	$7.95
The Bicycle Fitness Book	Rob van der Plas	$7.95
The Bicycle Repair Book	Rob van der Plas	$9.95
Bicycle Technology	Rob van der Plas	$16.95
Bicycle Touring International	Kameel Nasr	$18.95
The Bicycle Touring Manual	Rob van der Plas	$16.95
Bicycling Fuel	Richard Rafoth	$9.95
Cycling Europe	Nadine Slavinski	$12.95
Cycling France	Jerry Simpson	$12.95
Cycling Kenya	Kathleen Bennett	$12.95
Cycling the U.S. Parks	Jim Clark	$12.95
In High Gear (hardcover)	Samuel Abt	$21.95
In High Gear (paperback)	Samuel Abt	$10.95
The High Performance Heart	Maffetone/Mantell	$9.95
Major Taylor (hardcover)	Andrew Ritchie	$19.95
The Mountain Bike Book	Rob van der Plas	$10.95
Mountain Bike Magic (color)	Rob van der Plas	$14.95
Mountain Bike Maintenance	Rob van der Plas	$9.95
Mountain Bikes: Maint. & Repair*	John Stevenson	$22.50
Mountain Bike Racing (hardcover)*	Burney & Gould	$22.50
The New Bike Book	Jim Langley	$4.95
Roadside Bicycle Repairs	Rob van der Plas	$4.95
Tour of the Forest Bike Race	H. E. Thomson	$9.95
Tour de France (hardcover)	Samuel Abt	$22.95
Tour de France (paperback)	Samuel Abt	$12.95

Buy our books at your local book shop or bike store.

Book shops can obtain these titles for you from our book trade distributor (National Book Network for the USA), bike shops directly from us. If you have difficulty obtaining our books elsewhere, we will be pleased to supply them by mail, but we must add $2.50 postage and handling (as well as California Sales Tax if mailed to a California address). Prepayment by check (or credit card information) must be included with your order.

Bicycle Books, Inc.
PO Box 2038
Mill Valley CA 94941
Tel.: (415) 381-0172

In Britain: Bicycle Books
463 Ashley Road
Poole, Dorset BH14 0AX
Tel.: (0202) 71 53 49

* Books marked thus not available from Bicycle Books in the UK